# Frank Füredi

# THE SOVIET UNION
# DEMYSTIFIED
# A MATERIALIST ANALYSIS

junius

Published by
Junius Publications Ltd
BCM JPLTD
London WC1N 3XX

**British Library cataloguing in publication data**
Füredi, Frank
    The Soviet Union demystified: a materialist analysis
    1. Soviet Union — social conditions — 1917
    I. Title

    947.084.        HN523

ISBN 0-948392-03-7
ISBN 0-948392-05-3 Pbk

Copyright © Frank Füredi 1986

Set by
Junius Publications Ltd
Printed by
The Russell Press, Nottingham

Cover photo
**Vladimir Ilych Ulyanov (Lenin)** *convalescing at Gorki, August 1922*
*From the David King Collection*

# Contents

| | | |
|---|---|---|
| **Introduction** | | 1 |
| **Part I** | **The emergence of the Soviet Union** | 5 |
| 1. | The transition to communism | 7 |
| 2. | The demise of proletarian power | 27 |
| 3. | The emergence of the new society | 39 |
| 4. | Stalinism and destalinisation | 63 |
| **Part II** | **The Soviet social formation** | 79 |
| 5. | Economic regulation | 81 |
| 6. | Laws of motion | 109 |
| 7. | Counteracting chaos | 137 |
| **Part III** | **Class and international relations** | 163 |
| 8. | The bureaucracy | 165 |
| 9. | The working class | 187 |
| 10. | Foreign policy | 211 |
| **Conclusion** | | 249 |
| **Selected Bibliography** | | 257 |
| **Index** | | 265 |

# Introduction

Ever since the Russian Revolution of October 1917, the Soviet Union has been a constant source of controversy. Often ill-informed, this controversy has tended to fuel speculation rather than insight. Debates around the Soviet Union have been influenced by political motives to such an extent that those participating in them have often shown little respect for facts. In the West, anti-Soviet prejudices frequently overwhelm analysis, as Kremlinologists help to justify propaganda offensives against 'communist totalitarianism'. In the Soviet Union too, critical investigation has been vigorously discouraged. Studies of Soviet society have become little more than an apology for the status quo.

The Soviet Union needs to be demystified. Even the Soviet establishment now recognises that it lacks a clear understanding of how its own society works. Since 1983, when Andropov became premier, discussion of the nature of Soviet society has flourished inside the Soviet Union. Yet there used to be no such uncertainties: in 1961 premier Khrushchev was convinced that the Soviet Union was on the threshold of achieving its basic objectives. At the twenty-second congress of the Soviet Communist Party he confidently predicted that 'the present generation of Soviet people' would 'live under communism'.

A quarter of a century on from Khrushchev, however, communism has failed to materialise and the Soviet establishment has a lot of explaining to do. In the seventies the Moscow regime launched a veritable crusade to come up with an acceptable label for the sort of non-communist society that evidently still prevailed within the borders of the Soviet Union. The most popular label it could come up with was that it was a 'developed socialist society'. Other contenders were 'real existing socialism', 'mature socialism', and 'integral socialism'. Finding a name was relatively easy — explaining what it meant has proved to be more difficult. Soviet authors have failed to go beyond the rather banal observation that 'developed socialism' is a stage towards communism.

In the Soviet Union in the eighties there have been signs of a growing impatience with the old rhetoric. It is obvious to many that the constant manipulation of Marxist phrases has done little more than obscure the realities of Soviet life. The Soviet Communist Party's 1961 programme became an embarrassment which not even the most ardent party hack could relate to the realities of Soviet society. In November 1982 Andropov admitted: 'We have not yet studied properly the society in which we live and work.'

Three years later the draft of the Soviet Communist Party's new programme openly pleaded ignorance about the nature of Soviet society, observing that it was 'complex' and 'multi-faceted'. In particular the 1985 draft emphasises 'the immense importance of the general laws of development of socialism'. But what are these laws? It offers only a string of platitudes: 'The power of working people, with the working class playing the leading role: guidance of society's development by the Communist Party armed with the ideology of scientific socialism.'[1] Only in the specialist literature are Soviet writers prepared to admit that these 60-year-old formulations no longer ring true.

For their part, Western authorities brand the Soviet Union 'communist', 'socialist' or 'Marxist'. For them the Soviet Union confirms the view that communism is an inferior and malevolent social system. It serves too as a powerful argument against radical change in the West.

In the end, however, facts are always superior to name-calling. In recent years there has been a dramatic improvement in the quality of information available on the Soviet Union — both inside and outside its borders. We are now in a better position than ever before to find out about what is going on in the Soviet Union and to analyse the underlying dynamics of Soviet society. The purpose of this book is to investigate the movement of Soviet society from a Marxist point of view.

The Soviet Union presents a challenge to Marxism in a number of important respects. Of all historical developments, the Soviet Union is popularly seen as the most eloquent testimony to the failure of Marxism. It is true that the equation drawn by public opinion between Marxism and the Soviet Union cannot be counteracted by theoretical argument alone. Nevertheless, a critical investigation of Soviet society can help to rebut the prejudices against Marxism which provide the Western establishment with one of its most powerful sources of legitimacy.

The Soviet Union also poses a challenge to Marx's theory of

historical development. The main virtue of historical materialism is that it can grasp the objects under investigation in all their specificity and in their movement. The aim of this work is to explain the evolution of the Soviet Union and analyse the different phases of its development. The approach is therefore not merely historical, but historical-logical. The aim is to provide a logical reconstruction of the history of Soviet society to explain its main tendencies of development.

The structure of the book reflects its historical-logical approach. Part I outlines the historical background to the emergence of the Soviet Union as a distinct social formation. It extracts from history those moments that throw light on the specific forms of development of the Soviet Union. In Part II, the historical material is reworked to isolate what Marx calls the 'laws of motion' of society. Our aim here is to discuss social laws and to explain patterns of interaction which constantly reproduce themselves in Soviet society. In Part III, the previous discussion is extended and modified by taking into account class and international relations.

Many important topics are not discussed. Most importantly, regional variations and national minorities in the Soviet Union have been left aside. Our central focus here is on the developmental tendencies of Soviet society, not on the way these tendencies may be modified in certain circumstances. However, the elaboration of the fundamental laws of motion of Soviet society in Part II provides the basis for future research: into nationalism and racism, the position of women, and other vital questions.

Neither Soviet nor Western statistics on the Soviet Union can be regarded as reliable. In fact they tend to show similar patterns. Any figures in this book should be interpreted as broad markers of trends rather than as irrefutable facts.

Although this book was written in the West, the main influences that have shaped its conception lie elsewhere. In the late seventies I set about collecting material for a study of the history of the Hungarian Revolution of 1956. The impressions of this experience, which I lived through as a child, continued to influence my thinking and raised pressing questions about the nature of historical change. However, it soon became clear that such a study required a more thoroughgoing analysis of East European society and of the Soviet Union. East European Marxists have personally impressed upon me their frustration at the lack of progress in the study of the societies in which they live. Their views and my own research led to a change of direction towards an analysis of the Soviet Union.

The approach adopted in *The Soviet Union demystified* stands outside what is now known as mainstream Western Marxism. The authors that have strongly influenced this work do not belong to a coherent school but all have an important place in a critical reconstruction of Marxism. Grossman, Ilyenkov, Rosdolsky, Rubin and Zelený have, in different ways, developed and given expression to the critical and transformative dimensions of Marxism.[2] Of present-day Marxist writers on the Soviet Union, Ticktin has been the most useful and stimulating.[3]

Lastly, Marxist theory advances only through being tested against the practical problems of today. I have been fortunate to have a group of comrades and friends who have never let me forget this simple principle. Although the responsibility for this book is ultimately mine, Ann Burton, Mike Freeman, Mick Hume, Phil Murphy, Sabena Norton and Joan Phillips have helped provide the intellectual climate of critical discussion and debate essential for the completion of this work. Special thanks are due to David King and James Wood.

*Frank Füredi*
London
February 1986

---

1 CPSU (1985), p17.
2 See Grossman (1967), Ilyenkov (1982), Rosdolsky (1977), Rubin (1972) and Zelený (1980).
3 Ticktin's writings are published in the journal *Critique,* which he also edits.

# PART I
# The emergence of the Soviet Union

The first four chapters examine the evolution of the Soviet social formation in the twenties and thirties. There is no attempt here to provide a factual account of this period: there are numerous historical accounts and the new reader is advised to consult the bibliography at the back of this book. The object is to reconstruct the history of the Soviet Union to isolate the key moments in its development. Hence the material presented in this section in a sense presupposes the theoretical discussion in Part II. However, for the purposes of presentation the account is arranged in a more or less chronological sequence.

It is necessary to return to the discussions of Marx and Lenin on the problem of the transition from capitalism to communism and to Trotsky's critique of the development of Soviet society. Although these contributions have been extensively discussed, some of their key points have been misinterpreted or ignored. Our aim in reviving these aspects of the Marxist tradition is to stimulate contemporary discussion on these questions.

# PART I

# The emergence of the Soviet Union

# I. The transition to communism

The Russian Revolution and its subsequent course have strongly influenced contemporary attitudes towards the Marxist theory of the transition to communism. Unfortunately most of today's debates on the Soviet Union tend to be reactive and impressionistic. The negative outcome of the world's first working class revolution is widely used as an argument to discredit Marxism. To make matters worse, terms like 'socialism', 'communism' and 'the dictatorship of the proletariat' are used interchangeably: instead of representing precise concepts, they are used as rhetorical devices.

In a reaction against the coercive and anti-democratic features of Soviet society a whole literature has emerged which dismisses Marxism and Leninism as dangerous ideologies leading inexorably to totalitarian dictatorship. In France former leftists turned fashionable 'new philosophers' have made critiques of the Soviet Union which verge on demonology.[1] Even more circumspect left wingers can barely hide their revulsion against revolutionary Marxism. According to Claudin, the Spanish historian of the international communist movement, the October Revolution opened up a theoretical crisis in Marxism.[2] In what amount to outbursts of anti-Eastern chauvinism, others argue that Marxism belongs to the culture of the West, and therefore its Soviet variation is illegitimate. Thus for the British sociologist Bottomore 'communist orthodoxy' is 'a deviation, if not an aberration, engendered in peculiar social and historical conditions'.[3]

Critiques of the Soviet Union have generated much heat but little light. A serious critique must transcend moralism if it is to achieve some understanding of the way the Soviet system works. Given the prevailing confusion we must begin our analysis of Soviet society by reconstructing Marx's theory of the transition from capitalism to communism. It is essential to understand the goals of the Bolsheviks, or we will fail to understand how these goals were not achieved, or how the subsequent rulers of the Soviet state lost sight of them altogether.

## Marx on the proletarian dictatorship

Marxism developed as a distinct alternative to the romantic critiques of capitalism which arose in mid-nineteenth century Europe. Marx was not concerned simply to attack capitalist exploitation. Exploitation had existed in previous societies: though capitalists continued it, their system was still an advance on earlier forms of social organisation. Marx's critique of capitalism was based on the recognition that beyond a certain point the social relations of capitalist society created obstacles to the development of the forces of production. This failure to develop the forces of production systematically was the main target of Marx's attack. Marx's emphasis on the forces of production did not stem from an obsession with technology or production. For Marx, the liberation of humanity was inextricably linked to the development of the productive forces of society.

Many left wingers regard Marx's emphasis on the forces of production as crude and excessively materialistic. For Sirianni, the defects of what he calls 'productivist evolutionism' are self-evident.[4] Sirianni fails to grasp how Marx's preoccupation with the development of the forces of production arose from his commitment to the genuine liberation of mankind. Marx rejected the abstract conceptions of freedom that prevail in bourgeois society. For him, freedom meant freedom from want, freedom from the struggle for survival. He noted that freedom cannot be declared or conceded as an act of will:

> 'It is possible to achieve real liberation only in the real world and by real means....Slavery cannot be abolished without the steam engine and the mule jenny, serfdom cannot be abolished without improved agriculture, and...in general, people cannot be liberated as long as they are unable to obtain food and drink, housing and clothing in adequate quality and quantity.'[5]

People may imagine doing anything, but they cannot escape the material constraints that reality imposes on their behaviour. Marx continually highlighted the objective restrictions on human freedom and the need to overcome them to achieve human liberation: 'A development of the productive forces is the absolute premise, because without it want is generalised, and with want the struggle for necessities begins again, and that means all the old crap must revive.' Only by raising the productivity of labour can society generate enough surplus, enough disposable labour-time, to move from the 'realm of necessity' to the 'realm of freedom'.[6] The full development of the individual — the central project of Marxism — depends on the economic development of society. To express genuine individuality people need to have free time available so that they can make choices which are not limited by material constraints. Only when the development of the productive forces of society has eliminated hardship and shortages of basic goods can individuals make decisions which are conscious choices, rather than choices forced on them by the tyranny of necessity.

Marx's materialist approach to human liberation inspired his commitment to communism. Marx regarded communism as a worthy goal because it would provide the foundation for the unhindered development of the productivity of labour. In his view raising productivity was the key aim of all economic activity: 'Economy of time, to this all economy ultimately reduces itself.' Moreover, raising the productivity of labour was particularly important for a communist society. It was, Marx argued, 'the first economic law' of 'communal production'.[7]

Marx and Engels recognised that capitalism could not be transformed into communism overnight. A period of transition would be needed to build up the material prerequisites for communist society. They were well aware that the social system succeeding capitalism would 'in every respect, economically, morally and intellectually' be 'still stamped with the birthmarks of the old society from whose womb it emerges'.[8] They characterised this society — popularly known as 'socialism' — as 'the lower phase of communism'. In this phase class differences would persist, because the material foundations for equality would not yet be completed. During this transition period the working class would ensure its political control over society through 'the dictatorship of the proletariat'.[9]

The concept of the dictatorship of the proletariat has been under left-wing attack since the sixties, especially by Eurocommunists. Most critics have focused on its allegedly anti-democratic character and have promoted various notions of 'socialist democracy' as alternatives.[10] According to one Eurocommunist theoretician the fact that 'Marx and Engels tended to define the state solely in terms of class domination' is a fatal flaw in their work which leads to a serious underestimation of democracy.[11] Such criticisms, which amount to an explicit rejection of the Marxist theory of the state, reveal a misunderstanding of the relationship between democracy and the proletarian dictatorship.

Marx argued that democracy, like any form of political rule, could not exist in the abstract, in isolation from class interests. As long as classes exist, any form of political rule means the dictatorship of one class over another. Class dictatorship can assume a variety of political forms. In capitalist society, the rule of the capitalist class may be imposed through military dictatorship or fascism; or it may be exercised in a less coercive way through parliamentary democracy. But parliamentary democracy is simply one form of the dictatorship of the bourgeoisie. A classless democracy, without coercion and the institutionalised power of vested interests, exists only on the plane of abstract speculation.

In a famous letter, Marx summarised his views on the proletarian dictatorship, noting that 'this dictatorship only constitutes the transition to the abolition of all classes and to a classless society.'[12] Until humanity has overcome want, classes will persist. The proletarian dictatorship expresses the rule of one class — the proletariat — whose aim is to abolish all classes. However, class rule by definition means the application of force, and in this respect, as Engels noted, proletarian rule can be no different from the rule of other classes: 'So long as the proletariat still uses the state, it does not use it in the interests of freedom but in order to hold down its adversaries.'[13] Under the dictatorship of the proletariat, as under capitalism, state coercion may be mediated by participatory bodies and by consensus; but, whatever the political framework, it will be backed up by force. Under a proletarian state, force will be directed by the majority of society against the capitalist minority — the reverse of the situation under capitalism. The dictatorship of the proletariat will therefore provide a framework within which democracy can flourish as never before. It will mean the democracy of the masses, not the democracy of the slave owners of Athens or the charade tolerated under certain conditions by the capitalist class.

The establishment of the proletarian dictatorship and the destruction of the power of the capitalist class open up the road to communism. But, as Engels observed, the pace at which the proletarian dictatorship moves to take control of the economy, and the measures that it implements, depend on particular circumstances:

**'In general, the question is not whether the proletariat when it comes to power will simply seize by force the instruments of production, the**

raw materials and means of subsistence, whether it will redeem the property therein by small instalment payments. To attempt to answer such a question in advance and for all cases would be utopia-making.'[14]

To sum up: in the economic sphere the proletarian dictatorship must ensure the steady growth of the productive forces; in the sphere of politics the task of the state is to ensure that the working class stays in power.

## Lenin on planning

Marx and Engels considered the proletarian dictatorship primarily from a theoretical point of view. Lenin was obliged to tackle the practical problems confronting a newly formed workers' state. One of the key problems that will confront any proletarian state is that of building up the economy. The goal of a workers' state is to abolish value relations — the spontaneous distribution of labour-time through the capitalist market mechanism. In place of the market the proletarian state aims to distribute labour-time consciously, through planning. But what are the preconditions for the smooth operation of a social plan?

Even before the Russian Revolution, Lenin knew how difficult it would be to set up an effective system of planning. The backward character of the Russian economy, compounded by the low level of education, industrial skills and general culture, made it impossible for the Bolsheviks to introduce planning at once. Aware that it could easily confiscate capitalist property, but that running the economy would prove much more difficult, the new regime restricted the scope of nationalisation. Shortly before the revolution Lenin had noted that confiscation alone 'leads nowhere, as it does not contain the element of organisation'.[15] After 1917 he returned to this theme time and again.

For the Bolsheviks the first task of the proletarian dictatorship after the defeat of the capitalist class was to set up *workers' control* over the economy. 'The chief difficulty', Lenin wrote, 'is the establishment on a countrywide scale of the most precise and most conscientious accounting and control, of workers' control of the production and distribution of goods.'[16] Workers' control was not an end in itself: it was a precondition for successful planning — a system in which the economy came under direct *workers' management*.

Lenin identified workers' control and workers' management as two distinct stages in the battle for a communist society:

> **'Until workers' control has become a fact, until the advanced workers have organised and carried out a victorious and ruthless crusade against the violators of this control, or against those who are careless in matters of control, it will be impossible to pass from the first step (from workers' control) to the second step towards socialism, ie, to pass on to a workers' regulation of production.'**[17]

Lenin regarded workers' control as a transitional phase during which the proletariat would, through the exercise of political power, establish control over the economy. This power would then become consolidated through workers' management, which presupposed the capacity for the central regulation of economic affairs.

The Bolsheviks from the outset underestimated the difficulties involved in achieving workers' management. In 1918 and 1919, the years of 'war communism', Lenin suggested on several occasions that the Soviet Union was on the threshold of workers' management. However, it soon became apparent that simply setting up planning agencies was insufficient to guarantee genuine workers' management; in fact Lenin never lived to see workers' management of the Soviet economy. However, his awareness of the necessity for a transitional phase in which to strengthen the proletarian dicatorship is clear from the emphasis he placed on this problem in his writings. In his last years his energies were directed towards strengthening the control of the new state over the economy.

Today Lenin's analysis of workers' management is misunderstood or forgotten. His analysis shows that planning does not arise spontaneously. Establishing a conscious distribution of labour-time requires major social, cultural and economic changes — changes which can only be achieved through struggle. Yet, as one influential Bolshevik document argued, the progress of the proletarian dictatorship directly depends on how far it can manage the economy: 'In the economic sphere, the tasks of the proletarian dictatorship can be carried out only to the extent that the proletariat is able to create centralised organs for the management of production and introduce workers' management.'[18]

Constructing 'centralised organs for the management of production' is essential if production is to come under the conscious direction of society. Nationalisation, however, becomes progressive only insofar as the productive forces are socialised. Contrary to the widely held view, neither Marx nor Lenin regarded nationalisation itself as progressive. The communal ownership of industry is a step forward from private property insofar as it enhances the socialisation of labour and increases productivity. But apart from this, nationalised property has no special significance. Engels' witty remarks on left-wing illusions in nationalised property retain their relevance today:

'Of late, since Bismarck went in for state ownership of industrial establishments, a kind of spurious socialism has arisen, degenerating, now and again, into something of flunkeyism, that without more ado declares all state ownership, even of the Bismarckian sort, to be socialistic. Certainly, if the taking over by the state of the tobacco industry is socialistic, then Napoleon and Metternich must be numbered among the founders of socialism.'[19]

## Workers' control under the Bolsheviks

Shortly after the October Revolution the Bolsheviks discovered that if they were to preserve workers' power over society they had no alternative but to expropriate the bourgeoisie. The threat of economic sabotage by the capitalist class forced the hand of the new workers' government. Lenin regarded the confiscation of capitalist property not as an economic expedient, but as a political necessity:[20]

'The domination of the proletariat consists in the fact that the landowners and capitalists have been deprived of their property....The prime thing is the question of property. As soon as the question of property was settled practically, the domination of the class was assured.'[21]

The project of establishing a system of workers' management came up against a number of obstacles. The greatest problem facing the Bolsheviks was the fragmented character of the Russian economy, and the fact that it was dominated by small-scale agriculture. The country's economic backwardness limited the scope for state regulation and restricted the speed with which fundamental changes could be pushed through. Lenin recognised that Soviet society would have to undergo important changes before planning could begin. In one of his most important articles after 1917 he summed up the difficulties of the transition period:

'Theoretically, there can be no doubt that between capitalism and communism there lies a definite transition period which must combine the features and properties of these forms of social economy. This transition period has to be a period of struggle between dying capitalism and nascent communism — or, in other words, between capitalism which has been defeated but not destroyed and communism which has been born but is still very feeble.'[22]

In the transition period, the forces attempting to establish a planned society can expect to face continual rearguard resistance from the remnants of capitalist production relations.[23]

In Russia the economic problems were particularly acute. The combination of backward industry and a morass of peasant holdings meant that the social weight of state-run industry was relatively small. The failure of proletarian revolution outside Russia ensured that the new workers' state could not rely on economic assistance from the more developed countries of Europe. The only realistic option available to the proletarian dictatorship was to compromise with the peasantry and tolerate the existence of a capitalist market in agriculture. At the tenth congress of the Soviet Communist Party in March 1921 Lenin was candid: 'We know that so long as there is no revolution in other countries, only agreement with the peasantry can save the revolution in Russia.'[24]

The compromise formulated in the New Economic Policy (NEP) relied upon the market mechanism to reconstruct the economy. Foreign capitalists were given the right to invest in certain sectors and private traders and entrepreneurs were allowed to pursue their businesses. State power was the main guarantee that the proletarian dictatorship would not lose control over the activities of the capitalist sector. Thus in the NEP period workers' control assumed a peculiar form: the workers' state concentrated, not on planning the economy, but on keeping a firm grip on the capitalists and petty commodity producers. 'Growing capitalism will be under control and supervision, while political power will remain in the hands of the workers' state,' said Lenin.[25]

The Bolsheviks realised that the growth of capitalist production relations was a potential threat to the new government. But they felt that, through systematic control, the expansion of capitalism could be harnessed in the service of the working class. Lenin coined the phrase 'state capitalism' to express the regulation of capitalism by the proletarian state.[26] Unfortunately the state was ill-prepared to take on the *nepmen,* the entrepreneurs whose activities were given free rein by the new policy. The new state even had problems controlling the nationalised industries — those directly under its own administration.[27] One year after the introduction of NEP, Lenin was forced to admit that it had exposed the weaknesses of the Soviet state:

> **'The past showed quite clearly that we cannot run the economy. That is the fundamental lesson. Either we prove the opposite in the coming year, or Soviet power will not be able to exist.'[28]**

Lenin's warning was to prove prophetic. The policies introduced under NEP did help to stimulate economic recovery. However, much of the burgeoning economic activity remained unregulated, and as the prosperous peasants, or *kulaks*, grew stronger, so the state grew weaker. By late 1927 the *kulaks* had begun to hold back food from the cities. The crisis triggered by the conflict between the peasantry and the state reached a peak in June 1928 when violence and terrorism enveloped the countryside.[29] By April 1929 the system of voluntary food deliveries to the state distribution agencies had broken down. The NEP was abandoned as the state attempted to exert more direct forms of control over the rural economy.

## The disappearing proletariat

Under conditions of proletarian dictatorship, workers' control over the economy depends on a combination of centralised administration and local initiative.[30] The commitment and active participation of workers in economic life is essential to ensure that all aspects of the economy are run by the working class. Without this active involvement, neither the wide knowledge they have of work, nor their broader cultural and political experience, will find its way into the social plan. The creative spirit of the proletariat will be wasted and information vital to the planning process will not be forthcoming from the workplaces.

The forward movement of society under the dictatorship of the proletariat depends ultimately on the foresight of the working class. This was especially true of the Soviet Union in the difficult years of the early twenties, as Lenin was well aware:

> **'The proletarian state may, without changing its own nature, permit freedom to trade and the development of capitalism only within certain bounds and only on the condition that the state regulates...private trade and private capitalism. The success of such regulation will**

**depend not only on the state authorities but also, and to a larger extent, on the degree of maturity of the proletariat and of the masses of working people generally, on their cultural level.'**[31]

Lenin placed special emphasis on the role of the vanguard — the most active and politically aware section of the working class — in defending the proletarian state. He argued that the dictatorship of the proletariat could not be exercised by the whole of the working class because it was 'still so divided, so degraded, and so corrupted in parts' by capitalism that its consciousness remained uneven. Hence power could only be exercised by a vanguard that had 'absorbed the revolutionary energy of the class'.[32]

Both the working class and its vanguard underwent a major upheaval during the revolution and the years of turmoil that followed it. The invasion of the Soviet state by imperialist armies, ranged on several fronts, and the civil war that raged between 1918 and 1921, together had a catastrophic impact on the working class. In the five years following 1917 much of Soviet industry was destroyed, economic life came to a virtual standstill and the industrial proletariat was decimated. Hunger, poverty and unemployment drove workers into the countryside. According to the British historian Carr, the number of workers remaining in the Petrograd region at the end of 1918 was little more than half that employed there two years earlier. The number of industrial workers in the Soviet Union fell from three million in 1917 to 2.5 million in 1918, then to fewer than 1.5 million in 1920-21 and finally to fewer than 1.25 million in 1921-2.[33]

The sharp decline in the social weight of the working class dealt a hammer blow to the proletarian dictatorship. At a time when they might have hoped to extend workers' democracy through the system of soviets, the Bolsheviks were faced with the disintegration of their social base. The dissolution of the working class forced the Bolshevik Party to take direct responsibility for every aspect of social life. But the party itself could not remain immune from the consequences of the liquidation of the working class.

The Bolshevik Party paid the price of defending the revolution in blood. During the civil war all party members were declared eligible for service at the front and hence a disproportionate number of working class activists were killed. Although tens of thousands of workers flocked to join the party, the damage could not be undone. Indeed the influx of raw, inexperienced members, untrained in Marxism, had a tendency to lower the political standards of the party.³⁴ In March 1922 Lenin pointed out how fragile the party had become:

'If we do not close our eyes to reality we must admit that at the present time the proletarian policy of the party is not determined by the character of its membership, but by the enormous undivided prestige enjoyed by the small group which might be called the old guard of the party. A slight conflict within this group will be enough, if not to destroy this prestige, at all events to weaken the group to such a degree as to rob it of its power to determine policy.'³⁵

Even the party, the vanguard of the working class, lacked the political consciousness necessary to wield proletarian power. In practice, a few thousand individuals — 'the Old Bolsheviks' — were charged with overseeing the transition to communism.

## The transformation of the party

The coherence of the party was the ultimate guarantee of the survival of the proletarian dictatorship. Despite the deformations of the system of workers' democracy that resulted from the civil war, despite the destruction of the proletariat, the Bolsheviks rightly regarded the party as the agency that could still overcome the crisis faced by the young workers' state.

However, party life became stagnant in the immediate post-revolutionary period. The most experienced party members were drawn into full-time military, economic and administrative posts. By 1918 the party in Petrograd was almost bereft of experienced cadres; by the following year party and state machinery were virtually indistinguishable.³⁶ A sample of party members in October 1919 revealed that only 11 per cent were still working in factories. Sixty per cent were state or party employees and 25 per cent were in the Red Army.³⁷

The need to consolidate state control drew more and more Bolsheviks into the bureaucracy. At the eighth party congress in March 1918, Zinoviev argued for large-scale recruitment into the party on the grounds that more members were required to staff the various bodies of the state. The developing fusion between the party and the state apparatus had serious consequences for the proletarian character of the party. Party officials and state bureaucrats tended to merge into a new and distinct social stratum. As Zinoviev recognised, many people were now joining the party, not out of a commitment to communism, but to advance their career prospects:

> 'There have been cases in Moscow where a man turns up at the (district committee) at 8pm to take out party membership, and when he is told to come back the next day, he replies: "Do me a good turn, I am going for a job tomorrow and I need a party card right away." '[38]

In the circumstances that prevailed in the Soviet Union after the revolution, the emergence of a party bureaucracy and the abuse of position by certain individuals were inevitable. The Bolsheviks recognised these problems and, at their 1919 congress, introduced a selective method of recruitment that was weighted in favour of workers. In mid-1919 the party leadership launched the first major purge of inactive members and the pressures of the civil war also drove thousands of passive recruits out of the party. Nevertheless the trend towards bureaucratisation continued. During the period of the NEP, communists were increasingly drawn into state administration: only 12 per cent of new recruits in 1922 were genuine workers.[39] By this time an immense party bureaucracy had emerged: more than 15 000 people — one in every 25 party members — were engaged in full-time party work.[40]

Lenin was acutely aware of the dangers resulting from the coalescence of party and state and the last articles he wrote before he was disabled by a stroke early in 1923 were directed against this trend. However, there was an even greater problem: the Bolsheviks' preoccupation with military and administrative tasks destroyed the political life of the party. More and more local leaders were appointed rather than elected. In the chaos of civil war this was unavoidable — experienced personnel had to be posted to strategic areas at a moment's notice. But as the party apparatus expanded it assumed wider responsibilities and powers. Local officials were assimilated into the party machine and their promotion prospects became dependent on the party hierarchy. A layer of party officials emerged made up of individuals whose position depended more on the apparatus than on their standing in local cells.

In 1920 the party leadership set up the *Uchraspred*, a new section of the party secretariat, to supervise the appointment and transfer of members. In July 1923, the central committee drew up a list of 3500 posts which could only be filled by sanction from the party leadership, together with a further 1000 posts which had to be dealt with by the *Uchraspred*.[41] Since local secretaries relied on the central apparatus for their position, the *Uchraspred* could virtually control party life. In October 1923 Trotsky warned that the party appointment system was dangerously vulnerable to abuse:

**'Appointment of the secretaries of provincial committees is now the rule. That creates for the secretary a position essentially independent of the local organisation.'**[42]

Stalin, who rose to the head of the administration in 1922, used the independence of the apparatus from the party rank and file to advance his factional ambitions within the bureaucracy. By 1923 the apparatus was strong enough to ensure that only delegates it considered loyal were elected to the thirteenth party congress — and that all representatives of the party's Left Opposition were excluded. The vanguard party of the working class had become an instrument of bureaucratic manipulation.

## The administration and the old order

The disintegration of the working class and the bureaucratisation of the Bolshevik Party limited the effectiveness of the proletarian dictatorship. Another problem was the low cultural and educational level of the Soviet working class. Lenin recognised that, given the general lack of skill and training, the proletariat could not do without specialists from the old Tsarist regime:

**'The exploiters have been eliminated. But the cultural level has not been raised, and therefore the bureaucrats are occupying their old position.'**[43]

Much of the old state machinery remained intact and, as one Western scholar has observed, 'the structural changes were scarcely greater than those sometimes accompanying changes of government in Western parliamentary systems.'[44]

The civil war and other external pressures intensified the difficulties facing the early Soviet regime. Between 1918 and 1921 the Soviet state apparatus barely functioned in the countryside. A report by national commissar Podbelsky, who was sent in July 1919 to examine the soviets in the Tambov region, south-east of Moscow, summed up the situation that prevailed in most rural areas:

**'Strictly speaking, there is no soviet government in the majority of**

the (localities). At present soviets exist in most places only on paper: in reality, representatives of kulaks and speculators, or self-interested people, or cowards, who carry out the work without any definite direction, work under the name of soviets.'[45]

The precarious position of the proletarian state gave rise to tensions that could only be resolved by the party assuming direct responsibility for many aspects of administration. Given the weakness of the working class, the integration of party and state machinery was inescapable.

The Bolsheviks held state power, but in practice their capacity to exert effective control over the state apparatus was limited. Lenin put the problems starkly to the eleventh party congress in 1922:

'If we take Moscow with its 4700 communists in responsible positions, and if we take that huge bureaucratic machine, that gigantic heap, we must ask: who is directing whom? I doubt very much whether it can truthfully be said that the communists are directing that heap. To tell the truth, they are not directing, they are being directed.'[46]

Not only were the communist officials 'being directed', they were also coming under the ideological influence of the old bureaucrats.

Lenin pointed out that the social weight and ideological influence of the bourgeois and petit-bourgeois forces remained considerable:

'If the conquering nation is more cultured than the vanquished nation, the former imposes its culture upon the latter: but if the opposite is the case, the vanquished nation imposes its culture upon the conqueror. Has not something like this happened in the capital of the Soviet Union? Have the 4700 communists (nearly a whole army division, and all of them the very best) come under the influence of an alien culture? True, there may be the impression that the vanquished have a high level of culture. But that is not the case at all. Their culture is miserable, insignificant, but it is still at a higher level than ours.'[47]

In the last months of his life Lenin became acutely sensitive to the lack of control which the proletariat had over its state. In December 1922 he noted that in effect the Bolsheviks had merely taken over the old machinery of the state from the Tsar and the bourgeoisie.[48] Little had changed: the autocratic institutions had been 'slightly annointed with Soviet oil', but 'the apparatus we call ours is, in fact, still quite alien to us, it is a bourgeois and Tsarist hotch-potch'.[49]

The survival of much of the old state apparatus — a concern which haunted Lenin throughout his last months — was the inevitable consequence of the material conditions that prevailed in the Soviet Union. Only assistance from a victorious revolution in Europe could have counteracted the negative effects of economic backwardness. In these difficult circumstances the Bolsheviks' only option was to launch a campaign to renew the political life of a working class that had been worn out and to fight to raise the cultural level of the masses. It was on this problem that Lenin concentrated his final efforts. In his last two articles, both written in January 1923, he proposed that the power of the party's central control commission be increased with a view to stimulating political discussion in the party. He also proposed that the *Rabkin,* the workers' and peasants' inspectorate, should be strengthened to become a 'really exemplary institution, an instrument to improve our state apparatus'.[50]

For Lenin the top priority was to strengthen the institutions of workers' control so that they could counteract the pernicious influence of the bureaucracy. He also proposed more far-reaching measures which would involve 'thoroughly purging our government machine, by reducing to the utmost everything that is not absolutely essential in it'.[51] Lenin regarded his proposals as steps towards a broad 'cultural revolution':

**'This cultural revolution would now suffice to make our country a completely socialist country: but it presents immense difficulties of a purely cultural (for we are illiterate) and material character (for to be cultured we must achieve a certain development of the material means of production, must have a certain material base).'**[52]

## The last chance

Lenin correctly identified the bureaucratic character of the state and the lack of working class control over the apparatus. He also saw that the Bolshevik Party had become a fragile instrument for preserving proletarian power, relying on the authority of 'the small group which might be called the old guard of the party'. Given the insecure foundations of the world's first workers' state, only a rapid development of workers' political coherence and class consciousness of the working class could have prevented its degeneration.

Lenin's call for cultural revolution and party renewal came up against a formidable barrier. Even the old guard had ceased to be the true leadership of the party. The concentration of power in the apparatus meant that the top bureaucrats had become virtual masters of the situation. At the time when Lenin made his last proposals, the power of the bureaucracy was still far from total. A figure of his standing in the party could well have played a decisive role in reversing the growth of the apparatus. But Lenin lay speechless and paralysed from early 1923 until his death in January of the following year. He could no longer play an active part in the struggle.

Trotsky, to whom Lenin had entrusted the fight, played an undistinguished role at the twelfth congress of the Soviet Communist Party in March 1923. It was left up to isolated individuals such as Rakovsky, Kosior and Preobrazhensky to point out the grave threat to the workers' state posed by the burgeoning bureaucracy. Lenin's memorandum on the issue put Stalin and the bureaucracy he led on the defensive. But the lack of a real fight on the question meant that the apparatus escaped largely unscathed. Nevertheless, the apparatus was sufficiently vulnerable to criticism to make token gestures in the direction of democracy. In September 1923, the central committee set up a commission on the internal situation in the party.[53]

In October 1923, Trotsky at last began to take up the cudgels against the stagnation of party life. At around the same time a joint platform criticising the party regime was drawn up and signed by 46 prominent Bolsheviks and sent to the central committee. The party leadership was still not sure enough of its position to dismiss the criticisms. Stalin's tactic was to accept some of Trotsky's strictures, draw up a joint statement with him and thus try to downplay the conflict. Accordingly a resolution drafted by Trotsky, Stalin and Kamenev was unanimously passed at a joint session of the politburo and the presidium of the central control commission in December 1923. In this way the leadership hoped to isolate Trotsky from rank and file critics of the apparatus.

The joint resolution incorporated many of the criticisms of the apparatus and listed the dangers facing the party:

'**The sharp differentiation in the material situation of party members...in connection with differences of function, and the so-called"excesses"; the growth of a link with bourgeois elements and the ideological influence of the latter: an official narrowness of outlook, which should be distinguished from necessary specialisation, and the** consequent weakening of the link between communists engaged in different sectors of work: the danger of the loss of a broad view of socialist construction as a whole and of world revolution: the danger already noted by the congress of a degeneration under NEP of the section of party workers in closest contact, through the nature of their activity, with the bourgeois milieu: the bureaucratisation which has been observed in party offices and the threat arising therefrom of a divorce of the party from the masses.'[54]

The resolution sounded good, but its only practical consequence was to give the apparatus room to outmanoeuvre the opposition.

The December resolution was a prelude to the bitter struggle that broke out at the thirteenth party conference in 1924, when Lenin was on his death-bed. In the name of the apparatus Stalin launched a furious campaign against Trotsky and the opposition. This succeeded in isolating and decisively defeating the challenge to the bureaucracy. The conference went on to take a decision with long-term consequences for the party — the decision to launch a mass recruitment drive. After Lenin's death the apparatus carried through the 'Lenin levy' which brought 128 000 people into the party within three months. An influx of inexperienced recruits on this scale could only make a mockery of the internal life of the party.

The revolutionary wing of the party was reduced to a small minority. According to Carr only 10 000 'Old Bolsheviks', many of whom had become inactive, remained in the party.[55] Many of the new entrants were motivated entirely by self-interest. For the first time party membership conferred material privileges on the card holder. The growing passivity of party membership reflected the enhanced power of the bureaucracy. The thirteenth party congress was the last chance to revive the party, but unfortunately it merely ratified the defeat of the opposition and ended all realistic hope of revitalising the party.

A full decade later, in his major reassessment published in February 1935, Trotsky finally grasped the full implications of the events of 1924, drawing a striking parallel with the reaction which followed the French Revolution of the eighteenth century:

'The smashing of the Left Opposition implied in the most direct and immediate sense the transfer of power from the hands of the revolutionary vanguard into the hands of the more conservative elements among the bureaucracy and the upper-crust of the working class. The year 1924 — that was the beginning of the Soviet Thermidor.'[56]

Back in 1924 appearances were deceptive. Stalin had not yet assumed the role of the omnipotent public figure he later became. The leadership of the apparatus had still not come together to form a stable clique. Indeed the apparatus spent the rest of the twenties in internal disputes, realignments and purges. At the time Trotsky considered that the conflicts within the bureaucracy provided considerable potential for the growth of the Left Opposition. But the spasms of the apparatus merely reflected its instability, and struggles remained at the level of skirmishes among different sections of the bureaucracy. The Left Opposition itself failed to reach the rank and file and, even in its heyday in the mid-twenties, it remained tied to the institutions of the apparatus. While the battles were raging at meetings of the central committee, the party membership was consigned to the role of a passive observer.

## Notes

1   English speaking readers will find an illustration of this trend in Castoriadis (1980-81). A typical representative of this school is Glucksman (1983), pp67-9.
2   Claudin (1979), p138.
3   Bottomore (1983), p117.
4   Sirianni (1982). Sirianni ventures the opinion that the primacy that the Bolsheviks attached to the development of the forces of production leads logically to Stalin's maxim that 'technique decides everything', p254.
5   Marx (1976a), p38.
6   'The saving of labour-time is equal to an increase of free time, ie for the full development of the individual.' See Marx (1973), p711.
7   Marx (1973), pp172-3.
8   Engels (1968a), p319.
9   'Between capitalist and communist society lies the period of the revolutionary transformation of the one into the other. Corresponding to this is also a political transition period in which the state can be nothing but the *revolutionary* dictatorship of the proletariat.' Engels (1968a), p327.
10  See for example Carrillo (1977).
11  Sirianni (1982), p273.
12  Marx & Engels (1983), p63.
13  Marx & Engels (1975), p275.
14  Engels cited in Lenin (1972), p41.
15  Lenin 'Can the Bolsheviks retain state power?', *CW26*, p107.
16  Lenin *CW26*, p105.
17  Lenin 'The immediate tasks of the Soviet government', *CW27*, pp254-5.
18  Communist International (1980), pp43-4.
19  Engels (1975), p329.

20  Carr notes: 'The nationalisation of industry was treated at the outset not as a desirable end in itself but as a response to special conditions, usually some misdemeanour of the employers.' See Carr (1966), p87.
21  Lenin 'Report of the central committee, ninth congress of the RCP(B)', *CW30*, p451.
22  Lenin 'Economics and politics in the era of the dictatorship of the proletariat', *CW30*, p107.
23  In Lenin's words the Russian economy represented the 'struggle of labour, united on communist principles' against 'petty commodity production and against the capitalism which still persists'. *CW30*, p108. This dual character of the transitional economy, the struggle between *two different types of organisation of labour* is extensively analysed in the works of the Bolshevik theoretician Preobrazhensky (1967).
24  Lenin 'Report to the tenth congress of the RCP(B)', *CW32*, p215.
25  Lenin 'Report on the tax in kind', *CW31*, p298.
26  'The whole problem — in theoretical and practical terms — is to find the correct methods of directing the development of capitalism (which is to some extent and for some time inevitable) into the channels of state capitalism, and to determine how we are to hedge it about with conditions to ensure its transformation into socialism in the near future.' See Lenin 'Report on the tax in kind', *CW31*, p345.
27  Lenin wrote in May 1921: 'There is hardly any evidence of the operation of an integrated state economic plan. The predominating tendency is to "revise" everything, all branches of the national economy indiscriminately, even all the enterprises that we have inherited from capitalism.' See Lenin 'To comrade Krzhizhanovsky', *CW32*, p371.
28  Lenin 'Political report of the central committee of the RCP(B)', *CW33*, p274.
29  See Carr & Davies (1974), p62.
30  'The more resolutely we now have to stand for a ruthlessly firm government, for the dictatorship of individuals *in definite processes of work*, in definite aspects of *purely executive* functions, the more varied must be the forms and methods of control from below in order to counteract every shadow of a possibility of distorting the principles of Soviet government, in order repeatedly and tirelessly to weed out bureaucracy.' See Lenin 'The immediate tasks of the Soviet government', *CW27*, p275.
31  Lenin 'The role and functions of the trade unions under the NEP', *CW33*, p185.
32  Lenin 'The trade unions, the present situation and Trotsky's mistakes', *CW32*, p21.
33  Carr (1966), p197.
34  'Our party is less politically trained than is necessary for real proletarian leadership in the present difficult situation, especially in view of the tremendous preponderance of the peasantry, which is rapidly awakening to independent class politics.' See Lenin 'Conditions for admitting new members to the party', *CW33*, p256.
35  Lenin *CW33*, p257.
36  See Rigby (1979), p49.
37  Rigby (1968), p81.

38  Rigby (1968), p75.
39  Rigby (1968), p109.
40  Fainsod (1961), p159.
41  Carr (1970b), p220.
42  Trotsky (1975a), p2.
43  Lenin 'Eighth congress of the RCP(B), report on the party programme', *CW29*, p184.
44  Rigby (1979), p51.
45  Narkiewicz (1970), p64.
46  Lenin 'Political report of the central committee of the RCP(B)', *CW33*, p288.
47  Lenin *CW33*, p288.
48  Lenin 'Notes dictated December 1922 — January 1923', *CW36*, p597.
49  Lenin *CW36*, pp605-6.
50  Lenin 'Better fewer, but better', *CW33*, p489.
51  Lenin *CW33*, pp501-2.
52  Lenin 'On co-operation', *CW33*, p475.
53  Carr (1969), p113.
54  Cited in Carr (1969), p314.
55  Carr (1969), p362.
56  Trotsky (1971a), p174.

# 2. The demise of proletarian power

By 1924 only the remnants of the proletarian dictatorship survived. The mass dilution of the Bolshevik Party through the 'Lenin levy' rendered the strategy of party renewal impossible. The party apparatus was in full control and the leadership around Stalin moved swiftly to neutralise and then defeat the Left Opposition. The defeat of the German working class in 1923 shattered the hope that Europe would come to the assistance of the Soviet Union and strengthened conservative trends in the Bolshevik Party.

At the same time it appeared that the New Economic Policy was beginning to pay off. While relying on revolutionary developments abroad seemed increasingly unrealistic, national reconstruction under the guidance of the state apparatus appeared to be a viable alternative. Economic revival legitimised the authority of the newly-emerging bureaucracy and extended its influence in society.

The party apparatus did not consciously set out to destroy the proletarian dictatorship. It simply came up with administrative solutions to social and economic problems. It refused to wage a struggle to re-awaken the political consciousness of the working class, an option which would undoubtedly have generated unrest and threatened the institutions on which the bureaucrats' power rested. In the difficult economic circumstances of the time, Soviet leaders regarded their positions and privileges as too important to risk in an unpredictable cultural revolution. The passivity of the masses allowed the bureaucrats to get on with their day-to-day tasks, while the successful implementation of the NEP held out the promise of future prosperity.

To ensure its survival the party apparatus forged an alliance with the remnants of the Tsarist state machine, the *kulaks* and the *nepmen*. Because these forces ultimately sought the restoration of capitalism, their alliance with the party apparatus was a marriage of convenience. Their pragmatic unity of purpose in the reconstruction of the economy and the destruction of the proletarian dictatorship was overshadowed by a basic conflict of interests. The violent upheavals of the late twenties showed the instability of this alliance and forced the bureaucracy to transform the whole of Soviet social and economic life.

## The price of economic reconstruction

For Lenin, the NEP was a temporary compromise. It was designed to harness market forces to stimulate economic development — but market forces were to be kept under strict state control. Lenin was aware of the danger that market forces might get out of hand, and therefore advised the greatest caution in implementing the NEP.

The loosening of restrictions on private industry and agriculture under the NEP reversed the trend towards economic decline. The production of food increased and, between 1923 and 1924, even manufacturing output began to rise. The success of the NEP and the demands of the peasantry encouraged the bureaucracy to extend it, and to reduce state control over agriculture still further. In spring 1925 state regulation of grain purchasing prices was made more flexible; agricultural taxes were cut; the deadline for the ending of state-sanctioned land leasing was postponed; and wage labour, previously limited to the harvesting season, was allowed fuller sway. In addition, various administrative barriers to free trade were removed. There were signs that a significant section of the party bureaucracy wanted to go even further — even to the extent of denationalising land entirely.[1]

The extension of the NEP did not simply provide peasants with incentives to increase agricultural output. The greater economic independence conceded to the *kulaks* also increased their social power as they could now use their control over marketable grain to extract new concessions from the workers' state. By contrast, the condition of the working class continued to deteriorate. The subsidies the state paid to agriculture starved the Soviet regime of funds for industrial development: it was as late as 1926 before investment in industry overtook depreciation.[2] As market forces gained more of a grip on the factories, thousands of workers were made redundant. By October 1925 nearly 1.3 million workers were unemployed.[3]

## Crisis in the countryside

The Left Opposition opposed the extension of market forces. Preobrazhensky, the opposition's chief economic spokesman, pointed out that the NEP could only work if the state sector steadily encroached on private enterprise. In his major work, *The new economics*, he showed that what was at issue was a struggle between two laws active in the Soviet economy: the law of value and the law of primitive socialist accumulation.[4] With his colleagues in the Left Opposition, he argued that encouraging the *kulaks* would lead to the growth of private capital and would weaken the bond between the state and the peasant economy. Preobrazhensky argued that pushing ahead with the NEP would not strengthen socialist accumulation, but rather lead to the restoration of capitalism. Unless industry grew steadily, he maintained, the NEP would fail. While the state would simply be unable to provide the peasants with the goods they wanted, they would have no incentive to put their grain on the market.

The party apparatus ignored the danger to the Soviet state from those social strata that rallied around the spread of market forces. Bukharin's famous 'wager on the peasant' speech in April 1925 revealed how blind the bureaucracy had become to the growing threat of capitalist restoration:

> 'Our policy in relation to the countryside should develop in the direction of removing, and in part abolishing, many restrictions which put the brake on the growth of the well-to-do and *kulak* farm. To the peasants, to all the peasants, we must say: enrich yourselves, develop your farms, and do not fear that constraints will be put on you.'[5]

The party apparatus became fully committed to the course outlined by Bukharin and denounced the Left Opposition for 'underestimating the peasantry'. No sooner, however, did the bureaucracy put its wager on the peasantry than things began to go wrong. By mid-1926 the apparatus began to realise that industrialisation could not be sustained without further investment. For all the cash in their pockets, peasants experienced acute shortages of manufactured goods. They therefore threatened to withhold grain from the cities. In November of the same year the party leadership, including Bukharin, came to the conclusion that investment in industry had to be stepped up to avert a crisis in the countryside.[6] But this discovery came too late. In 1927 the *kulaks* started withholding grain and in practice confirmed the Left Opposition's warning about the erosion of the bond between state and countryside.

At the fifteenth party congress in December 1927 the bureaucracy was forced to change tack. It now portrayed its former allies in the countryside as enemies of the system and began to curb the activities of the *kulaks*.[7] However in early 1928 the grain situation temporarily improved and the bureaucracy held back from further measures. But the *kulaks* continued to withhold their grain and by April 1928 the cities were threatened with famine. The bureaucracy was forced to requisition grain from rich peasants, disrupting the market relations developed under the NEP and provoking widespread violence in the countryside. However, the party's central committee remained cautious: as late as July 1928, it resolved to restrain the offensive against the *kulaks*. But as disruption in the countryside went further and further out of control, the abandonment of the NEP became inevitable.

The grain crisis came at the same time that relations between the Soviet Union and the imperialist powers again began to deteriorate. Between 1922 and 1926 the Soviet Union had come under little external pressure, but towards the end of 1926 Poland, backed by France, started to make menacing noises and Britain too joined in the threats. By spring 1927 Soviet society was, with considerable justification, gripped by war panic. British-backed forces attacked the Soviet legation in Peking and in May Britain broke off diplomatic relations with the Kremlin. When the Soviet representative in Warsaw was assassinated in June, Stalin's military aide Voroshilov expressed the insecurity of the Soviet bureaucracy:

**'If I personally am of the opinion that a war this year is improbable, events develop so rapidly that we cannot predict with certainty what awaits us in the immediate future....It can come in two years or in one year, but it is possible, though not probable, that the delay might be only a few months.'**[8]

The challenge to the security of the Soviet Union heightened the regime's awareness of the need to build up industry. Converging external and internal crises pushed the Soviet regime into launching an industrialisation drive. As the supply of grain dwindled the bureaucracy became panic-stricken. By 1929 the system of voluntary grain deliveries had broken down and the bureaucracy was forced to organise expeditions to plunder the countryside for grain. These raids were haphazardly transformed into a programme of forced collectivisation.

Collectivisation was an irrational policy because Soviet agriculture was too backward to allow collective farming methods to work effectively.[9] However, the central motivation behind the establishment of collective farms was not the quest for higher agricultural productivity, but the need to maintain political control of the countryside. Forced collectivisation led to the liquidation of the *kulaks* and to years of chaos and stagnation in agriculture. This was the final consequence of pushing ahead with the NEP without a policy of curbing the effects of market forces.

## Workers' control usurped

The fusion of the party apparatus with the state bureaucracy pushed the working class to the margins of political life. By 1924 the bureaucracy was so independent of proletarian pressure that it could pursue its interests without resistance. Over the next five years the consolidation of the bureaucracy was given maximum assistance by the other beneficiaries of the NEP—the former Tsarist specialists, the intelligentsia, the *nepmen* and the *kulaks* were all firmly behind the new regime. This alliance only fell apart when the conflicting interests of its constituent elements could no longer be reconciled within the existing system.

The power of the party apparatus rested on its control over industry and its monopoly over the state's repressive apparatus. At the same time the NEP and all the services required in economic reconstruction gave the other beneficiaries of the system considerable social power. But while in the short run the aims of the professionals and entrepreneurs corresponded with those of the bureaucracy, in the long run, as Carr notes, their interests lay in the restoration of capitalism: 'Under NEP the bureaucracy, the managers, the technicians, and the intelligentsia — the "officer corps"of the new society — were predominantly, almost exclusively, made up of elements alien to the regime.'[10] The influence of the traditional intelligentsia remained considerable. They still had a big say in running industry, and retained significant authority within the state machine. In 1929 less than 12 per cent of state employees were communists: former Tsarist officals made up 52 per cent of the staff of local government in Leningrad and a higher proportion still in the provinces. In the commissariats of finance and labour they made up respectively 37 and 27 per cent of personnel.[11]

The social position and influence over the state of the pro-capitalist forces, although important, were not however their most important strength. As long as the state owned the means of production, maintained its monopoly over foreign trade and controlled the instruments of coercion, the party bureaucracy could keep a firm grip on Soviet society. The key influence of the pro-market forces was the political sway they came to exert over the ruling party. During the twenties the party developed close links with these forces, and, as a result, conservative tendencies were greatly strengthened.

The party continued to pay lip-service to revolutionary politics, but was compelled to develop an ideology that corresponded to its real interests. Stalin's theory of 'socialism in one country' held out the possibility of economic development in the Soviet Union in isolation from the rest of the world; it gave the bureaucracy a coherent social outlook. The elaboration of this theory was significant, because it showed that sections of the party apparatus had evolved a consciousness of their distinct — and distinctly narrow — interests.

The bureaucracy faced little working class opposition. It succeeded in assimilating the more advanced workers into its ranks, while the privileges that went with party membership, marginal though they were, allowed it to pull together a base of support among a key layer of worker aristocrats.[12] The party and the trade unions actively defended the sectional interests of the better-off workers against the unemployed and the less skilled layers of the working class. Conservative traits were particularly striking in the rural areas, where rich peasants predominated among party members, rapidly forming a 'new communist elite...consisting of local officials and relatively well-to-do farmers'.[13] Rigby's study of party membership also suggests that rural members saw the Bolsheviks as the 'party of encouragement for private peasant enterprise'.[14]

In the early twenties the party bureaucracy was merely a distinct layer that relied on administrative rather than political means to defend the Soviet regime. By the end of the decade it had become an elite which was aware of its sectional interests and deeply suspicious of proletarian revolution. The transformation was gradual because, despite the depoliticisation of the rank and file, the party bureaucracy itself was far from homogeneous. While the Left Opposition remained influential in the higher echelons of the party until the late twenties, another section — particularly susceptible to pro-capitalist influences — crystallised into the Right Opposition in 1929.

Although there was considerable factional strife within the apparatus, all sections of the party leadership were united in their commitment to preserve the existing regime. The lack of serious opposition strengthened the power of the bureaucracy even when — as in its persistence with the NEP in the late twenties — its own policies led to disaster. In the end, however, the Stalinist bureaucracy discovered that, while its policies could depoliticise the working class, they could not guarantee the survival of its rule.

In the years of the NEP the revolution was destroyed, but the question of who would rule remained unresolved. The period was marked by a temporary alliance between the old and the new, but the inherent instability of that alliance forced the bureaucracy in a direction over which it had no control.

## The Left Opposition

Through much of the twenties the Left Opposition fought to salvage the gains of the October Revolution. It campaigned relentlessly for the adoption of revolutionary policies and put forward a systematic critique of the bureaucracy's programme. The opposition however consisted mainly of well-known revolutionary figures who had assumed important posts in management, administration or in the army; it lacked a mass base in the working class. The depoliticisation of the party membership and the growing climate of conservatism meant that there was little wider resonance for the opposition's critique of the bureaucracy. As a result its struggle was conducted largely within the framework of the apparatus.

The Left Opposition's strategy and tactics doomed its supporters to playing the role of permanent oppositionists within the bureaucracy. Aware of the fragile hold of the party over the state, the opposition feared the consequences of a split at the highest level of the party. The opposition leaders' longstanding commitment to the revolution inhibited them from taking any steps which might, even temporarily, weaken the party. To some extent the opposition underestimated the extent of the degeneration of the party itself, identifying external factors such as the old Tsarist officials or the *kulaks* and *nepmen*, rather than the party leadership itself, as the source of the problem.

It was as late as 1926 before the opposition took stock of how far the working class had been weakened. Writing in November 1926, Trotsky observed how things had changed for the worse since 1917: 'The proletariat today is considerably less receptive to revolutionary perspectives and to broad generalisations than it was during the October Revolution and in the ensuing few years.' Trotsky noted that quiescence and passivity in the working class now constituted 'the basic political background of party life':

> **'These are the moods which bureaucratism — as an element of "law and order" and "tranquility" — relies on. The attempt of the opposition to put the new problems before the party ran up against precisely these moods.'**[15]

Before 1926 the Left Opposition limited its critique to the problem of the bureaucratisation of the party, while also putting forward detailed proposals for industrialisation. It adopted a fairly narrow focus because it considered that the cause of party unity made a showdown out of the question. But the result was that it was outmanoeuvred by the leadership around Stalin. For his part, Trotsky took a back seat in many of the controversies right up until the formation of the United Opposition in spring 1926. It was Zinoviev who made the first public attack on Stalin's theory of 'socialism in one country' in October 1925. Trotsky delayed until the fifteenth party conference in November 1926 before launching his devastating critique of Stalin's theory.

By late 1926, however, the rapid pace of events compelled the Left Opposition to drop its diplomatic tactics and go on the offensive. But while Trotsky was aware of the reactionary nature of the bureaucracy, he still tended to overestimate the revolutionary potential of the party. His writings on the dangers of counter-revolution in the mid-twenties projected into the future problems that were already a reality. In December 1927 he noted the growth of 'elements of Thermidor', but asserted his faith that the party could still reform itself:

> **'Power has not yet been torn from the hands of the proletariat. It is still possible to rectify our political course, remove the elements of dual power and reinforce the dictatorship by measures of a reformist kind.'**[16]

One month after Trotsky's expulsion from the party and one month before he was to be exiled by Stalin, the Left Opposition still hoped that the party could be revived.

To its credit, the Left Opposition did attempt to broaden out its struggle, particularly in late 1927. In October and November, at risk of imprisonment or exile, the opposition leaders organised scores of meetings and demonstrations. But all this was too little and too late. Moreover the opposition remained tied to the view that the main danger came from the right of the party. It consistently underestimated the threat from Stalin, the centre and the apparatus.

The end of the NEP era in 1928 and the bureaucracy's subsequent 'left turn' caused further confusion within the Left Opposition. Trotsky misinterpreted the new policies as an unconscious struggle against capitalist elements, and, along with his comrades, regarded the Shakhty showtrial in March 1928 and the drive against the *kulaks* as moves necessary for the defence of the revolution. Trotsky appealed for critical support for the group of bureaucrats around Stalin. He considered that their fight against the right made them a 'centrist' force:

'A break between the centre and the rights would mean a class fissure, with the propertied elements dragging Rykov much further to the right, and the workers dragging Stalin much further to the left. In the long term, there could be a civil war between us and the army of the rights and a common front between us and the army of the centrists.'[17]

Despite his misgivings about the centre, Trotsky saw its leftward shift as a result of working class pressure — as a positive response to events. His overestimation of the leverage of the working class on an essentially reactionary bureaucracy threw him off course.

In September 1929 Trotsky identified a bureaucratic twist of policy as a struggle to retain the last vestiges of proletarian power:

'Stalin found himself driven, simultaneously with the crushing of the Left Opposition, to plagiarise partially from its programme in all fields, to direct his fire to the right, and to convert an internal party manoeuvre into a very sharp and prolonged zigzag to the left. This shows that despite everything the proletariat still possesses powers to exert pressure and that the state apparatus still remains dependent on it. Upon this cardinal fact the Russian Opposition must continue to base its own policy, which is the policy of reform and not of revolution.'[18]

It was not working class pressure that forced the bureaucracy to change course, but rather its instinct for self-preservation. The party was already an empty shell and the working class posed no problems for the state apparatus. The *nepmen* however were a serious threat to the bureaucracy: they had to be eliminated.

The Left Opposition's confusion arose from its analysis of the growth of the bureaucracy. Trotsky and his colleagues focused on the influence of the old bourgeois forces on the course of events. This influence was real enough — but it was always held in check by the party apparatus. The apparatus itself was the real problem. The bureaucratisation of the party was the result not merely of external forces, but of the growing differentiation of a working class aristocracy from the rest of the proletariat. The ruling bureaucratic stratum was not a foreign body grafted on to a healthy proletariat, but was thrown up by the working class itself. As proletarian power disintegrated, the working class split into different sections and the leading stratum was transformed into a distinct social layer closely integrated into the state machine.

Among the leaders of the Left Opposition, only Rakovsky probed the problem of the proletarian base of the bureaucracy. In August 1928, in his famous letter 'On the "professional dangers" of power', he focused on the differentiation within the working class:

> **'When a class takes power, one of its parts becomes the agent of that power. Thus arises bureaucracy. In a socialist state, where capitalist accumulation is forbidden by members of the directing party, this differentiation begins as a functional one: it later becomes a social one.'**[19]

Rakovsky argued that the Soviet bureaucrats had 'changed to such a point that not only objectively but subjectively, not only materially but also morally, they have ceased to be a part of this very same working class'.[20]

Rakovsky's line of inquiry was not pursued further. The opposition was too closely bound up with the past and too integrated into the party to see the need to conduct its struggle outside party channels. It paid a bitter price for its confusion. When Stalin shifted leftwards the opposition was thrown into disarray — many of its members recanted and joined the apparatus. Only the most fervent exponents of proletarian internationalism such as Trotsky were able to stand up to the pressure of the bureaucracy.

## Notes

1  According to Rousset, in 1925 'the commissar for agriculture of Georgia, with Stalin's connivance, lodged a project for the abolition of the nationalisation of land'. See Rousset (1982), p30.
2  Carr (1970a), p367.
3  Carr (1970a), p389.
4  Preobrazhensky (1967), pp136-46.
5  Carr (1970a), p286.
6  See Cohen (1973), pp244-6.
7  Carr & Davies (1974), p39. It is significant that the expulsion of Trotsky and Zinoviev from the party on 14 November 1927 coincided with the worsening of the grain situation.
8  Carr (1978), p9.
9  Of the area under grain in 1928, 10 per cent was still ploughed with the wooden plough, 75 per cent was sown by hand, half the crop was harvested with scythe and sickle and 40 per cent was threshed by hand. See Carr (1978), p232.
10  Carr (1970a), p130.
11  Carr (1970a), p130.
12  Carr notes: 'In spite of manifold shortcomings, the availability of a ladder of promotion and the opening of the party ranks to a relatively large number of workers sufficed to create a nucleus of approval for the regime among the more advanced and articulate sectors of the proletariat, and the improvement, however gradual and halting, of material standards of life kept the mass of workers docile, if not actively sympathetic to the regime. After 1923 few signs appeared of any widespread proletarian discontent with the new order.' Carr (1970a), p124.
13  Rigby (1968), p171.
14  Rigby (1968), p172.
15  Trotsky (1980), p170.
16  Trotsky (1980), p189.
17  Trotsky (1981), p288.
18  Trotsky (1975b), p286.
19  Rakovsky (1980), p126.
20  Rakovsky (1980), p130.

# 3. The emergence of the new society

The social upheaval precipitated by the shortage of grain in 1927 and 1928 revealed that the marriage of convenience between the party bureaucracy and the *nepmen* had broken down. The bureaucracy was at first slow to grasp the gravity of the crisis, but once it realised that its very survival was at stake it reacted with a frenzy. A programme originally drawn up to increase industrial capacity was transformed into an all-out drive to restructure the economy. The first five year plan, launched in April 1929, sought to provide the Soviet economy with a secure industrial base. The plan projected wider state control over the economy and the destruction of market relations.

The bureaucracy could no longer rely on its old allies and, to preserve its own rule, it turned to crush their influence. Stalin's new theory of 'the intensification of the class struggle' showed his willingness to use revolutionary rhetoric to mobilise working class support for the drive against the *kulaks* and the traditional intelligentsia. In March 1928 the state prosecutor announced the discovery of a 'counter-revolutionary economic conspiracy' in the Shakhty region of the Donbass. The ensuing showtrial was the signal for an all-out offensive against the old specialists, the intelligentsia and the former Tsarist bureaucrats. As a result of the purge in the Donbass, by 1931 50 per cent of all engineering and technical workers had been arrested.[1]

The bureaucracy also set out to destroy the power of the *kulaks* and the *nepmen*. Forced collectivisation destroyed the power of the *kulaks* and plunged the countryside into chaos. Millions of peasants were uprooted and more than a million homesteads were exiled under the 'dekulakisation' campaign.[2] The attack on the *nepmen* led to the eviction of around 500 000 merchants and millions of others were deprived of their civil rights.[3] By 1931 the end result of these moves was that the capitalist sector of the economy was in ruins.

The immediate objective of the bureaucracy was to destroy the social forces which had thrived under the NEP. Its long-term goal was industrialisation and the establishment of an economic base under its direct control. What actually emerged was the product of improvisation and reaction to the exigencies of maintaining state control over Soviet society.

## Industrialisation

The destruction of the NEP sector meant that the Soviet Union was deprived of its central mechanism for the allocation of labour-time. From the early twenties the state-controlled market had been the driving force behind economic recovery. As a result of the erosion of working class control and the disappearance of even rudimentary organisations of workers' democracy, conscious planning played little role in the Soviet economy. The effect of the industrialisation and collectivisation drives was that the bureaucracy was left with neither a market nor the capacity for the conscious direction of resources through planning. The only way it could now organise the distribution of labour-time was through direct political control and coercion. The central bureaucracy and the police force had to become involved in every detail of economic life to gain even a semblance of control over economic development.

The economic recovery during the NEP period provided the basis for further industrialisation. By 1928 the working class had recovered its pre-First World War numbers.[4] Moreover, although there was a pressing need for new investment, industry was still not working at full capacity. According to a leading economist of the period, unused capacity in industry in 1928 was around 30 per cent.[5] Much of the initial spurt in industry under the five year plan took place through the more efficient utilisation of already existing plant.

The industrialisation drive still required considerable investment in plant and machinery. In the course of capitalist development the source of industrial investment has generally been the surplus transferred from agriculture. But the collectivisation drive created such an upheaval in the countryside that agricultural production and productivity actually fell. Losses of livestock between 1928 and 1933 were catastrophic, accounting for almost 27 per cent of the total capital stock in 1928, according to one estimate.[6] By 1932 famine ravaged the Soviet Union, leading to more than five million deaths over the next two years.

It is impossible to sustain the traditional view that the collectivisation of agriculture provided the funds for industrial investment: 'Measured in 1928 prices, the net agricultural surplus was small before collectivisation (four per cent of national income in 1928) and fell to negligible levels (0.5 per cent of national income on average in 1930-2) as a result of collectivisation.'[7] In all probability agriculture actively impeded industrialisation during the first five year plan. In fact the investment fund for industrialisation was provided by the sweat and toil of the working class.

The industrialisation drive depended on the mass recruitment of peasants into industry. Between 1928 and 1932 more than eight million peasants were drawn into the factories and, by 1934, the size of the working class had doubled in five years to reach nearly 23 million. The employment of millions of new workers at real wages considerably lower than 1928 levels was the secret source of the funds for industrialisation. A sharp fall in living standards meant that an extraordinarily large proportion of society's output was available for investment. The share of capital accumulation in the national income rose from 19.4 per cent to 30.3 per cent in 1932.[8]

The combination of spare capacity, mass migration from the countryside, poverty-line incomes and the intensification of labour provided the basis for Soviet industrialisation. At the time Rakovsky recognised the key role of the exploitation of labour in the Stalinist industrialisation drive:

'**The decisive factor in this growth has not been the increase of fixed capital or the expansion of industry's technological base, but the more intensive utilisation of old fixed capital which comes, on the one hand, from the rise in the number of workers and on the other hand, from the greater intensification of labour.**'[9]

The bureaucracy also began to purchase foreign technology on a large scale during the period of the first five year plan, but it only began to have an impact after 1934, when it contributed to very high growth rates over the next three years.[10]

Industrialisation transformed Soviet society, but at a terrible price. The bureaucracy could drive peasants into the factories and force them to raise output, but the spectacular growth rates of the early thirties mystified the essential processes at work. Industrial output rose by between 35 and 45 per cent in the three years up to 1932, but this performance was achieved through an 89 per cent increase in the industrial workforce. In terms of output per head, this amounted to a drop of more than 30 per cent.[11] Jasny has pointed out the secret of industrialisation — the massively increased exploitation of the working class.

'Instead of increasing by 110 per cent in five years, as foreseen in the first five year plan, output per man in industry declined by perhaps 25 per cent in the last three years of operation. Only the very large decline in real wages may have prevented an increase in production costs in industry (in real terms).'[12]

The blind drive to achieve ever higher production targets culminated in disaster in 1933, when industrial output itself began to decline and the bureaucracy was forced to call the 'all-out drive' to raise output to a halt.

The 1933 slowdown, leading to an unplanned 14 per cent drop in investment, revealed that Soviet industry could not yet absorb the investment funds that were available. Fortunately for the bureaucracy the investments it had made earlier, particularly in foreign technology, were beginning to have an effect on industrial growth. Between 1933 and 1936 output per man increased by more than 30 per cent. As consumption remained minimal, funds for investment grew.[13] Soviet industry entered its boom years — by 1937 the Soviet Union could boast enough heavy industry to build a modern arms sector.

In 1937 stagnation set in once again. The bureaucracy's lack of control over the economy limited the process of cumulative growth. The great purges of that year and the pressures to prepare for war prevented balanced industrial development. The bureaucracy had proved that it could establish heavy industry, but, as it was unable to plan society's resources, it could not control the forces it had unleashed.

## The consolidation of the bureaucracy

Whatever the costs, industrialisation guaranteed the survival of the bureaucracy. Despite the devastation wrought by the Second World War, total output in 1955 was nearly four times that of 1928.[14] This achievement required the destruction of the petit bourgeoisie in the countryside and the fierce repression of the working class. The bureaucracy used terror systematically to create a modern industrial sector.

During the thirties the Soviet working class was virtually enslaved. The task of recruiting new workers and keeping the rest under firm control became the major preoccupation of the bureaucracy. The decline of real wages and the deterioration in working conditions, housing and social services provoked considerable unrest in the factories. Workers voted with their feet and went from one factory to another looking for better conditions. In 1930 the average duration of employment in mining and iron ore production was about four months.[15]

The bureaucracy was obliged to use force because it could offer no economic incentive to attract workers into the factories or to keep them working. Its only solution to high labour turnover was terror. Every year the authorities introduced new laws to discipline workers, bringing in labour passports, work books and stringent regulations on absenteeism. A 1939 regulation proclaimed that anybody who was more than 20 minutes late for work was liable to be charged with unjustified absence. A 'reform' introduced in June 1940 made absenteeism a criminal offence.[16]

The bureaucracy, however, could not guarantee its survival through terror alone. Even at the height of the first five year plan it began to attempt to create a social base of support for the emerging order. The working class membership of the party furnished the bureaucracy with a distinct layer committed to the new regime. Party membership now became a passport to social advancement. During the first five year plan, more than 100 000 party members — nearly one tenth of the total — entered higher education.[17] The bureaucracy was determined to forge a new intelligentsia that was drawn from the party ranks and hence loyal to the new regime.

Industrialisation and collectivisation created tremendous scope for upward mobility. Specialists, technicians, supervisors and directors were in great demand in industry, agriculture and state administration. The purge of the old specialists meant that party members could be rewarded with leading positions in industry.[18] Between May 1930 and October 1933 the proportion of party members among directors and deputy directors of industrial undertakings rose from 29 to 70 per cent. A similar process took place in administration and government.[19]

The new intelligentsia provided the bureaucracy with a degree of support in society. From an early stage this layer of privileged party members was aware of its separate sectional interest. As early as 1931 Stalin openly proclaimed that this 'new stratum of working class' was indispensable for the survival of the system:

> 'Our country has entered a phase of development in which the working class must create its own industrial and technical intelligentsia, one that is capable of upholding the interests of the working class in production as the interests of the ruling class.
>
> 'No ruling class has managed without its own intelligentsia. There are no grounds for believing that the working class of the USSR can manage without its own industrial and technical intelligentsia.'[20]

By the early thirties the bureaucracy felt sufficiently confident to rehabilitate many of the old specialists. Yesterday's 'wreckers' now worked 'hand in hand with the working class'.[21]

As the bureaucracy consolidated its grip the rhetoric of 'class struggle' receded into the background. In 1936 Stalin reported 'the victory of socialism': in the Soviet Union, he argued, the elimination of exploiting classes and exploitation itself now rendered the class struggle obsolete. To justify the status quo Stalin redefined class relations, insisting that the working class could no longer be called the proletariat because it now owned the means of production. This attempt to create an image of social harmony by juggling terms aimed to legitimise the position of the new intellectual elite. For Stalin the intelligentsia was 'now an equal member of Soviet society, in which side by side with the workers and peasants, pulling together with them, it is engaged in building the new, classless, socialist society'.[22]

The composition of the party came to reflect the social weight of the new stratum of directors, specialists, technicians, supervisors and administrators. Recruitment was directed towards the intelligentsia and the proportion of working class party members dropped steadily. In 1929 around 81 per cent of the recruits came from the working class, but by 1939-41 this figure had dropped to 20 per cent. Some 70 per cent of the intake came from the intelligentsia and white collar personnel.[23]

The new ruling stratum created through the industrialisation drive was determined to maintain its privileges. The new hierarchical relations were justified on the grounds of technical efficiency. Egalitarianism, particularly in the sphere of wages, was denounced as a petit-bourgeois deviation.

To expand the base of support of the bureaucracy still further, skilled workers too were given special benefits. Documents from Soviet archives reveal that the vast majority of unskilled and semi-skilled workers were made to bear the burden of the industrialisation drive.[24] The growing exclusiveness of education was yet another sign that the new intelligentsia intended to monopolise all routes to power in Soviet society. In the twenties all workers had been positively encouraged to go into higher education; by 1935 admission had reverted to criteria based on merit.

By the end of the thirties the intelligentsia could ensure the perpetuation of its privileges. At the eighteenth party congress in March 1939 key speakers referred to the intelligentsia — not the working class — as the leading section of society. Molotov observed that in the Soviet Union it was 'the most advanced people who set the mark'. 'Who are these foremost people? They are politically conscious communists, non-party Bolsheviks, Stakhanovites, those in the lead on the collective farms and members of the socialist intelligentsia.'[25] The bureaucracy modified its ideology to uphold the leading role of its main social bulwark.

According to figures released at the eighteenth party congress, the Soviet intelligentsia numbered almost 10 million people. Families of the intelligentsia included, this layer made up no less than 13 per cent of the population. As the table below shows, the intelligentsia was a heterogeneous stratum composed of factory directors, doctors and teachers who enjoyed widely varying access to privileges and wealth. By no means all members of the intelligentsia were committed to the new regime; yet a significant number had sufficient privileges guaranteed by it to have a stake in its preservation.

Given the grinding poverty of Soviet society in this period, even relatively minor privileges — such as access to decent housing — acquired enormous importance. The most loyal supporters of the bureaucracy were to be found among the 1.8 million executives in industry and agriculture, many of whom had risen from the ranks of the proletariat to the heights of industry. Their positions and privileges were directly dependent on the patronage of the new regime.

### Composition of the Soviet intelligentsia, in January 1937 (by profession)[26]

| | |
|---|---:|
| Directors and other executives of establishments, institutions, factory departments, state farms, collective farms etc | 1 751 000 |
| Engineers and architects (exclusive of directors and other executives of establishments and factory departments) | 250 000 |
| Intermediate technical personnel (technicians, construction chiefs, foresters, railroad station masters and others) | 810 000 |
| Agronomists | 80 000 |
| Miscellaneous scientific personnel for agriculture (land surveyors and persons specially trained in land improvement, scientific farming and stock breeding) | 96 000 |
| Scientific workers (professors, university faculty members and others) | 80 000 |
| Teachers | 969 000 |
| Cultural workers (journalists, librarians, club managers and others) | 297 000 |
| Art workers | 159 000 |
| Physicians | 132 000 |
| Intermediate medical personnel (feldshers, midwives and trained nurses) | 382 000 |
| Economists and statisticians | 822 000 |
| Book-keepers and accountants | 1 617 000 |
| Judiciary and procurator staffs (judges, procurators, investigators and others) | 46 000 |
| University and college students | 550 000 |
| Miscellaneous groups of intellectuals (inclusive of the intelligentsia in the armed forces) | 1 550 000 |
| **Total** | **9 591 000** |

## Limits to the consolidation of the bureaucracy

The new intelligentsia provided an essential social base for the Soviet bureaucracy. However, economic backwardness and chaos imposed severe limits on the creation of a stable ruling stratum. The economy was too fragmented and too far out of control to allow the new relations among different sections of society to stabilise and become self-perpetuating. The fact that repression was the only reliable means of regulating the economy and controlling society meant that there was permanent conflict within the bureaucracy. Even the beneficiaries of the new regime could not feel secure.

The thirties was the era of the purges. Because of the spectacular scale of the showtrials and the mass executions, commentators have concentrated attention on conspiracies and evil deeds. Without in any sense underestimating the horror of the purges, or the responsibility of the Stalinist regime for the atrocities it carried out, it is essential to take a wider and more dispassionate view of the purges. Force was the only instrument available to the Soviet bureaucracy to maintain the coherence of the new social formation.

Terror was essential to discipline the working class and also to keep the bureaucracy itself in line. The regime had to have a means of controlling officials who might be driven by circumstances to take decisions at variance with the requirements of the central apparatus. The centre demoted or transferred officials at regular intervals to prevent individuals from building up sectional or regional power bases. But as such measures had only limited effect, the regime needed to deploy more far-reaching deterrents.

Terror could not eliminate chaos (indeed it often exacerbated it) but it could curb some of the consequences of economic fragmentation and ensure that factory directors and other officials would not ignore the directives of the central bureaucracy. The climate of fear created by the purges discouraged autonomous action and ensured maximum subordination to the dictates of the bureaucracy. However, the purges were no more consciously planned than the economy, and as force was the bureaucrats' answer to every problem, they responded to every new problem with even more force.

The purges enabled the Stalinist regime to eliminate the last vestiges of the Bolshevik tradition. By liquidating the Old Bolsheviks, Stalin ensured that the bureaucracy's links with the past were severed and that its members owed their position in every respect to the new society. The regime also used the purges in an attempt to give it wider popularity. Stalin sought to channel workers' dissatisfactions with the new society against the victims of the purges, who were blamed for all prevailing social problems.

Many observers have drawn attention to the apparently irrational aspects of the purges and showtrials — the continual invention of new enemies, the destruction of the officer corps of the Soviet army, etc. It is true that by 1937 the system of purges had become so far out of hand that they threatened the bureaucracy itself. However, it would be mistaken to reduce the purges to the influence of irrational forces or to the peculiarities of Stalin's personality. The purges were the outcome of the irrational social formation that emerged in the thirties. Stalin did not consciously set out on a campaign of mass terror; this was the consequence of a system of bureaucratic power which could not be exercised through a framework of rules and regulations, but only through *reactive* force.

## The new order

The achievements of the industrialisation drive should not be underestimated. According to revised Soviet figures published in the sixties, industrial output grew at an annual rate of 19.2 per cent in the first five year plan, 17.8 per cent in the second, and 13.2 per cent in the prolonged third plan.[27] A heavy industrial sector was created which went on to sustain the Soviet military machine throughout the Second World War. The massive investment in industry meant that, by 1937, 80 per cent of industrial output was produced by plants that were either newly built or completely restructured.[28]

These achievements were all the more significant because the bureaucracy lacked the means to regulate the labour-time of society. Despite its claims, it could not genuinely plan the Soviet economy. The drive to industrialise and collectivise agriculture was out of control from the beginning. The original 1929 plan targets were consistently revised and the decision to go for wholesale collectivisation made the original targets for agricultural output redundant. As Molotov noted in 1929, talking about the five year plan in agriculture was a 'useless affair'.[29]

During the first five year plan the bureaucracy simply stepped up its targets and hoped for the best. In this way forced industrialisation could compensate for the lack of economic regulators. This method of progress was very costly: it widened the Soviet Union's industrial base, but by a colossal squandering of resources. In 1939 Stalin revealed that the bureaucracy was well aware of the consequences of forced industrialisation:

'We were confronted by a dilemma: either to begin with the instruction of people in technical grammar schools and to postpone for ten years the production and mass utilisation of machines, until technically trained people are turned out by the schools: or to proceed directly to the building of machines and to develop a mass utilisation of machines in the national economy so that in the very process of building and utilising machines people would be taught technique and trained cadres would be turned out. We chose the second alternative. We proceeded openly and consciously to the inevitable outlays and over-expenditures associated with the shortage of sufficiently trained people who know how to handle machines. True, we destroyed many machines at the same time. But at the same time we won the most important thing — time — and we created the most precious thing in the economy — cadres.'[30]

Stalin's bureaucracy was prepared to destroy 'many machines' to realise its objectives.

However, destroying machines was no passing phenomenon: the misuse of resources was a defining feature of the social system. Bureaucratic control over the economy could only influence the *quantity* of output, not its *quality*. From the beginning the new system proved incapable of producing products of the right quality. Hence while output increased throughout the thirties, the quality of goods continued to deteriorate. The bureaucracy's failure to solve this problem led to the enactment, in July 1940, of a decree on 'the production of low quality or incomplete goods and non-fulfilment of official standards'. Under this decree, directors, engineers and inspectors of technical control could receive up to eight years in jail if found guilty of producing poor quality, incomplete or substandard goods.[31]

The threat of imprisonment may have put fear into factory directors, but it could not establish a framework for the efficient allocation of resources. Directors were forced to meet physical targets — what happened to their products after they left the factory was not their concern. They did not have to sell their products, they had to meet targets. Often meeting targets meant producing shoddy goods, products that were not use values, but quantities of things that could be added up to meet the plan targets.

The bureaucracy's only real sanction over the directors was the central system for allocating materials, the *mattekhsnab*.[32] The *mattekhsnab* gave a semblance of consistency to the state's distribution of resources, and gave the bureaucracy the power to determine economic priorities and establish new sectors of production. But control over material resources could not guarantee consistency in the distribution of resources. At best it was a form of negative control — the power to withhold inputs.

Once resources were distributed, the state had no mechanism for ensuring that they were deployed in accordance with its objectives. In 1933 and again in 1937 it became apparent that the bureaucracy had lost control over its investments. In these years investment could not be absorbed by the economy and projects, once begun, were often left uncompleted.

## Growth without harmony

Despite the inefficient allocation of society's labour-time, the Soviet Union managed to industrialise. It succeeded largely because the bureaucracy's utilisation of labour-time was unimpeded. Under capitalism, the process of exchange establishes the social average of labour input into commodities and only labour which is socially necessary counts as value-creating labour. The distribution of labour-time is thus regulated through the exchange of commodities.

By contrast, in the Soviet Union in the thirties, the market had been destroyed and value relations no longer restricted the distribution of labour-time. Labour was not required to create values — it had only to create useful products (use values). The only limit on the distribution of labour-time was the total number of workers, the total physical labour available. Even without conscious planning, the Soviet bureaucracy managed, through the deployment of vast reserves of labour, to raise output and establish new industries. In the Soviet Union factories may have required three or four times as much labour to build them as in the USA, but they were still built. What a capitalist society — or a workers' democracy — would have regarded as a waste of labour, the Soviet bureaucracy viewed as the inescapable price of industrialisation.

The rapid growth of the industrial workforce is a common feature of societies undergoing the early stages of industrial development. But the further progress of industry depends on raising the productivity of labour. Higher productivity demands the utilisation of new machinery or techniques which lead to an increase in the output of each individual worker. Forced industrialisation in the Soviet Union relied on manpower growth rather than growth in productivity. The frantic search for new sources of labour from the late thirties onwards revealed a central barrier to Soviet industrial development.

The destruction of the market in the Soviet Union allowed the bureaucracy to distribute resources without considering the criterion of profitability. Just as labour could be freely distributed, so the bureaucracy could choose where to invest both the products of labour and the rich natural wealth of the Soviet Union. Investment resources were often mismanaged; but high rates of investment ensured that new plant and machinery were built, and that at least some new industries were established. Given its ineffective allocation of resources, and its low levels of productivity, the system needed a high rate of investment to achieve a modest degree of growth.

High rates of investment in the Soviet Union presupposed low levels of consumption. Bureaucratic terror ensured that the consumption and living standards of the working class remained at subsistence levels. As late as 1950 food consumption per head was still below 1928 levels.[33]

The final important component of Soviet industrial growth was foreign technology. The state monopoly of foreign trade allowed the Soviet Union to select technology from abroad. Foreign firms, desperate for sales during the world slump of the inter-war years, competed fiercely to sell their wares to a single customer—the state trade commission. This was the only sphere in which the bureaucracy could plan sales and purchases.[34] Moreover, the unified system of resource allocation made sure that foreign technology was rapidly assimilated into Soviet industry. One important study draws a direct link between foreign technology and industrial growth, concluding that 'those sectors with high rates of growth had high levels of technical assistance.'[35]

The mass mobilisation of manpower reserves and other resources, harsh constraints on consumption and the rapid assimilation of foreign technology together ensured the development of Soviet industry. But even during the thirties industrial growth was problematic. The inefficient distribution of labour-time meant that low quality and productivity soon became deeply entrenched. However, while industry was restricted to a few sectors and the division of labour was fairly limited, the bureaucracy could maintain a degree of control. The high growth rates of physical outputs disguised the limitations of this form of industrial development.

The apparent link between booming industrial growth and a centrally planned economy in the Soviet Union — at a time of worldwide capitalist stagnation — seemed to vindicate Stalin's theories and methods, especially abroad. Most foreign observers were impressed by the growth statistics and the grand plans drawn up by the bureaucracy. They did not see the state of controlled chaos that prevailed in Soviet factories.

## Critics in the wilderness

From his position in exile during the thirties, Trotsky followed developments in the Soviet Union closely. His writings provide the most developed analysis of Soviet society available at the time. Written from a solid foundation in the Bolshevik tradition, Trotsky's theory contains insights which remain valuable; however his assessment also contains a number of defects. A reappraisal of Trotsky's theory is worthwhile because many of its defects are evident in contemporary Marxist literature. Trotsky's main fault was that he regarded the pattern of Soviet society in the thirties as the mere continuation of trends established in the twenties. Failing to appreciate that profound changes had taken place, Trotsky perceived Stalin's bureaucracy as the simple extension of the party apparatus of 1924, rather than as a newly emerging stratum of society.

Trotsky's analysis of the Soviet Union went through several stages. The period between 1928 and 1933 may be regarded as the low point of his theory. As we have seen, Trotsky and the Left Opposition failed to grasp the significance of the 1929 turn, firmly believing that this tragic finale to the 1917 Revolution was forced on the bureaucracy by working class pressure. As late as 1931, after market relations had been thoroughly destroyed, Trotsky believed that the tension that had existed between the state-controlled and the market sectors in the twenties still existed:

'The relationship of forces between the socialist and the capitalist elements of the economy has undoubtedly been shifted to the benefit of the former.'[36]

Even in the early thirties Trotsky still identified the *nepmen* and the pro-market sectors as the main threat to Soviet society. He was thus inclined to accept the bureaucracy's rhetoric about saboteurs and wreckers. Sadly, Trotsky took at face value 'the saboteurs' trial' in 1930, and accepted the validity of the confessions of the so-called 'industrial party'.[37] Similarly he accepted the confessions of the 'Menshevik centre' at the 1931 showtrial.[38] Trotsky believed much of the confessions at these trials, not only because he lacked factual information, but because his own analysis predisposed him to see a threat from the pro-capitalist elements rather than from the bureaucracy itself.

Trotsky remained bitterly critical of the bureaucracy and its turn towards industrialisation. He correctly condemned the 1929 turn as economic adventurism and understood that mass collectivisation in agriculture was nonsense.[39] Nevertheless, once industrialisation began in earnest, Trotsky was carried away with its apparent success. Thus in November 1930 he observed that 'successful socialist construction is proceeding in the USSR', if 'under the influence of hostile forces'.[40] Four months later he enthused about the 'gigantic successes of the Soviet economy' and the 'superiority of the Soviet form of production'.[41] In 1931, at a time when agriculture was in a state of near collapse, Trotsky wrote that 'in the field of agriculture...the regime of the proletarian dictatorship also succeeded in revealing a mighty creative power.'[42]

Trotsky's optimism can only be explained by his desire to retrieve the gains of the Russian Revolution. Thus, while he attacked the bureaucracy, he also tried to discover some progressive potential in the Soviet system. He recognised that the Bolshevik Party had been destroyed, but, as he indicated in March 1933, he believed that the dictatorship of the proletariat still survived:

**'No new revolution is necessary to save and strengthen the dictatorship. Profound and all-sided fully thought-out reform will completely suffice.'**[43]

Because Trotsky found it difficult to sustain his strategy of reform, his discussion became contradictory and often idealist. How was the strategy of reform to be implemented? In January 1933 Trotsky's attempt to sustain this approach seemed to lead him around in circles:

**'There is nothing irreparable in the country's economy. Only something is needed to repair it. What is needed is a party. There is no party in the true sense of the word now.'**[44]

But if there was no party how was the strategy of reform to be put into practice?

In March 1933 Trotsky pondered the possibility of 'reviving the party' with the return of the Left Opposition.[45] His desperation was obvious in the article 'We need an honest inner-party agreement' which marks the nadir of his analysis. Here he attempted a metaphysical resolution of the tension between the reality of the counter-revolution and his vain hope for reform:

**'It is perfectly true that Stalin has destroyed the party, smashed it in pieces, scattered it in prison and exile, diluted it with a crude mass, frightened it, demoralised it. But at the same time, it remains a very real historical factor. This is proved by the continuing arrests of Left Oppositionists.'**[46]

The party which had been 'destroyed' Trotsky brought back to life in his writings as a 'very real historical factor'. The 'scattered, fettered, frightened elements of the real Bolshevik Party' in Trotsky's mind came together to revive party democracy. He did not discuss how this could happen and in the end sheer fantasy overtook his analysis: 'The revival of the party by democratising it involves undoubted risks, but it still opens the only thinkable way out.'[47] What was the 'only thinkable way out' in March 1933 became unthinkable by October, for by that time new events had forced Trotsky to reconsider. Ironically it was the rise of Hitler in Germany, rather than an appreciation of developments in the Soviet Union, which forced Trotsky to jettison much of his reformist strategy. The collapse of the German Communist Party and its cynical manoeuvres before the Hitler coup were unmistakable evidence of the reactionary character of Stalinism.

'The class nature of the Soviet state' was the first serious assessment of the Soviet Union in the thirties. Trotsky concluded that the bureaucracy could only be removed by force, abandoned the strategy of democratising the Soviet Communist Party and called for the establishment of a new revolutionary party and a new international.[48] However, Trotsky still held that no social revolution was necessary — a view he retained throughout the thirties.

Trotsky made a distinction between the political regime, which was reactionary and needed to be destroyed, and the economy, which was progressive and had to be preserved:

**'The anatomy of society is determined by its economic relations. So**

long as the forms of property that have been created by the October Revolution are not overthrown, the proletariat remains the ruling class.'[49]

Trotsky emphasised Soviet property relations as the abiding achievement of the revolution:

'The bureaucracy derives its privileges not from any special property relations peculiar to it as a "class", but from those property relations that have been created by the October Revolution and that are fundamentally adequate for the dictatorship of the proletariat.'[50]

Trotsky regarded the bureaucracy not as the creator of the new social system, but as a parasitic excrescence on an essentially healthy economy. The removal of the parasites would be sufficient to allow the dictatorship of the proletariat to flourish. Trotsky characterised the bureaucracy as 'centrist', as a force vacillating between the demands of the working class for the defence of the existing property relations, and the capitalist forces seeking its overthrow.[51]

In his overestimation of the positive role of the bureaucracy, Trotsky was even prepared, in March 1934, to praise the achievements of the Stalinist regime:

'It would be criminal to deny the progressive work accomplished by the Soviet bureaucracy. With no initiative, with no horizons, with no understanding of the historical dynamic forces, the bureaucracy, after a stubborn resistance, found itself compelled by the logic of its own interests to adopt the programme of industrialisation and collectivisation.'[52]

There was an element of uncertainty in Trotsky's assessment of the bureaucracy as a centrist force. In February 1935 he admitted that his previous discussion on the threat of counter-revolution 'served to becloud rather than to clarify the question'.[53] But he insisted that the dictatorship of the proletariat survived—even though it found a 'distorted but indubitable expression in the dictatorship of the bureaucracy'.[54] His discussion of the bureaucracy remained contradictory and imprecise. In a letter to the leader of the American Left Opposition in October 1937 Trotsky only added to the confusion:

'Some comrades continue to characterise Stalinism as "bureaucratic cretinism". This characterisation is now totally out of date. On the international arena, Stalinism is no longer centrism, but the crudest form of opportunism and social patriotism.'[55]

*The revolution betrayed* published in 1937 represents a synthesis of Trotsky's thoughts on the Soviet Union. Here the analysis is presented in a clear and rigorous form and the text provides a useful survey of the new social system. It is a powerful critique of the Stalinist bureaucracy and clearly exposes its reactionary role. However, there is little theoretical development over the previous discussion.

In *The revolution betrayed* Trotsky insisted that nationalised property relations defined the Soviet Union as a 'proletarian state'.[56] He depicted the bureaucracy as a parasitic layer which enforced its interests through its control over consumption — it 'draws off the cream for its own use', he wrote. Industrialisation had raised the productive forces and hence also increased the privileges available to the bureaucracy: 'That is the first reason why the growth of production has so far strengthened not the socialist, but the bourgeois features of the state.'[57] Access to consumption goods had shaped the bureaucracy as a caste with independent interests.

Insofar as the bureaucracy developed the forces of production it formed the basis for socialism. Insofar as it sought to consolidate its own privileges through its bourgeois form of distribution, the bureaucracy opened the way for the return of capitalism:

'Two opposite tendencies are growing out of the depth of the Soviet regime. To the extent that, for the benefit of an upper stratum, it carries to more and more extreme expression bourgeois norms of distribution, it is preparing a capitalist restoration. This contrast between forms of property and norms of distribution cannot grow indefinitely. Either the bourgeois norm must in one form or another spread to the means of production, or the means of distribution must be brought into correspondence with the socialist property system.'[58]

For Trotsky the main contradiction was between the 'socialist property system' and 'bourgeois norms of distribution'.

Trotsky pointed to certain dangers. Although the means of production belonged to the state, the state belonged to the bureaucracy. If these as 'yet wholly new relations should solidify, become the norm and be legalised', Trotsky argued, 'they would, in the long run, lead to a complete liquidation of the social conquests of the proletarian revolution'.[59] Trotsky was also aware that the bureaucracy was more than just the bureaucracy of the dominating class (that is, of the proletariat): 'In no other regime has a bureaucracy ever achieved such a degree of independence from the dominating class.'[60] In his later writings Trotsky shifted his emphasis, arguing that the Soviet Union was more progressive than capitalism because of its planned economy.

He contrasted 'the nationalised and planned economy of the USSR' to capitalist stagnation.[61] He argued that the conflict between socialist property relations and bourgeois norms of distribution would eventually explode, leading either to the restoration of capitalism or to a socialist system.[62]

## Trotsky's inconsistencies

Trotsky's proposition that the Soviet Union was a workers' state, albeit one that had become wholly deformed, was derived from the view that nationalised property relations and planning constituted the economic basis for socialist construction. He fully recognised the reactionary character of the Stalinist bureaucracy — this is why he called for a political revolution. Yet he insisted that the existing economic relations were progressive and that a social revolution was unnecessary.

Trotsky drew a close link between nationalised property relations and the dictatorship of the proletariat. He emphasised that as long as the nationalised forms of property created after the revolution had not been overthrown, 'the proletariat remains the ruling class'. Trotsky considered that the proletarian dictatorship could take different political forms, and could even find an 'expression in the dictatorship of the bureaucracy' — so long as nationalised property relations remained intact. 'The regime which guards the expropriated and nationalised property from the imperialists is, independent of political forms, the dictatorship of the proletariat.'[63]

Trotsky's identification of the dictatorship of the proletariat with nationalised property relations is unconvincing and contradicts much of his own writing on the subject. For the Bolsheviks, as we have seen, the confiscation of capitalist property was essential if the bourgeoisie was to be deprived of its economic power. In this sense nationalisation is a component part of the establishment of the proletarian dictatorship. However, in the transition period between capitalism and communism, nationalised industry has no inherent virtues. The key factor in strengthening the proletarian dictatorship is not nationalised property in itself, but the establishment of workers' management. Workers' management, the centralised direction of the economy and the conscious direction of labour-time, was the only progressive alternative to capitalism, and the only real safeguard for the proletarian dictatorship.

From a Marxist point of view social relations, not property relations, are decisive. According to Marx a particular form of property can only be understood in the context of social relations. 'To try to give a definition of property as of an independent relation, a category apart...can be nothing but an illusion of metaphysics or jurisprudence.'[64] The justification for the proletarian dictatorship is not that it nationalises the means of production but that it increases the productivity of labour above the level possible under capitalism. For Marx, Engels and Lenin, this was central. The fact that Trotsky shared this view is apparent from his important early analysis of the Soviet Union, *Towards capitalism or socialism?* published in 1925.

Trotsky noted that the viability of the Soviet Union would be determined by its capacity to raise the productivity of labour.[65] In 1940 he returned to this theme. 'It is necessary to compare year by year the movement of labour productivity in the USSR and the capitalist countries to determine whether the present economic system in the USSR has justified itself or not.'[66] In the Marxist tradition, Trotsky linked social advance directly to the development of the productive forces. He concluded an article written in 1937 with the words 'Marxism teaches us, does it not, that the productive forces are the fundamental factor of historic progress.' As if to resolve his dilemma he added that 'the same applies to the USSR. Whatever its modes of exploitation may be, this society is by its very character superior to capitalist society.'[67] It was superior because 'on the basis of nationalised property' the bureaucracy had 'ensured a development of productive forces never equalled in the history of the world'.[68]

For Trotsky, the progressive character of the Soviet Union was 'assured' by its ability to develop the forces of production. Trotsky now shifted his position and identified nationalised property with the capacity to develop the forces of production. Here Trotsky was on shaky ground. The historical evidence shows that Soviet industrial growth never reached a level at which it could compete with that of capitalism. Moreover the productivity of labour tended to rise slowly, always behind the growth of total output. Perhaps

Trotsky can be excused on the grounds that he was misled by the misinformation published by the bureaucracy in the thirties. But with the evidence that is available to us today there can be no excuse for repeating this mistake.

Much of Trotsky's assessment of the Soviet Union was based on the belief that the bureaucracy could plan the economy. He was aware of many of the defects of bureaucratic planning—he stressed, for example, the failure of the bureaucracy to solve the problem of quality. But in the end Trotsky had no reservations about characterising the Soviet Union as a planned economy. Trotsky never provided any arguments to back up his case, nor could he. The disparity between planned targets and real output — even in the thirties — indicated the fictitious character of planning.

It is surprising that Trotsky considered the bureaucracy capable of planning. The Bolsheviks never reduced planning to a technical function; they understood that it depended on a specific social relationship — workers' management. Without this, planning could be nothing more than administrative regulation. From a Marxist perspective, a social revolution against the bureaucracy was needed to install workers' management of production.

Trotsky's final writings show signs that he was beginning to move away from his preoccupation with nationalised property relations. Commenting on the Soviet invasion of Poland in 1939, he noted that 'the statification of the means of production is, as we said, a progressive measure. But its progressiveness is relative: its specific weight depends on the sum total of all other factors'. On balance, Trotsky concluded that the 'evil far outweighs the progressive content of Stalinist reforms in Poland'.[69]

Much of Trotsky's analysis was based on abstract formulas and analogies. Even *The revolution betrayed* contains only a superficial assessment of the bureaucracy. However, Trotsky correctly noted that the bureaucracy was not a class. He saw the bureaucracy as a caste, a 'commanding stratum' whose 'appropriation of a vast share of the national income has the character of social parasitism'.[70] Here Trotsky failed to grasp how the bureaucracy was in part the creator, and in part the creation, of the new social system. The bureaucrats may have been greedy and rapacious, but they can hardly be considered mere parasites on an otherwise healthy body. The system as it existed in the thirties could not have survived without the bureaucracy, and vice versa. It almost appears as if Trotsky feared to probe the bureaucracy too closely in case he revealed the structural defects of the system.

Trotsky defended the Soviet Union to the end, but with less and less conviction. Written in 1940, his last notes provide a clue to the direction of his thinking shortly before his assassination. He defended the Soviet Union against the imperialist powers not because it was more progressive, but because imperialism was by far the greater evil:

'When Italy attacked Ethiopia...I was fully on the side of the latter, despite the Ethiopian negus for whom I have no sympathy. What mattered was to oppose imperialism's seizure of this new territory. In the same way now I decisively oppose the imperialist camp and support independence for the USSR, despite the negus in the Kremlin.'[71]

Trotsky's forthright defence of the Soviet Union was based on no false claims for its progressive qualities. Rather it was founded on the recognition that it was imperialism, not the Soviet Union, that was the main threat to the international working class. Such an approach distanced him from his previous analysis and clearly placed him within the Marxist perspective.

Throughout his life Trotsky remained an uncompromising opponent of the Soviet bureaucracy. But his attachment to the October Revolution constantly blinded him to the thoroughgoing changes that the Soviet Union underwent in the thirties. At the outbreak of the Second World War, the darkest moment for the working class this century, he sought to retrieve the irretrievable — the gains of the Russian Revolution.

## Notes

1 Bailes (1978), p150.
2 See Lewin (1978), p58.
3 Lewin (1978), p59.
4 Schwarz (1953), p7.
5 Cited in Jasny (1961), p54.
6 Karcz (1971), p38. Ironically, this decrease in livestock led to a 50 per cent decline in the number of animals consuming grain which meant that the marketable portion of grain production increased.
7 Ellman (1975), p853. Ellman's figures are based on the important work carried out by Barsov (1969).
8 Nove (1982), p196.

## The emergence of the new society 61

9   Rakovsky (1981), p18. This article written in internal exile was based on the very limited resources available to Rakovsky. To some extent Rakovsky underestimates the limited but important transfer of technology that was beginning to percolate from the West. See Sutton (1971).
10  Foreign technology allowed the industrialisation drive to be completed. In 1932, 78 per cent of all machine tools installed were bought abroad. See Nove (1982), p230.
11  Jasny (1961), p104.
12  Jasny (1961), p72.
13  Jasny (1961), p146-50.
14  Bergson (1961), p216.
15  Schwarz (1953), p86.
16  Schwarz (1953), pp91-106.
17  Fitzpatrick (1979), p187.
18  According to one study, as late as 1934, 50 per cent of directors in heavy industry only had primary education. See Granick (1954), chapter 3.
19  See Rigby (1968), p200.
20  Stalin (1947), p369.
21  Stalin (1947), p371.
22  'On the draft constitution of the USSR', 25 November 1936, Stalin (1947), p545.
23  Rigby (1968), p225.
24  See the circulars referred to in Fainsod (1958), pp318-21.
25  Molotov (1939), p111.
26  Molotov (1939), p109.
27  Cited in Lewin (1973), p116.
28  Baykov (1947), p286.
29  Cited in Lewin (1962), p274.
30  Cited in Berliner (1957), pp138-9.
31  Baykov (1947), p291.
32  See the discussion on the *mattekhsnab* in Lewin (1973), pp106-7.
33  See Kuznets (1963), p362.
34  One admirer of Soviet industrialisation noted: 'It is no exaggeration to say that the planning of the foreign trade proved to be more successful and technically more adequate than the planning of the home-trade turnover.' Baykov (1947), p273.
35  Sutton (1971), p339. Access to foreign technology was closely linked to the development of foreign relations. See chapter 10.
36  'Draft thesis of the ILO on the Russian question', Trotsky (1973), p210.
37  'What is to be learned from the "saboteurs" trial?', Trotsky (1973).
38  'The real disposition of the pieces on the political chessboard', Trotsky (1973).
39  'The new course in the Soviet economy', Trotsky (1975b), p109.
40  'Thermidor and Bonapartism', Trotsky (1973), p73.
41  'Draft thesis...', Trotsky (1973), p203.
42  'Draft thesis...', Trotsky (1973), p203.
43  'Alarm signal', Trotsky (1972b), p112.
44  'The dangers of Thermidor', Trotsky (1972b), p78.

45 'Alarm signal', Trotsky (1972b), p112.
46 'We need an honest inner-party agreement', Trotsky (1972b), pp165-6.
47 Trotsky (1972b), p166.
48 'The class nature of the Soviet state', Trotsky (1972c), p118. It should be noted that the call for a new party was justified on the grounds that the tragic events in Germany had finally discredited Stalinism, rather than on a reassessment of internal developments in the Soviet Union.
49 Trotsky (1972c), p104.
50 Trotsky (1972c), p112.
51 Trotsky (1972c), p116.
52 'The Stalinist bureaucracy and the assassination', Trotsky (1971a), p130.
53 'The workers' state, Thermidor and Bonapartism', Trotsky (1971a), p168.
54 Trotsky (1971a), p174.
55 See footnote 49 in Trotsky (1971a), p329.
56 Trotsky (1972a), p248.
57 Trotsky (1972a), p113.
58 Trotsky (1972a), p244.
59 Trotsky (1972a), p249.
60 Trotsky (1972a), p248.
61 'Once again: the USSR and its defence', Trotsky (1976), p33.
62 Elsewhere Trotsky noted: 'The historic alternative, carried to the end, is as follows: either the Stalin regime is an abhorrent relapse in the process of transforming society into a socialist society, or the Stalin regime is the first stage of a new exploiting society.' Trotsky (1979b), p9.
63 'Not a workers' and not a bourgeois state', Trotsky (1976), p62.
64 Marx (1976b), p197.
65 'Towards capitalism or socialism', Trotsky (1979a), p345.
66 'Fragments on the USSR', Trotsky (1979b), p862.
67 'Once again: the USSR and its defence', Trotsky (1976), p35.
68 Trotsky (1976), p35.
69 Trotsky (1970a), p19.
70 Trotsky (1972a), p250.
71 Trotsky (1979b), p885.

# 4. Stalinism and destalinisation

The Soviet Union of today is the product of the thirties. Although much has changed over the past 50 years, the essential social relations established at the height of the Stalin era remain unaltered. The process of 'destalinisation' initiated by Khrushchev in the mid-fifties was a major attempt to reform and rationalise the system. Destalinisation failed, not because of any lack of will on the part of Khrushchev, but because of the deep-seated resistance of the Soviet social formation to any policy of change.

## The achievements of the Stalinist regime

The strength of the Soviet system under Stalin lay in the way it overcame constraints on the mobilisation of resources. To realise its objectives, Stalin's regime could draw on a vast reservoir of natural resources and labour. Through the use of terror the regime also eliminated much of the demand for consumer goods, thus diverting funds for accumulation. Stalin's regime was more successful in mobilising resources than it was in using them efficiently, but in the thirties and forties the consequences of the inefficient allocation of society's labour-time were not widely apparent. Indeed the exigencies of the Second World War revealed the strengths rather than the weaknesses of the Soviet system.

The invasion of the Soviet Union by more than three million German troops in 1941 precipitated a major economic crisis. Within weeks German troops took over strategic sectors of the Soviet economy. They held hostage 65 per cent of Soviet coal production, 68 per cent of iron, 60 per cent of steel and aluminium, 40 per cent of railway equipment, 84 per cent of sugar and 40 per cent of cereals.[1] The German invasion cut Soviet industrial output in half and held captive no less than 40 per cent of the population.[2]

Yet, despite the military and economic collapse of 1941, the Soviet economy was able to rise to meet this threat to its very survival. By 1943 the Soviet Union had transformed itself into a full-scale war economy: 'For every combat aircraft, cannon and tank produced in 1940, in 1944 Soviet industry produced four, eight and ten respectively.'[3] The Soviet regime succeeded in rallying its economic reserves to sustain a vastly expanded military machine.

The secret of Stalin's wartime success was the freedom the bureaucracy enjoyed in mobilising resources. It is true that Western aid, weapons and technology greatly assisted the Soviet war effort. By 1944 the USA was financing up to a quarter of Soviet defence expenditure.[4] Nevertheless most of the resources deployed in the war economy were internally generated. According to one estimate some 55 per cent of the Soviet Union's national income was allocated for military purposes.[5]

The Soviet war economy operated on the principles adopted by the Stalinist bureaucracy in the thirties. As Harrison notes, the policy of all-out mobilisation whatever the cost was pushed with renewed vigour in wartime:

**'As a method of mobilising resources under extreme pressure, it shared many features in common with previous peace-time episodes of rapid economic mobilisation....It carried these common features to a new extreme.'[6]**

The system of forced industrialisation developed in the thirties was ideally suited to the conditions of war.

The period of post-war reconstruction also demonstrated the durability of the Soviet social formation. The fourth five year plan, from 1945 to 1950, succeeded in doubling industrial output. Despite the devastation of war, total output in 1955 was more than three times that of 1928; production grew during this period at an average rate of 4.7 per cent a year. These achievements allowed the Soviet Union to emerge as an industrial power second only to the USA.

The key to success was, once again, the vast mobilisation of society's resources. Despite the loss of millions of lives in the war, the labour force in 1950 was 23 per cent larger than in 1940.[7] Consumption was still restricted: nearly all resources were concentrated in heavy industry. Only 12 per cent of industrial investment was directed towards light industry, consumer goods production and food processing. In the textile sector, for example, employment of manual workers in 1950 still lay below pre-war levels.[8]

Throughout the fifties high levels of investment sustained industrial growth. Between 1950 and 1958, investment grew at an average of 12.9 per cent each year. Soviet sources suggest that this gave the economy an average annual growth rate of 7.1 per cent; CIA studies estimate a lower growth rate of 5.5 per cent.[9] But, while figures for this period remain a matter of controversy, even the CIA's estimate indicates an impressive pace of economic development.

The Soviet economy reached its high point in the late fifties. There were still a number of unresolved problems: agriculture remained stagnant and the consumer goods sector continued to lag behind all others. However, in general the economy continued to grow — enough for the bureaucracy to begin to attempt to raise living standards. In 1957 the launch of Sputnik, the world's first space satellite, appeared to place the Soviet Union at the threshold of a new era.

## The price of growth

The methods of the Soviet bureaucracy achieved accelerated industrialisation and growth, but at a price. Growth took place at the expense of economic equilibrium and internal coherence. Instead of planning, the bureaucracy was constantly forced to improvise — and, in particular, to improvise links between one branch of production and another. But, even when it was backed up by terror, improvisation could only minimise chaos, not eliminate it. The central bureaucracy controlled only the material resources, not how they were used.

Improvisation undermined planning. During the war even formal 'paper' planning had to be abandoned as wartime dislocations forced the bureaucracy to allow local enterprises to fall back on their own devices to make ends meet. Enterprises were encouraged to draw on local resources to reduce the strain on the centre.[10] Nor did planning improve in the post-war period. One study of the years between 1945 and 1953 shows that plan targets for heavy industry were always over-fulfilled. By contrast, targets for light industry were under-fulfilled, while schemes for regional development were out of control.[11]

The failure of planning led to inefficiency and low productivity. Because enterprises were faced with a continuous shortage of inputs, investment resources were tied up for years: when — if —

they did get used, it was often at less than their full capacity. From the late forties and throughout the fifties the Soviet press regularly drew attention to the scale of the planning problem. *Pravda* provides a typical example of this trend. Two major tractor plants in Stalingrad and Kharkov, it reported, were bogged down because they lacked the enamel to paint their products. The plants were also short of tractor belts: they had been unable to make any deliveries of finished tractors for days.[12] Poor planning exacted a particularly high cost in the Soviet construction industry. Here investment resources were spread over a large number of unfinished projects, which in total represented 73 per cent of total annual investment in construction.[13]

The bureaucracy's poor planning and its habit of resorting to improvisation were already evident in the thirties. However, they were compounded by a number of new problems that emerged only after the war. Resource mobilisation worked best at an early stage of industrialisation: when there were only a few industrial sectors, the central bureaucracy could retain a degree of control over the direction of resources. But, as the number of sectors increased and industry became more complex, it became more difficult to keep things balanced. The bureaucracy had no choice but to preoccupy itself with a few top priority sectors, and leave the rest to fend for themselves.

The defects of the bureaucracy's strategy were particularly apparent in sectors where some advances had been made in the thirties. Then the assimilation of new technology had been a key achievement. Now, as industry became more complex, it became more difficult to develop and integrate new techniques. In the thirties, the bureaucracy itself supervised the introduction of technology. In the fifties, in the absence of central direction of technological innovation, many of the new industries of the thirties stagnated. Thus Universal tractors, first produced in 1924, and Moskvich cars, designed in 1936, were temporarily put back into production after the war to boost output while new designs were drawn up. They were still being produced in 1955.[14]

The Soviet economy also lagged behind in its absorption of Western technology. In the thirties the Soviet bureaucracy was not only able to absorb new technology but also to copy it and replace imports with its own products.[15] In the post-war years this capacity to assimilate technology decreased dramatically.[16] Granick has shown the bureaucracy's difficulties in absorbing and substituting foreign pipe and chemical equipment in the fifties. The fact that the

Soviet Union continued to import these products revealed its incapacity 'to achieve the degree of new product mastery that was accomplished during the thirties'.[17]

For a time high growth rates could mask the defects of Soviet industrialisation. But by the late fifties the inherent limitations of the strategy of simply throwing resources at industry could no longer be disguised. As the technical division of labour became more complex, massive investments brought diminishing returns. Investment could stimulate growth, but could not compensate for incoherence and inefficiency. By 1958, the rate of growth of the Soviet economy began to decline. This tendency towards economic contraction has been the dominant feature of the Soviet system ever since.

The slowdown in the rate of growth is a symptom of the inefficiency of investment. It means that each unit of new investment produces a smaller increase in industrial output. The decline in what Soviet researchers label the 'dynamics of the efficiency of industrial production' is not simply an expression of the inefficiency of investment. It shows that the Soviet system cannot systematically raise the productivity of labour through new investment. Between 1951 and 1955 the productivity of the Soviet worker grew by an average of 7.6 per cent a year. Between 1956 and 1960 it grew by an annual average of 6.3 per cent. Between 1961 and 1965 the figure was down to 4.8 per cent and it has subsequently fallen further still.

The inefficiency of investment and the difficulty of raising productivity point to the limited potential of Soviet industrialisation. High growth rates have resulted, not from efficiency, but from a unique freedom to dispose of society's resources regardless of any criterion of efficiency. It was not the economic system that guaranteed growth, but a combination of external factors: rich reserves of natural resources, a large reservoir of cheap labour, and foreign technology.

The Soviet bureaucracy could not rely forever on such factors. By the late fifties it realised that what it called 'extensive growth' had to be turned into 'intensive growth', through reforms of the system. By 1961 the rate of increase in investment was four per cent, down from 16 per cent in 1958. Yet although alarm about the economy's slowdown still persists, little has really changed. Economic growth today continues along the lines laid down in the thirties. Every year since 1958, the Soviet leadership has made its obligatory denunciations of the persistence of extensive growth; every year, too, it has exhorted industry to develop intensively. In subsequent chapters we examine why the Soviet bureaucracy has proved incapable of shifting to a new pattern of development.

## The Stalinist order

For many Western observers the repressive and authoritarian features of the Soviet Union are its defining characteristics. The concept of 'Soviet totalitarianism' is the logical conclusion of the idealist approach of Western political analysis, which examines repression in the Soviet Union independently of its social relations. Repression is used to explain Soviet society, rather than the reverse. Since Soviet society is distinguished by the prevalence of repression, then its particular form of historical development becomes irrelevant. Thus Carrère D'Encausse has discovered that 'Stalinism is in no way specific to Russia. The main characteristics of this political system were also repeated at the time in Hitler's Germany.'[18] From this point of view the Soviet Union is Hitler's Germany, and Hitler's Germany is the Soviet Union — only the dogma of totalitarianism is real.

The myth of totalitarianism retains considerable influence among anti-Soviet propagandists in the West. The renewal of East/West tensions has revived Western obsessions about the forces of Stalinist repression, their methods — and their victims. In a recently published history of the Soviet Union, Hosking even attempts to explain the process of destalinisation as the response of the post-Stalin leadership to pressures for change from dissidents held in prison camps.[19] However, the totalitarianism thesis retains few adherents among less prejudiced academic and official Western observers of the Soviet Union. They have replaced the concept of totalitarianism with other concepts, such as 'pluralism', 'corporatism' and 'pressure groups'.[20] But this sort of sociological analysis offers little more than the insight that conflicts of interest exist in the Soviet Union. This truism is supplemented by anecdotal accounts of conflicts among randomly selected cliques.

It is a testimony to the enduring strength of the totalitarianism thesis that new 'discoveries' about conflicts of interest can still be treated as major revelations. The modern approaches of Western political science still depend on looking at institutions and personalities in isolation from the underlying socio-economic trends. As a result the analysis remains narrowly political and major events in the Soviet Union are discussed in terms of faction-fights and personality clashes. This method not only fails to go beyond speculative journalism, it also addresses the wrong problems.

In the seventies the question that preoccupied the academic literature, especially in the USA, was the search for a successor to Brezhnev. As recently as 1983, the most comprehensive Western survey of the Soviet Union contained an article which argued in all seriousness that 'the biggest problem, one fraught with danger for the Soviet system, is the political succession.'[21] Three party leaders later it should be obvious that the particular personality occupying the office of head of state was the least of the Soviet bureaucracy's worries. To understand the nature of Stalinist rule we have to go beyond the field of political speculation.

In fact the totalitarian model of the Soviet Union has never corresponded to the real state of affairs: even under Stalin total control always eluded the bureaucracy. Stalin and the party politburo could dominate but never fully control society. This was particularly evident in economic affairs — and a bureaucracy which could not regulate the economy could only react to events, not dictate the pace of social change.

There can be no doubt about the scale of terror that prevailed in the Soviet Union in the thirties. Yet this was not a matter of choice for the bureaucracy, but a necessity imposed on it by the forces unleashed in the construction of the new social formation. There were no administrative, technical or economic strategies at hand for building a new society; it required the direct intervention of the bureaucracy. The new order was created through force and could only be consolidated by more force.

The use of terror is not peculiar to the Soviet Union under Stalin. Ancient Greece and Rome relied on conquest and slavery; modern South Africa and Brazil owe their existence to systematic violence. What distinguishes the Soviet Union from other modern societies is that force proved to be the bureaucracy's central mechanism for cohering the new social formation. The Stalinist regime was not the natural outcome of social or historical forces. It was an artificial creation that could only be sustained by repressive methods.

The absence of any other mechanism of economic regulation or social cohesion explains not only the scale but also the form of Soviet state terror. Despite the vast bureaucratic apparatus, repression was not administered in any systematic way. Western Kremlinologists tend to read history backwards and portray the colossal apparatus of repression as the outcome of a conspiracy. But coercion, like everything else in Stalinist society, developed in a makeshift fashion. In the thirties the strategy of terror did not emerge as a conscious plan. On the contrary, the terror campaign was improvised in response to social forces outside the control of the bureaucracy. Each new development required the further application of force.

The highly subjective character of bureaucratic domination explains apparently irrational events such as the Stalinist purges. Under a system which gave such wide-ranging powers to officials, there was no effective framework to contain coercion. Not only were rules and procedures violated: they lost all operational meaning. The purges created a climate in which nobody could feel immune from the arbitrary exercise of power. Despite the austere figure of the all-powerful Stalin, Soviet society was not so much totalitarian as out of control.

The Stalinist bureaucracy built up its network of secret police and prison camps in response to its lack of information about what was going on in society. The secret police cannot be understood in terms of their repressive function alone. They evolved into a vital channel of communication — one which provided the bureaucracy with information essential to the exercise of its rule. The secret police were pushed into a closer involvement in running the economy, until they became a unit of economic administration in their own right. The well-documented involvement of labour camps in productive work is only an extreme example of how the repressive and economic functions of the secret police were intertwined.

It is clear in retrospect that the Stalinist era, especially between 1930 and 1950, was a period of tremendous tensions within the Kremlin and the party. Because the bureaucracy could only survive through showtrials and mass executions, it failed to evolve a procedure to regulate its own affairs. Although the leadership could eliminate its opponents, it lacked the means to establish a coherent framework of social domination. That one individual, Stalin, could exercise such influence was itself a symptom of the internal tensions within the bureaucracy.

Stalin the all-powerful dictator is as much a myth as the totalitarian Soviet state. As head of state, Stalin did exercise considerable power, but this was not because of any characteristics of his personality. The bureaucracy produced an autocratic ruler because it had no more serviceable way of running society. Stalin's influence was constrained by the need to maintain the cohesion of the bureaucracy. At the same time his grip over the Kremlin apparatus allowed him to intervene on key questions, modify proposals and determine the fate of individual bureaucrats.

The exaggerated significance attributed to Stalin as an individual is particularly misplaced after the Second World War. From 1946 onwards Stalin was in poor health and could no longer maintain a high level of involvement in day-to-day affairs of state. During the post-war period Stalin made only two speeches in public and left major areas of responsibility to his colleagues. In the latter years of Stalin's rule there was a major change in the attitude of the bureaucracy. It was no longer prepared to tolerate any individual exercise of arbitrary powers. With the stabilisation of Soviet society after the war, the bureaucrats began to sort out their own affairs at last. They were particularly keen to protect themselves from the random purges of the pre-war years.

## Shifts in the apparatus

The changing attitude of the Soviet bureaucracy towards the Stalinist order was not readily apparent before Stalin's death. After the war a brief interlude of relaxation was followed by renewed repression. The purge of the Leningrad party organisation in 1948 and a wider national clampdown appeared to confirm that not much had changed since the thirties. However, behind the scenes important developments were taking place. Step by step relations within the bureaucracy improved. While Stalin was alive this process could not be formalised, but the underlying trend, towards modifying repression and preventing the arbitrary removal of individuals from positions of responsibility, gathered momentum.

Between 1934 and 1936, some 25 to 34 per cent of enterprise managers in heavy industry left their posts within 12 months.[22] The average tenure of industrial enterprise directors in the thirties was only three years. By 1953 directors tended to stay in the same post for 10 years.[23] A similar pattern emerged in appointments to party and administrative posts. A growing body of officials wanted curbs on arbitrary arrest and most bureaucrats favoured a more limited role for the secret police.

Although the bureaucracy had no objections in principle to the use of force against the rest of the population, it became increasingly aware of the contradiction between repression and the development of a modern industrial society. Force had been the essential lever for industrialisation, but proved a blunt instrument when more efficient production at a higher technological level was required. That this was widely recognised in the post-war period is evident from the Soviet leadership's experiments with material incentives to reward work. In discussion of the new five year plan in 1946, leading bureaucrats like Molotov and Zhdanov even spoke out in favour of encouraging the production of consumer goods.

Two government decrees in November and December 1946 indicated that the bureaucracy was ready to pump more resources into the production of consumer goods. *Pravda* commented that increasing the output of consumer goods was now 'one of the highest priorities and most urgent tasks of the whole state'.[24] This priority was not met. The bureaucracy no longer opposed raising workers' living standards, but simply could not direct investment where it wanted.

Nobody in the Soviet bureaucracy interpreted these attempted modifications in the exercise of state rule as a fundamental break with the past. On the contrary, they were rightly seen as efforts to consolidate the social system that had emerged in the thirties. However, transitions in the form of political domination never take place smoothly. It was not until 1956, three years after Stalin's death, that these changes in the bureaucracy and its policies could be publicly ratified.

Between 1953 and 1956 the symptoms of change were evident. In announcing the regime's new economic policy in August 1953, with its emphasis on the provision of consumer goods and liberalisation measures, Malenkov marked an important departure from the past. Party and state organs which had become defunct in the previous two decades were reactivated in an attempt to institutionalise the bureaucracy's political rule. Repression was now reduced: in 1953 and 1955, limited amnesties were declared, the Soviet press was allowed occasionally to denounce cases of arbitrary repression, and a number of restrictions on intellectual life were loosened.

The twentieth congress of the Soviet Communist Party in February 1956 ratified the shift towards a less coercive form of bureaucratic rule. Although Khrushchev's open denunciation of the excesses of the Stalinist era came as a shock, there was no fundamental break with the past. Khrushchev's rejection of some of the methods of Stalin was the logical conclusion of the process of change within the apparatus which had begun a decade earlier.

## From Khrushchev to Gorbachev

Events in Soviet politics are generally presented as the culmination of trials of strength between prominent individuals or between factions of 'hardliners' and 'liberals' in the Kremlin. In the Soviet Union, as in every society, power struggles take place and influence the course of political events. However, fundamental policy changes cannot be explained as the chance outcome of interactions within the bureaucracy. Personality factors can only influence superficial aspects of policy-making. Key decisions are imposed on the bureaucracy by forces outside its control, by the need to respond and adapt to changing social conditions.

Khrushchev was the Soviet leader who became publicly associated with the policy of destalinisation; but, sooner or later, whoever ran the bureaucracy would have had to strike out on a similar path. Khrushchev did influence the form of the destalinisation process, but the impulse for change came from the changing requirements of the Soviet social order. Whatever the peculiarities of Khrushchev's political approach, destalinisation was necessary for the consolidation, and ultimately even for the survival, of the Soviet social formation.

Khrushchev's famous speech criticising Stalin was followed by a general relaxation of social and political life in the Soviet Union. The more overt forms of Stalinist terror were pushed into the background and most people experienced a less oppressive life. Many contemporary observers interpreted Khrushchev's speech as little short of revolutionary in its implications. At the time, even an exceptionally prescient observer such as Deutscher thought that it marked a fundamental change:

> '**The break with Stalinism is now apparent in almost every field of Soviet domestic policy, not merely in the denunciation of the leader-cult. It is a deep and radical break, especially in social policy.**'[25]

Khrushchev's statement was a major departure, but it was no 'radical break': subsequent events showed that the substance of the bureaucracy's domination remained unaltered. What then did destalinisation really represent?

Khrushchev's social and economic policies were designed to foster a new consensus in a society in which stability would rely on rising living standards rather than on fear. Khrushchev held out the prospect of wage increases and the reduction of the working week as a prelude to more reforms. The repeal of harsh labour laws and the relaxation of controls over travel contributed to a less coercive climate. Most welcome of all were a series of state decrees curbing the arbitrary powers of the secret police.

Destalinisation was not however a fundamental break with Stalinism. The mass repression that had mobilised investment resources in the thirties was no longer appropriate: instead of promoting industrial growth, technological development and the production of quality goods, it bred apathy and inefficiency. But destalinisation merely implied a different sort of terror — terror of a more selective kind.

For most Soviet people this meant the end of direct coercion. Yet they were still faced with the implied threat of coercion if they stepped out of line. The ending of arbitrary repression removed a major source of insecurity and, in this sense, it did indeed appear that the Stalinist era had come to an end. But while the excesses of Stalinism had been removed, the basic relationship between society and the bureaucracy had not changed. The rationalisation of repression did not amount to the restoration of basic rights and liberties. Khrushchev's reforms concerned solely the terms on which the bureaucracy exercised its rule: repression had become better organised, not expunged.

Destalinisation can thus be seen as the rationalisation of the Stalinist order. In the fifties it provoked considerable enthusiasm for the future; the intelligentsia in particular believed that the abatement of Stalinist terror would be the point of departure for more far-reaching reforms.[26] In the sixties too there was a surge of confidence and optimism among Soviet intellectuals.[27] But the main beneficiary of destalinisation was the bureaucracy itself. In the years before the twentieth congress, the bureaucracy had succeeded in stabilising its position. Khrushchev sealed this process by his anti-Stalin campaign. His attack on Stalin represented above all the bureaucracy's concern to safeguard itself against arbitrary terror. Khrushchev had no objection in principle to Stalin's methods — his only concern was how they were applied and against whom. He was careful to avoid criticising Stalin's pre-1934 crimes, which were directed against the whole population. His criticisms were levelled at the repression experienced within the bureaucracy itself in the late thirties. Indeed Khrushchev praised Stalin for crushing the Left and the Right Oppositions. The formal target of Khrushchev's denunciations was Stalin's 'cult of the individual'. The real target was the havoc Stalin caused within the bureaucracy.

Under Khrushchev the central bureaucracy acquired a considerable degree of autonomy from the secret police, removing a major source of insecurity for leading bureaucrats. The new atmosphere of security was underlined in 1957, when Khrushchev dismissed his main opponents. Molotov, Malenkov and Bulganin were demoted; but they were not purged, imprisoned or executed, as they would have been under Stalin. They were even allowed to keep the privileges associated with high bureaucratic positions. A new era of stability within the bureaucracy had arrived.

The new stability gave the bureaucrats a chance to get on with the job of accumulating status and privileges, bringing out some of their most conservative characteristics. Appointments began to acquire the status of sinecures. According to Hough, the annual turnover rate of the Soviet council of ministers was 67 per cent in the years between 1956 and 1961, only to drop to 45 per cent in the sixties and to 10 per cent by 1971.[28]

In the Brezhnev era of the late sixties and early seventies the bureaucracy carried its concern for self-preservation to new extremes. Indeed one of the main impulses behind the demotion of Khrushchev in 1964 was the hostility of the top bureaucrats towards his populist approach, which they considered a threat to their job security. A particular irritant was the compulsory rotation of personnel, which Khrushchev introduced in the party platform in 1961.[29] Brezhnev was a personal symbol of the primacy of job security for the bureaucracy.

From a materialist point of view, destalinisation was the political aspect of the drive to rationalise and modernise the Soviet social formation. Further development could no longer be sustained within the framework of the old political order. A system based on arbitrary arrest, torture and mass imprisonment and executions no longer corresponded to the requirements of Soviet society in the fifties.

In the end, however, destalinisation could not get at the roots of the problem. But it is not for want of trying that the bureaucracy has made so little progress; it is the difficulty of transforming the social relations established in the thirties which accounts for the limited nature of the changes that have occurred in the Soviet Union since 1956. Without generating a new dynamic of social development, the Soviet bureaucracy can do little more than embark on modest reform programmes. Yet despite its ambitions for reform, it cannot get far because it senses the irreformable nature of its system. This is why the destalinisation reforms have achieved such limited results.

Even on the ideological level, little has been achieved: the re-emergence of the Stalin cult in the seventies highlighted the superficial nature of destalinisation.

The Soviet 'gerontocracy' has become a subject of widespread discussion both West and East. The bureaucracy's conservative reputation is the price it has to pay for preserving stability. This conservatism is not some innate psychological or personality trait of the Soviet bureaucrat. In their own way Soviet leaders have been open to experimentation and have tried out a wide assortment of policies to deal with economic problems. Objective constraints, not lack of will, are the real problem. Within the existing framework of social relations the bureaucracy can do little else but mark time. Critics of the conservatism of the bureaucracy miss the essential point. Although the bureaucracy was the active agent in the creation of the Soviet social formation, it is now very much its product. Its conservatism reflects a realistic appreciation of the limited scope for change in the Soviet system.

Granick contrasts the heroic thirties, when purges spurred the bureaucrats on, with the conservatism of the sixties and seventies. He bemoans the fact that 'the previous practice of widespread and rapid demotion was abandoned' and argues that 'insofar as industrial managers are concerned, the Soviet system has stabilised into comparative ossification'.[30] To blame the stagnation of the Soviet social formation on lack of managerial flair is to turn things upside down. Re-introducing a strict career ladder may make life difficult for managers, but it cannot provide the system with the dynamic it lacks.

The conservatism of the Soviet bureaucrat is the product of the system's failure to overcome its fundamental defects. Soviet reformers too are concerned about tackling the problem of conservatism: this is the understandable response of apologists for the system. It is easier to blame conservative bureaucrats for the lack of progress than to target the basic social relations of the Soviet Union as the source of the problem.

In the fifties destalinisation was the bureaucracy's response to the immobility of the Soviet social formation. For all its weaknesses, it was a genuine attempt to modify the methods of organising Soviet society. In the eighties, under first Andropov and then Gorbachev, the bureaucracy has reduced its ambitions to merely changing its image. Gorbachev projects himself as a youthful and competent manager — this is the message of the bureaucracy in the eighties. In a system which has exhausted all its possibilities for social advance, the Soviet leadership can offer no more than cosmetic changes. To understand why the system has reached this impasse we must look at the social relations that prevail in the Soviet Union.

## Notes

1. Carrère D'Encausse (1981), p80.
2. Nove (1982), p272.
3. Harrison (1985), p110.
4. Harrison (1985), p150.
5. Nove (1982), p279.
6. Harrison (1985), p101.
7. Dunmore (1980), p127.
8. Dunmore (1980), p127.
9. Lane (1985a), p52.
10. See Harrison (1985), pp204-9.
11. Dunmore (1980).
12. *Pravda*, 12 January 1949.
13. Schwartz (1965), p136.
14. *Pravda*, 8 February 1955.
15. See Sutton (1971).
16. This point is developed in Sutton (1973), chapter 3.
17. Granick (1983), pp249-50.
18. Carrère D'Encausse (1981), p213.
19. Hosking (1985), pp326-32.
20. See Hough (1983) and Bunce & Echols (1980).
21. Cook (1983), p13.
22. Granick (1983), p240.
23. Dunmore (1980), p17.
24. Cited in Dunmore (1980), p107.
25. Deutscher (1970), p55.
26. Werth (1961).
27. See Bushnell (1980), p182.
28. Hough (1979), p75.
29. Bunce & Echols (1980), p8.
30. Granick (1983), pp244-50.

# PART II
# The Soviet social formation

The next three chapters discuss the laws of development of Soviet society, focusing on the unique relations of production that prevail and the way the economy is regulated. The central emphasis is on the difficulty encountered by the Soviet social formation in reproducing itself. The absence of any effective mechanism for distributing the labour-time of society is the most striking expression of this fundamental deficiency of Soviet society.

The lack of any dynamic of development in Soviet society is its most distinctive feature. The permanent involvement of the Soviet bureaucracy in all aspects of social life is necessary to compensate for the absence of any internal dynamic. The final chapter in Part II examines the ways the bureaucracy seeks to regulate forces which are in fact beyond its control.

# PART II
# The Soviet social formation

# 5. Economic regulation

'The materialist conception of history has a lot of dangerous friends nowadays, who use it as an excuse for not studying history....In general, the word "materialist" serves many of the younger writers in Germany as a mere phrase with which anything and everything is labelled without further study, that is, they stick on this label and then consider the question disposed of.' Engels[1]

Much of the analysis of the Soviet Union by writers who claim to be Marxists has served as an excuse for not studying history. Instead of looking at history as a social process which has to be examined in its specificity, many Marxists have resorted to the use of comparisons and mechanical analogies. As a result most of the debate has focused around different labels and typologies.[2] The starting point of this debate is not the real movement of history but a set of concepts; participants begin by asking whether the Soviet Union is 'socialist', or 'capitalist', or 'something in between' and proceed to list features which enable them to fit it into the designated slot.

Some Marxists try to justify their method on the grounds that Marx analysed history as a succession of stages, and that therefore the study of the Soviet Union demands the characterisation of this society in relation to Marx's stages. This comparative approach is most apparent in the writings of Mandel, who tries to legitimise his studies of the transition to socialism by drawing out similarities with the process of transition in past epochs. Mandel invokes the 'transitional epoch from slave-owning society to feudalism' to argue that 'the society transitional between capitalism and socialism must be treated according to the same method'.[3]

Mandel and other writers forget that Marx's theory of history is not distinguished by the doctrine of the historical succession of economic stages. Early bourgeois political economists such as Sismondi and Jones had noted this phenomenon long before Marx.[4] What distinguished Marx's history was his insistence that every social system was governed by laws that were specific to it. Marx's rejection of general historical principles should serve as a warning against the comparative approach to studies of the Soviet Union. Transitions from one society to another in the past tell us very little about social change in the present.

The process of change which Marx analysed cannot be reduced to a ready-made model of history, or, as Mandel would put it, to a 'method'. Marx observed that the transition to one system from another takes place when the social relations of production become a fetter on the development of the forces of production. But this important insight into the unfolding of history provides a guide to the investigation of the particular society in question, not a substitute for such an investigation. Marx noted that the interactions between the relations and forces of production are not fixed, that they have to be investigated as part of the movement of history. As Marx put it, the 'dialectic of the concepts productive force (means of production) and relations of production' is 'a dialectic whose boundaries are to be determined'.[5] These boundaries are not given *a priori* but require rigorous inquiry into the specific features of the society under investigation.

To apply the same concepts to the study of the transitions from feudalism to capitalism and from capitalism to communism is to assume the existence of a universal process of historical change. Yet history denies the existence of any such universal laws: the forces that effect social transformation are different in different forms of society. In the early stages of capitalist development the advance of the forces of production proved in itself more or less sufficient to stimulate profound changes in social organisation. The human agency was required to play a much less significant role in building capitalist society than was required in advancing towards communism in the Soviet Union after the revolution. Unlike in the transition to capitalism, the transition to communism presupposes human consciousness as the decisive factor and as the key to the development of the productive forces. Any method of analysis which seeks to provide insight into the evolution of Soviet society must capture the specific features of this particular process of historical transition.

The failure to study the relations specific to Soviet society has led to a discussion of the applicability of abstract concepts to the subject. Instead of deriving laws from the study of the Soviet Union, concepts are simply assumed to be relevant and made the starting point of the analysis. Thus virtually all the Marxist studies of the Soviet Union either consciously or unconsciously rely on the concepts of Marx's *Capital* to explain Soviet society. <u>This violation of the principle of historical specificity — the understanding that different social formations are governed by specific laws and therefore require analysis through the elaboration of specific concepts — has become the standard approach</u>.

For example, Marxists who designate the Soviet Union as 'state capitalist' have no inhibitions about using the categories of *Capital* because of the apparent similarities between capitalism and Soviet society. In defending the state capitalist thesis, the British socialists Binns and Haynes identify the declining growth rates of the Soviet economy as proof that this society is indeed capitalist. It seems to these writers that the phenomenon of declining growth rates despite increasing investments in the Soviet Union is very similar to the tendency of the rate of profit to fall under capitalism:

> '**This decline is a symptom of something much more fundamental; the decline in the rate of profit. For it has taken place in circumstances of increasing investment.**'[6]

The absurdity of this comparison is evident on even a perfunctory survey of Soviet society.

The slowdown in economic growth in the Soviet Union means that each new input of investment leads to a smaller rise in new use values produced. In certain cases — coal and steel — there has been an absolute drop in output. Under capitalism, by contrast, the decline in the rate of profit has nothing to do with the decline in the rate of production of use values. Indeed the rate of profit falls as productivity increases and more use values are produced than ever before. The slowdown in the West results, not from an insufficiency of use values, but from the difficulty of maintaining capital accumulation at a profitable level. Whereas in the Soviet Union there are continuous shortages of resources, in the West resources are available in abundance but cannot be invested profitably. However for Binns and Haynes the observation that a decline is a decline is sufficient to justify the conviction that two different societies must be experiencing similar problems.

Even writers who reject the view that the Soviet Union is capitalist often base their analysis on an indiscriminate use of the concepts of *Capital*. Thus <u>Mandel recognises that the law of value does not regulate the Soviet economy</u>, but finds in the distribution of consumer goods the invisible hand of the market and hence the form of value, exchange value. Why should the law of value govern the distribution of consumer goods? Because a 'portion of these products may prove unsaleable. Their use value cannot be realised if their exchange value is not realised.'[7] But if certain products are unsaleable this does not prove that they are commodities.

Unsaleable goods are not peculiar to the capitalist market — they may also appear under a system of barter or in the Soviet Union. In the Soviet Union it is not the invisible hand of the market or the much-acclaimed laws of supply and demand that lead to the production of unsaleable products. In contrast to the West, there is always demand, but not always the supply. If products remain unsold on the shelves it is not because there is no demand for them, but because they are of such low quality that they will not serve as use values.

As a result of their ahistorical approach Marxist writers have continually discovered and rediscovered the categories derived from an analysis of capitalist society in the Soviet Union. Even when such writers claim that the Soviet Union is not capitalist, they often do so for the negative reason that traditional Marxist categories seem not to fit Soviet society. To move away from this obsession with fixed concepts and formal definitions we need to reconstruct the Marxist approach to the study of social development.

## Marx on the development of society

Historical materialism developed through a critique of the static science that equated knowledge with the classification and definition of social phenomena. For Marx social phenomena existed in relation to others and were subject to constant change. This is why definitions serve social science so inadequately. As Grossman pointed out, social phenomena 'have no "fixed" or "eternal" elements or character but are subject to constant change. A definition fixes the superficial attributes of a thing at any given moment or period, and thus transforms these attributes into something permanent and unchanging.'[8] Marx's method provides a dynamic approach, one which surveys interaction, social process and movement. Marx derived his science 'from a critical knowledge of the historical movement'.[9]

The object of Marx's theory of capitalism was to discover the laws of motion which governed this form of society. He saw 'social movement as a process of natural history, governed by laws...independent of human will'.[10] Although 'independent of human will', social laws are not eternal or natural but vary with different forms of social organisation. But why are social laws 'independent of human will'?

Social laws evolve from natural laws through the mediation of man's interaction with nature. To survive, man is forced to interact with nature; but until society begins to control nature, it dominates man as an alien force. The laws of nature compel man to work as a necessity for survival. For man labour is a social act, even though its basis lies in the natural world. Marx explained the emergence of human society through man's action on nature: 'By thus acting on the external world and changing it, he at the same time changes his own nature.'[11] Social evolution is closely linked to the development of man's understanding and control of nature.

Social development does not abolish natural laws but, as time passes, these laws assume an increasingly social form. Take work, the basis for human existence. The progress of history does not free humanity from the need to work:

'So far therefore as labour is a creator of use values, is useful labour, it is a necessary condition, independent of all forms of society, for the existence of the human race, it is an eternal nature-imposed necessity, without which there can be no material exchanges between man and nature; and therefore no life.'[12]

The 'eternal nature-imposed necessity' expresses itself in changing forms of social organisation. The development of the social organisation of labour marks real historical advance:

'To the extent that the labour process is solely a process between man and nature, its simple elements remain common to all social forms of development. But each specific historical form of this process further develops its material foundations and social forms.'[13]

Marx argued that society can be understood from two points of view: the technical-natural and the social-historical. The laws of nature, mediated through society, are expressed in social laws specific to the particular stage of development of society. Marx emphasised this point in his explanation of the historical materialist approach:

'In the social production of their existence, men inevitably enter into definite relations, which are independent of their will, namely relations of production appropriate to a given stage in the development of their material forces of production.'[14]

Natural laws exist independently of the will of man. To the extent that society — through which the nature-imposed necessity of work is mediated — has yet to succeed in controlling nature, social laws continue to operate independently of human will:

> '**Natural laws cannot be abolished at all. What can change in historically different circumstances is only the form in which these laws assert themselves.**'[15]

The discovery of the particular social forms in which natural laws assert themselves, the laws of motion of particular human societies, is the object of study in Marxist theory.

## The social history of work

Every society has to work, produce and consume to reproduce itself:

> '**Labour is the everlasting nature-imposed condition of human existence, and is therefore independent of every form of that existence, or rather it is common to all forms of society in which human beings live.**'[16]

But the forms in which labour is organised — as slavery, serfdom, the peasant economy, wage labour — are historically specific, governed by the special laws arising from particular relations of production.

The development of the productivity of labour is the most striking manifestation of historical progress. Higher productivity leads to a wider social division of labour, which allows society to reproduce itself with less work and to create a larger surplus product. For Marx, the increase in the surplus product was the key to development. The struggle for survival becomes less intense as natural necessity becomes less immediate. Human society experiences this change as the replacement of natural needs by historically created needs. As Marx put it: 'Hunger is hunger: but the hunger that is satisfied by cooked meat eaten with knife and fork differs from the hunger that devours raw meat with the help of hands, nails and teeth.'[17]

Marx's emphasis on the reduction of labour-time shows how

central the growth of productivity and the forces of production were to his theory. For Marx, freedom from necessity, from the domination of nature, is achieved through economies in the deployment of the time available for work:

'**The less time society requires to produce wheat, cattle etc, the more time it wins for other production, material or mental. Just as in the case of an individual, the multiplicity of its development, its enjoyment and its activity depends on economisation of time.**'[18]

No society can escape the operation of this basic law: 'Economy of time, to this all economy ultimately reduces itself.'[19]

The historical transformation of social labour is apparent in the combined development of the division of labour and its socialisation. Before the capitalist epoch, social relations were characterised by the isolated productive activities of families and local communities. In general the division of labour was restricted to activities within a family in the local community. 'The product of labour bore the specific social imprint of the family relationship with its naturally evolved division of labour.'[20] The products of labour were social products, but only within the confines of the family and the community.

The parochial and atomised character of pre-capitalist society acted as a barrier to the development of social labour. Links among communities were restricted and self-sufficiency prevailed. Under these conditions the concept of labour-time applied only to the particular labour of an individual. A more universal application of the concept of labour-time was retarded by the underdeveloped division of labour: 'It was the distinct labour of the individual in its original form, the particular features of his labour and not its universal aspects that formed the social ties at the time.'[21]

Capitalism broke down the existing production relations and established a new division of labour. Under capitalism social ties are not restricted to local communities. Production is directed outward, through the market, to other communities and other parts of the world. Under these conditions the labour of every individual becomes a part of the labour of society and, through the exchange of products, the universal aspect of labour becomes relevant. The most progressive feature of capitalism was that it destroyed parochial obstacles and gave an impetus towards the development of a universal form of society.

Grossman explained how the socialisation of labour under capitalism was evidence of its historic mission:

> 'This process begins with the "scattered private property arising from individual labour"; it continues with the "centralisation of the means of production and socialisation of labour"; and it ends with the transformation "of already socialised production into socialised property" — a result that looms only at the end of a long historical transformation of social labour.'[22]

Marx's theory of value was designed to explain the distribution of labour-time in capitalist society. Under capitalism, the distribution of labour-time takes place automatically through the mechanism of the market. Individual producers exist within a division of labour in which the connections are only established through exchange. The social links between individual producers are established through commodities. These exchange on the basis of their equivalence as the products of equal amounts of labour-time — their possession of equal values: 'The form in which this proportional distribution of labour operates, in a state of society where the inter-connection of social labour is manifested in the private exchange of the individual products of labour, is precisely the exchange value of these products.'[23]

Under capitalism the distribution of labour takes place automatically. Products are not produced for a specific social want — for their use value — but for the market. The invisible hand of the market, the so-called law of supply and demand, regulates the distribution of labour-time and the products of labour. Atomised individual producers are brought together in a unified division of labour through a socially recognised regulator, the law of value. The products of labour, commodities, assume the form of value and are equated to each other on the basis of the amount of labour-time embodied in them.

In his excellent discussion of Marx's theory, Rubin portrayed value as a transmission belt that allows independent, private producers to adjust to each other:

> 'This adjustment is only possible if one part influences another through the movement of prices on the market, a movement which is determined by the law of value. In other words, it is only through the "value" of commodities that the working activity of separate independent producers leads to the productive unity which is called a

social economy, to the interconnections and mutual conditioning of the labour of individual members of society. Value is the transmission belt which transfers the working processes from one part of society to another, making that society a functioning whole.'[24]

The regulation of production through the market imposes a discipline on producers. The market has no compassion for losers and demands efficiency — the economy of labour-time. The inefficient use of labour is penalised through the operation of the law of value. The expenditure of inefficient labour does not enter into the calculation of the value of a commodity. The value of a commodity is determined, not by the quantity of labour, but by the amount of socially-necessary labour-time that it embodies.

The magnitude of socially-necessary labour-time is 'that required to produce an article under the normal conditions of production, and with the average degree of skill and intensity prevalent at the time'.[25] Any time expended above that which is socially necessary does not count as social labour and therefore adds no value to the commodity. The market acts as a regulator of the distribution of labour and for its efficient use. Capitalist development has brought about a decrease in the magnitude of socially-necessary labour required to produce commodities and allowed continuous reductions in the deployment of human labour-time.

By comparison with earlier forms of society the capitalist market is an efficient regulator of society's labour-time. Nevertheless capital imposes limits on the socialisation of labour: market relations, which proved such an advance as a means of distributing labour-time, also impose an element of chaos on society. Capitalist society acquires a productive unity through the interconnections created by the operation of the law of value. But these connections are continually put under strain by the autonomous activities of independent production units. The profound contradiction between the social character of labour and its private appropriation results in periodic breakdowns in the efficacy of the market, leading to crisis and stagnation.

Under capitalism labour becomes social indirectly, through the exchange of commodities; the labour of private individuals acquires its social character only through exchange. Labour-time is distributed automatically through the operation of the law of value which operates independently, 'behind the backs' of producers. It operates 'as a blind law of nature' maintaining 'the social equilibrium of production amid its accidental fluctuations'.[26]

A continuous tension between private and social labour leads to disruptions in the distribution of society's labour-time, revealing the historic limits to the capitalist mode of production. The further transformation of social labour and the removal of all obstacles to the socialisation of labour requires the elimination of capitalist relations of production. Only through the elimination of private capitalist property and the market can the restrictions on the further socialisation of labour be removed.

By eliminating capitalist production, the element of chaos can be removed and society, rather than the invisible hand of the market, can determine the distribution of labour-time. Production can become predetermined rather than being unconscious, and 'the labour of the individual is posited from the outset as social labour'.[27] The difference between capitalist and communist society can be best understood by looking at the all-important change that occurs in the regulation of labour-time.

The anarchy of capitalist production is a barrier to the socialisation of labour. The 'blind law' of the market can only be eliminated through a social revolution. In a planned economy labour is directly organised and becomes directly social. The link between individual producers is no longer made through the market, but through a social plan. Conscious regulation replaces unconscious reaction to the movement of the capitalist market. Society can acquire greater control over its resources and remove the existing obstacles to the socialisation of labour.

## Beyond the law of value

Marx's rejection of capitalism was not merely a personal response to the inequalities generated by capitalist exploitation. Marx advocated social revolution because he understood that capitalism itself threw up barriers to the systematic development of the forces of production. For Marx, human liberation meant overcoming the 'realm of necessity'. This required economy of labour-time, which in turn demanded the removal of the private appropriation of the products of labour and of the relations of production based upon it.

The creation of a communist society is intimately tied up with the socialisation of labour and the economy of labour-time. As we noted in Chapter 1, Marx was categorical on this point: the 'economy of time, along with the planned distribution of labour-time among the various branches of production, remains the first economic law on

**JOSEPH STALIN:** *once the hero of the international communist movement, now derided as a villain East and West, he symbolises the autocratic character of the Soviet regime*

**LEON TROTSKY:** *the commander of the Red Army addresses the troops fighting Western intervention in the Soviet state*

**LENIN:** *the blurred image at the centre of attention at the opening of the second congress of the Communist International in July 1920*

**A NEW DECADE — A NEW SOCIETY:** *trucks display the achievements of industrialisation, while peasants gaze at caricatures of their new class enemies –* **the** *kulaks*

**STALINIST ARITHMETIC:** *'more enthusiasm from the workers' exhorts this poster promoting the first five year plan which tried to cram five years' industrial production into four*

**THE STALIN SCHOOL OF FALSIFICATION:** *a faked photograph of Stalin sharing a bench with Lenin, to stress a bogus continuity between his policies and those of his predecessor*

**EDUCATION AS SOCIAL ENGINEERING:** *despite the scepticism of the women of Central Asia, the Soviet bureaucracy won new allies by training a layer of skilled workers*

**RED GUARDS RECRUITING:** *the decimation of the working class in the years of war paved the way for the takeover of the bureaucracy*

**THE REVOLUTION ABORTED:** *a gigantic lightbulb finished by hand symbolises the archaic design and technique of the Soviet economy and its failure to raise the productivity of labour*

**THE REVOLUTION UPHELD:** *the leaders of the Left Opposition with Trotsky (centre) after Stalin's clampdown*

**EUGENII PREOBRAZHENSKY:** *the bureaucracy's most rigorous critic in the realm of economic policy* the basis of communal production'.[28] This emphasis stemmed from the realisation that human development was intimately bound up with the increase in society's disposable labour-time: 'The saving of labour time (is) equal to an increase of free time, ie time for the full development of the individual, which in turn reacts back upon the productive power of labour as itself the greatest productive power.'[29]

It is readily apparent that the planned distribution of labour-time is antithetical to the automatic regulation of labour-time through the law of value. The law of value is a social law, specific to the capitalist mode of production, which regulates the interaction of unconscious individual producers. Planning, on the other hand, is a system of conscious regulation of economic life. It is therefore surprising to find that many writers on the Soviet Union argue that the law of value continues to regulate economic life under socialism, the type of society which Marx called the lower stage of communism.

The notion that the law of value operates in the Soviet Union was first popularised by Stalin. He argued that the law of value was 'not a bad thing, since it trains our business executives to conduct production on rational lines and disciplines them'. He continued:

**'It is not a bad thing because it teaches our executives systematically to improve methods of production, to lower production costs, to practice cost accounting, and to make their enterprises pay. It is a good practical school which accelerates the development of our executive personnel and their growth into genuine leaders of socialist production at the present stage of development.'**[30]

Stalin's equation of the law of value with socialism may be dismissed as no more than an apology for the state of affairs in the Soviet Union. What he called 'not a bad thing' was simply the unconscious and capricious operation of market forces.

Conscious regulation cannot replace the market overnight. Spontaneous forces may well influence and even dominate a post-capitalist society for some time. But in that case spontaneity will not be seen as a socialist regulator, but as an obstacle to planning. Let us now turn to the problem of economic regulation in the Soviet Union.

## The emergence of a new society

The Marxist approach of working out the laws of motion of Soviet society through an analysis of the changing material conditions has been widely disregarded in radical circles in the West. Armed with ready-made definitions, left-wing writers have tried to fit the Soviet Union into their categories, rather than examine the problem in its specificity. Cliff provides a typical example of this method:

> 'When Trotsky defined Russia as a society in transition, he emphasised correctly that as such it must by its own immanent laws lead either to the victory of socialism, or to the restoration of private capitalism. If the latter is ruled out, one of three possibilities remains.'[31]

This sort of speculation, which begins from 'one of three possibilities' or asks 'is it this or is it that?', inevitably fails to analyse the specific features of the society under investigation.

No society in transition can be analysed in abstraction from the prevailing material conditions. Marx and Engels anticipated the speculative mode of thought when they combated attempts to characterise socialist society by means of a series of fixed definitions. Engels scornfully dismissed discussion on the methods of distribution which would prevail under socialism. He argued that the form of distribution would depend on the development of the forces of production, on 'how much there is to divide up':

> 'But strangely enough it has not struck anyone that, after all, the method of distribution essentially depends on how much there is to distribute, and that this must surely change with the progress of production and social organisation, and that therefore the method of distribution will also change. But everyone who took part in the discussion described "socialist society" not as something continuously changing and advancing but as something stable and fixed once and for all.'[32]

Vulgar Marxists have continued to pursue this approach of general analysis and general definitions.

One of Preobrazhensky's great merits was that he tried to break from the tradition of vulgar Marxism and its general theories of the transition to socialism. He rigorously criticised rote definitions and platitudes about the conflict between planning and the law of value in the Soviet Union in the twenties. Highlighting the inapplicability of this simplistic approach to the complex post-capitalist societies of the future, Preobrazhensky asked:

> 'Is it possible that with regard to such different situations, such different technical and production relations, such different systems of ties between the organised economy and the private economy, we should be satisfied with one and the same general phrase — which will, of course, remain true for twenty or forty years, but just for that reason will always be empty of content?'[33]

Little did Preobrazhensky think that more than 60 years later 'the same general phrase' would be offered as an adequate analysis of the laws of motion of the Soviet Union.

To work out the laws of motion of Soviet society it is essential to approach it in terms of its specific historical evolution. We have to isolate those tendencies which appear to regulate the Soviet social formation. Western Sovietologists, Soviet social scientists and Marxist critics of the Soviet Union all agree that the basic relations of contemporary Soviet society were established in the thirties. We begin, therefore, by looking at the circumstances that gave rise to the social formation of the thirties.

## Collectivisation and industrialisation

There is a consensus that Stalin's campaign to collectivise agriculture and build up industry marked a major break with the previous patterns of Soviet development. What were the forces that helped to make this break?

The central challenge facing the post-revolutionary regime was to find a satisfactory method of economic regulation to replace the market. The defeat of the European revolution and the devastation resulting from the civil war made this problem even more acute. Building a new society based on a national division of labour, in face of a hostile world economy, imposed severe restrictions on the advance of the revolutionary process. By 1921, the leadership of the Bolshevik Party decided on a tactical retreat. The New Economic Policy was a compromise programme which recognised the need for a breathing space until revolution broke out elsewhere.

The Bolsheviks' emphasis on world revolution was not the product of some wild internationalist fantasy. It was a pragmatic recognition of the fact that the division of labour within one country could not surpass the efficiency and productivity of the international division of labour established through the capitalist world market. In the Soviet Union the potential for the socialisation of labour was restricted and, worse still, the capitalist-dominated world economy was a direct threat to the new society. The national constraints on the revolution forced the Bolsheviks to make a deal with the peasantry and allow market forces to operate in agriculture, sections of international commerce and in small-scale manufacturing.

Many studies of the Soviet Union have ignored the problem of national constraints. This is largely because of the popularity of the Stalinist dogma of 'socialism in one country', which justified the strategy of 'the national road to socialism'. Whatever view one takes of Stalin's strategy, it was certainly alien to Lenin's thinking. When he advocated the New Economic Policy in 1921, Lenin said:

> 'We know that so long as there is no revolution in other countries, only agreement with the peasantry can save the socialist revolution in Russia ....Basically the situation is this: we must satisfy the middle peasantry economically and go over to free exchange: otherwise it would be impossible — economically impossible — in view of the delay in the world revolution, to preserve the rule of the proletariat in Russia.'[34]

The delay in the world revolution forced the Bolsheviks to introduce 'free exchange' — market relations — in important areas of the economy.

The aim of the NEP was to use market forces as an incentive for the peasants to produce more food. Relying on the peasant's instinct for self-preservation, the Bolsheviks hoped to make the market raise the forces of production. They understood that this strategy carried the danger of encouraging capitalist forces, but under the circumstances they reckoned that this was a risk they had to take. In Chapter 2 we looked at the role of the NEP in destroying the gains of the revolution. Here we are concerned only with the problem market forces caused for the regulation of the Soviet economy.

The NEP succeeded in promoting economic recovery. Its very success, however, exacerbated the tension between the Soviet state and the free market sector. It was Preobrazhensky who first examined the conflict between the two sectors and their different forms of regulation. Preobrazhensky and the Left Opposition held that the conflict between the two modes of economic regulation could only be favourably resolved through the steady encroachment of the state sector on private production. Unless this occurred, market forces would strengthen and the law of value would gain influence over Soviet society.

In fact the policy of the Soviet leadership after Lenin's death allowed the NEP to become, by the late twenties, a serious threat to the Soviet regime. Growing prosperity in the countryside created a steady demand for industrial goods. The inability of industry to meet this demand created a 'goods famine'. The shortage of industrial goods increasingly alienated the peasantry from the Soviet regime. There was no incentive for peasants to sell their produce for money when money could not buy the goods they required. Thus peasants began to hoard grain and produce less food, moves which led to shortages in the towns and cities. The grain crisis of 1928 and 1929 showed that the regime was in serious danger of losing control over the countryside.

There is no doubt that the Soviet leaders faced tremendously difficult decisions. The state sector was confronted by the market relations of peasant agriculture and the enormous power of a hostile world capitalist economy. No matter what course of economic development was adopted, these pressures would have created major difficulties. Nevertheless Stalin and Bukharin made a critical blunder when, in 1924, they rejected Trotsky's proposals. Trotsky recommended diverting state resources into industrial investment, so that enough industrial products could be made to meet the demands of the countryside.[35] This was the only realistic option for the Soviet Union at the time.

The blindness of Stalin and Bukharin to the dangers arising from the operation of the law of value stemmed from a failure to come to grips with the problem of economic regulation. This becomes clear in the writings of Bukharin, the key theoretician of 'socialism in one country'. Bukharin took a narrow, technical view of the question of economic regulation. He denied that the law of value was specific to capitalist society and argued that this law had a 'material content' valid for every form of society. This 'material content' was 'the need to distribute the existing labour force proportionately between different areas and branches of the economy'.[36]

Bukharin was right to suggest that every society needs to distribute its labour-time. But by posing the question in such a general way, he ignored not only the specific character of the distribution of labour-time through the law of value under capitalism. He also neglected the way the law of value came into conflict with the attempt to regulate labour through planning in a society attempting to move beyond capitalism towards communism.

Bukharin's ahistorical approach led him to see the problems of the Soviet Union as merely a variant of the problems of capitalist society. Hence he dismissed the crisis of the Soviet economy in 1930 as a local manifestation of the crisis in the capitalist world:

'At the same time, however, the growth of our economy and the indubitable advance of socialism are accompanied by peculiar "crises", which despite the obviously decided difference between the laws governing our development and that of capitalism, apparently "repeat" the crises of capitalism, even though in a distorted mirror. Here as there, we see a disproportion between production and consumption.'[37]

Bukharin's timeless formula about the disproportion between production and consumption ignored the real conflict between the law of value and planning in the Soviet Union. Indeed, Bukharin bitterly criticised Preobrazhensky and the Left Opposition for always discussing the two modes of regulation in terms of conflict. Bukharin argued that the 'principle of spontaneity' and the 'planning principle' not only struggled, but also 'co-operated' within the framework of the law of value.[38] This optimistic view of the harmonious relation between the market and planning led to the policies which eventually resulted in the grain strikes of the late twenties.

While Bukharin and Stalin could dismiss theoreticians who argued that the law of value presented a threat, they could not ignore its practical effects. From 1928 onwards the predictions of the Left Opposition began to be borne out by events. As market forces came into their own, the state lost much of its power over the economy. Industry remained paralysed by backwardness, and food shortages became widespread as the countryside passed out of control. The earlier warnings of Preobrazhensky to the effect 'that we accumulate not on the basis of or parallel with the operations of the law of value, but on the basis of a desperate struggle against it'[39] went unheeded. By 1929, the Stalinist bureaucracy could not avoid a struggle against the influence of the law of value without risking the destruction of the Soviet regime.

The Soviet regime had lost precious time and its options had narrowed severely. It was now faced with a political as well as an economic crisis. To solve the problems of economic regulation, the regime had introduced a system of market incentives. Now this system had broken down and no further incentives were available. Since the Stalinist bureaucracy had no means of encouraging the peasants to produce, it had only one alternative — to force them. This was the meaning of collectivisation.

Many authors have commented on the panic which led, virtually overnight, to the policy of forced collectivisation. Yet while the new policy was implemented in a frenzy, it was the outcome of underlying material forces. Collectivisation was not merely an economic policy: it was a survival strategy designed to compensate for the lack of an economic regulator. The bureaucracy now set about organising the Soviet economy through the exercise of terror. The repressive apparatus required to coerce the representatives of market forces could also be used to reassert political control over the countryside.

There is a growing body of literature about the contribution made by mass collectivisation to the subsequent development of the Soviet economy.[40] However, the question of whether or not collectivisation provided a surplus for development is of secondary importance. The aim of collectivisation was to retain political control by breaking the influence of the law of value.

Collectivisation led to the destruction of the agents of the market forces and gave the Stalinist regime the freedom to carry out its plans with little regard to incentives, the availability of consumer goods or the consumption needs of the peasantry. The 'demand' side of the market was effectively suppressed and the state could pursue its policies with a new autonomy. For Stalin the collapse of agriculture was a small price to pay for this freedom to manoeuvre.

The industrialisation drive which was launched in parallel with mass collectivisation aimed to achieve industrial self-sufficiency. The rapid pace of Soviet industrialisation was motivated by the awareness that time was running out. This fear was confirmed, not only by the internal instability of the Soviet Union, but by the awareness that hostile imperialist forces would not forever keep their hands off the Soviet Union. The break in diplomatic relations between Britain and the Soviet Union in 1927 marked the beginning of a new phase of anti-Soviet hostility from the Western camp.

The industrialisation programme of the first five year plan introduced in 1929 was designed in part as a response to the foreign threat. The destruction of the market represented a major break with earlier forms of economic regulation. The state emerged as the main organiser of economic activities. There was no more talk of co-operating with the law of value. Leading Soviet economists declared the spontaneous forces of the market dead and argued that state planning could be the only regulator of the economy.[41] This new emphasis on 'the will of the state' indicated the desperate desire to escape the havoc wrought by the law of value.

## The foundations of the new order

The elimination of the market gave the Soviet state a degree of control over the resources of society. In practice the bureaucracy's control was limited by its lack of detailed information and expertise in managing different aspects of the economy. Yet it succeeded in acquiring overall control over the physical resources of society. Moreover, the absence of constraints gave the Soviet bureaucracy considerable power to allocate resources in line with state policies.

Control over physical resources did not resolve the problems of economic regulation. But by mobilising raw materials and labour on a vast scale, without regard to the efficient deployment of society's labour-time, the bureaucrats succeeded in putting off problems for a time. Once policy objectives were established, they could ensure that the necessary resources were made available. The limits to the utilisation of resources that prevailed under capitalist market forces could be ignored. The inefficient use of resources was regarded as a price well worth paying to achieve the central goal of industrial growth.

Soviet industrialisation was achieved, not through effective economic management, but by sweeping aside all the social and political obstacles that stood in its way. By capitalist criteria many of the bureaucracy's investment decisions made no sense. In terms of rational planning, the industrialisation drive lacked conscious direction and appeared more like a form of planned anarchy. But whatever its policy defects, the bureaucracy's programme removed all barriers in the way of industrialisation. How did it succeed?

The death of the capitalist market also meant the passing of the law of value as the regulator of society's labour-time. Labour no longer had to create values — it had only to produce useful products. Instead of the market, a chain of command now determined the allocation of resources. The ultimate limit on the distribution of labour-time was the total physical labour available to Soviet society.

This labour was used inefficiently because Soviet planning was not a conscious process. But even in the absence of conscious planning, the elimination of the market gave the Soviet bureaucracy the freedom to deploy resources which would not have been mobilised if the criterion of capitalist profitability had still been in operation. The

Soviet experience showed that even the grossly inefficient application of labour could lead to the establishment of new industries. The new industries may have been built with two to three times as much labour as would have been required in the capitalist world, but built they were. Labour on a scale which would have been regarded as wasteful in a capitalist society, or under a consciously planned socialist society, was essential to develop industry under the peculiar conditions of the Soviet Union under Stalin.

The main advantage of the Soviet social formation was the freedom it had won from the restrictions imposed by capitalist market relations. The success of the industrialisation drive depended on the bureaucracy's liberty to deploy resources in a manner not feasible in any other society. The availability of vast resources and the freedom to use them with little regard for efficiency was the secret behind the growth of Soviet industry. The Soviet Union's considerable natural reserves of minerals and other sources of energy and raw materials was vital for its industrial development. But the most important resource of all was the army of labour that was drafted from the countryside into the factories. Cuts in living standards provided more resources for investment and made it easier for the bureaucracy to ignore social demand.

Whatever the social costs, the growth of Soviet industry stood in sharp contrast to the depression enveloping the rest of the world. In the thirties the Soviet experiment won an international reputation for its progressive character: even its critics could barely hide their envy. The British ambassador in Moscow noted that 'whatever the prejudice or the political anxiety that might arise from a dislike of Bolshevik methods, the experiment in itself is one of the most important and most far-reaching that has ever been undertaken.'[42]

The achievements of Soviet industrialisation were widely hailed as the results of socialist planning. This mistaken view confused the legal form of the plan with the results of industrialisation. Both Soviet and Western experts now concede that industrial development took place despite planning targets rather than because of them. The key instrument for developing the forces of production was the bureaucracy's central control over material allocation and its freedom to pursue policy priorities regardless of the cost. To this day it is this control that gives the Soviet social formation its coherence — a point well understood by contemporary Soviet economists. In July 1965 academician Aganbegyan, director of the Novosibirsk economics institute and a frequent contributor to *Pravda* and specialist publications, paid tribute to the centralised distribution system:

> 'Our systems of planning, establishing incentives and managing industry were established in the thirties. Ever since then nothing has changed except the names given things....Our prices and our monetary-value relationships serve no purpose at all. The thing held most important is centralised distribution.'[43]

The irrelevance to real life of the plans drawn up by the Soviet administration indicates the absence of a system of economic regulation. This problem is today the subject of open discussion in the Soviet Union, where experts generally agree that no mechanism exists with which to govern society's labour-time. Professor Beloysov summed up the new consensus at a symposium on national planning in 1982: 'Strange as it may seem, there is still no clear understanding as to what criterion should be used for evaluating performance results and the utilisation of resources for the national economy as a whole or for individual branches, regions or enterprises.'[44]

While the Soviet bureaucrats have not managed to create a planned economy, they have, in line with policy objectives, succeeded in concentrating resources in priority areas. By identifying priority sectors the Soviet Union has been able to establish new industries and make breakthroughs in fields such as space technology. Pouring everything into specially-designated sectors was a crucial aspect of the industrialisation drive of the thirties. It stimulated the assimilation of new technology in key branches of production and helped provide the Soviet Union with an outstanding military capability: 'The strength of the central planning mechanism lies in its ability to concentrate resources in priority areas, and in this respect the defence sector has historically been the main beneficiary.'[45] Central control over resources and the capacity to concentrate them in key areas enable the Soviet bureaucracy to reach some of its key objectives.

At the same time the bureaucracy's dependence on priority allocation reveals the fragility of the social formation. The very existence of priority allocation amounts to admitting that plan mechanisms have failed. In practice the priority system means that the bureaucracy cannot maintain momentum throughout the economy: non-priority sectors are simply allowed to languish. Thus the late seventies decision to concentrate investment in primary and extractive industries had a devastating impact on metallurgy and machine building. In 1979 production in the much-vaunted steel industry fell for the first time in Soviet peacetime history — only to fall again in 1980.

The tension between priority allocation and the regulation of society's resources is not new. Even in the thirties, when industry was less complex, practical economic policy-making was synonymous with priority allocation. One observer, who worked with the economic research institute of the planning ministry *Gosplan* in Moscow in the late thirties, noted that instead of coherent planning there was a simple system of priorities, and that these were limited 'to products and services important enough to merit decisions by the politburo and its permanent staff'.[46] Since the central bureaucracy could only directly supervise a small portion of the economy, the few priority sectors were forced to exist in an environment of chaos.

## The limits of priority allocation

Any sort of planned society will require a system of priority allocation. In a socialist society, priorities decided by social consensus will become an important influence on planning. In the Soviet social formation, however, priority allocation has become a substitute for economic regulation. Let us look at this question more closely.

As the Soviet bureaucracy has discovered, it is fairly easy to destroy the operation of the law of value, but much more difficult to acquire mastery over society's resources. Any alternative to economic regulation through value relations must confront the problem of spontaneity. Spontaneous or unconscious forces are the socially mediated way in which nature-imposed necessity is experienced by society. The capitalist market is one form of social organisation through which spontaneity reminds humanity of its lack of control over its own creations. This is why the Marxist tradition has always placed such an emphasis on conscious control. The central problem of the transition to communism is that unless conscious regulation is established, the elimination of the market will lead to the destruction of capitalist regulation, but the forces of spontaneity will continue to wreak havoc.

Worse still, there is the danger that post-capitalist society is left with all the disadvantages and none of the advantages of capitalism. The market at least gives coherence to the division of labour through the process of exchange. If this is not replaced with an alternative form of regulation, the spontaneous distribution of labour-time can easily become even more anarchic than it is under the discipline of the market. This is precisely the problem that has dogged the Soviet bureaucracy: <u>the law of value has been destroyed, but the tendency towards the spontaneous distribution of labour-time has not</u>.

The elimination of the law of value gives the Soviet bureaucracy <u>control over the distribution of material resources without being subject to the constraints of profitability</u> or efficiency. This is the main advantage of the Soviet social formation, one it shares with any post-capitalist system. The drawback, however, is that physical control cannot be translated into conscious direction and development because of the strength of the forces of spontaneity. Isolated individuals and production units make things in an increasingly random manner without any effective mechanism for regulating input or output. Meanwhile, in the planning offices, the bureaucrats can distribute, but not regulate, society's resources. As we shall argue, this leads to a structural inability to socialise society's labour-time.

In the absence of economic regulation, the Soviet social formation has no inherent tendency to socialise labour or to establish a national division of labour. While the exchange of commodities provides capitalism with a mechanism for extending the social division of labour, the Soviet Union has no such mechanism at its disposal. Although there is no capitalist market, the Soviet producers still remain isolated from one another. In technical terms the Soviet division of labour appears similar to that of Western industrial societies. But this formal similarity obscures the lack of a cohering mechanism between different units of production.

The attempt to give coherence to the economy through a plan and the use of success indicators establishes only a technical unity among producers. Different producers depend on each other for particular products, giving the Soviet division of labour a semblance of coherence. But a technical relationship is not a substitute for a social division of labour. It does not solve the problem of the efficient utilisation of social labour, nor does it necessarily lead to harmony or co-operation. This is why, ever since the thirties, there has been a tendency towards the breakdown of the technical division of labour in the Soviet Union.

From the start, plans for Soviet industrialisation projected increased specialisation and a growing division of labour, but in fact the opposite has taken place. To secure raw materials and components, each industry has diversified vertically into more backward areas, rather than reaching out to establish links with other sectors at the same or higher levels of development. In his study of the Soviet metal-fabricating industry, Granick has summarised the trends:

**'From the early 1930s on, Soviet metal-working practice developed along the opposite line of vertical integration within individual factories — technological development was distorted....Various early attempts to break out of the mould were unsuccessful and had to be abandoned. Thereafter, the solidified pattern of vertical integration was regularly condemned, its inefficiencies were pointed out and, in fact, open defenders of the existing structure were rare. Nevertheless despite all this verbal agreement as to the fundamental faults of the existing organisation of production, practical attempts to develop interplant division of labour, rather than increasing, grew fewer and more feeble.'**[47]

The phenomenon of 'empire-building' is a symptom of the tendency towards the fragmentation of the existing division of labour. The response of individual production units to the problems caused by the absence of economic regulation is to strive for a measure of self-sufficiency. Thus instead of a mutually beneficial division of labour *between* enterprises, industries and regions, the pattern is for the division of labour to be reproduced *within* each sector of the economy.

Spontaneous elements which lead towards fragmentation can only be neutralised through conscious planning. In the absence of the social relations that would make planning possible, the Soviet bureaucracy has been forced to fall back on its own devices. Only through its direct political control can it give any coherence to the economy. In practice this means that only a limited range of sectors can come under its inspection, and that the elements of spontaneity acquire considerable influence elsewhere.

As a strategy, priority allocation has restricted scope. It is therefore likely to be more effective at an early stage of industrialisation than when the technological division of labour becomes more complex. As the number of sectors increases, priority allocation has less of an impact over industry as a whole. This happens not only because of the increased sophistication of industry, but because of the difficulty in spreading over a large number of sectors the high input of labour-time that priority allocation demands. Although this system can achieve considerable results, it does so only at a very high price.

Even in the thirties the establishment of new priority sectors required the massive mobilisation of resources and an indifference to standards of efficiency and quality. The main defect of the priority system was that it depended on the mobilisation rather than on the saving of resources. This method of management has been singularly unsuccessful in raising the productivity of labour and increasing the labour-time available to society. Thus priorities acclaimed with every five year plan — the conservation of metal and other raw materials, the reduction of manual labour or increased production of consumer goods — are seldom realised.

Priorities which require resources to be *saved* have never been realised throughout the history of the Soviet Union. Such objectives, which imply the more intensive and efficient use of existing investment, cannot be achieved through central directives and allocations without a fundamental change in social relations. The more efficient use of resources in this way requires a dynamic of development immanent in the process of production, not external pressure. This is why it is easier to establish a new priority sector than to modernise an existing sector. A new priority sector requires merely an abundance of resources, not that these resources are efficiently used.

The limits to priority allocation ultimately reflect the prevailing obstacles to the socialisation of labour in the Soviet Union. One of the main advantages of a planned economy is the directly social character of labour. Under capitalism the social character of labour is realised only indirectly, through exchange, leading to misuse and inefficiency in the distribution of labour. In the Soviet social formation the character of labour is different from that which prevails in either a planned or a capitalist society.

Although the capitalist market does not exist in the Soviet Union, spontaneity survives. Through the state, the bureaucracy tries to curb the effects of spontaneity and to establish a degree of coherence among different production units. These units do not produce commodities for the market, but products in line with the bureaucracy's directives. Ideally they produce use values for others and, since the object and direction of labour is decided in advance, labour acquires a directly social character. However, this ideal is contradicted by the elements of spontaneity in the system — the lack of control over the distribution of resources and the absence of economic regulation.

Since no regulating mechanism exists in the Soviet Union there is no way of ensuring that the products of labour become use values. In practice neither producers nor consumers can be certain that the goods they produce or purchase will serve the purposes for which they are intended. Within a single enterprise the problem can be resolved through close inspection and the products of one department can be used as useful inputs to another. In priority sectors the problem is resolved through a system of incentives and careful supervision. Other industries confront the problem by minimising purchases from outside and producing many of their inputs themselves. But all these attempts underline the difficulty in realising the social character of labour. Without these measures the element of spontaneity would prevail and the social character of labour would not be realised at all.

The existence of a considerable apparatus between producer and consumer to ensure that products of labour actually become use values is another hallmark of the lack of economic regulation. This is the only way the Soviet social formation can realise the social character of labour. In effect it means that the Soviet bureaucracy is forced to organise around the spontaneous element in society to curb its effects.

The strength of spontaneity is revealed by the way that it shapes the existing division of labour — despite the best efforts of the Soviet state. Because of the tendency towards autarchy, each industry and region seeks the maximum level of autonomy from the unpredictable national division of labour. Every major Soviet leader since the thirties has demanded an end to this tendency. As early as 1931 a high-ranking Soviet official complained:

**'Our own business leaders...themselves want to possess everything — their own foundry, boiler shop and smithy — and often these efforts are supported by the working mass: everyone tries to get control over whatever he needs and to live in a self-serving, semi-naturalistic economy.'**[48]

The same point has been reiterated by Malenkov, Khrushchev, Brezhnev, Andropov and Chernenko. The fragmentation of the division of labour remains a central theme of economic discussion in the Soviet Union today.

Fal'tsman and Kornev complain about the prevailing forms of autarchic management:

'Some enterprises try to reduce external economic relations to a minimum by developing their own instruction and repair facilities, their own motor pool, their own computers, etc. The attempt of every economic unit to function with a maximum degree of autonomy naturally results in the loss of investment resources.'[49]

The same point is emphasised by Kheiman in his study of the machine-building industry. He comments on the prevalence of 'gigantic autarchy' in this sector and indicates that even medium-sized plants 'use their own personnel to produce the auxiliary equipment they absolutely need and a broad range of blanks, component assemblies and parts, a large mix of tools, and almost all production accessories'.[50]

The tendency to strive for local self-sufficiency at the expense of a wider national division of labour expresses the obstacles to the socialisation of labour in the Soviet Union. Individual units try to restrain the spontaneous elements and compensate for the incoherence of the economy by establishing their own division of labour — one within which the social character of labour can be realised. Under these circumstances the overall, national division of labour acquires the form of a sophisticated system of barter, which is kept together by the centre through its control over the distribution of material resources and the method of priority allocation.

The widely-discussed issues of waste and economic irrationality in the Soviet Union are symptoms of the problem of realising the social character of labour. Even Soviet scholars now more or less concede this problem. Thus, in an assessment of the Soviet economy written for a closed seminar organised by the economic department of the central committee of the Soviet Communist Party, Zaslavskaya has taken scientists to task for taking as given 'the direct social nature of socialist labour'.[51] Zaslavskaya recognises empirically the strength of the spontaneous elements in the Soviet economy. But, following the anti-working class prejudices she shares with much of the Soviet intelligentsia, she blames the influence of spontaneous forces on the workers, or, more specifically, on the lack of regulation over the labour market. According to this theory the Soviet Union has a planned economy, but the working class upsets it:

'The role of the spontaneous, that is not regulated, behaviour of the workers in the development of the socialist economy has many ramifications. Several aspects of it often infringe upon its planned

**character, cause disproportions and lower the rate of production development.'**[52]

Castigating the Soviet working class is the bureaucrats' instinctive response to the persistence of spontaneity. To explore the problem of the distribution of labour-time would reveal the historical limits of the Soviet social formation.

## Notes

1  Marx & Engels (1983), p393.
2  See Bellis (1979).
3  Mandel (1974), p7.
4  See the brilliant essay on this subject by Grossman (1943).
5  Marx (1973), p109.
6  Binns & Haynes (1980), p39.
7  Mandel (1977), p11.
8  Grossman (1943), p517.
9  Marx & Engels (1975), p145.
10  Marx (1974), p27.
11  Marx (1974), p173.
12  Marx (1974), p50.
13  Marx (1971), p883.
14  Marx (1970), p20.
15  Marx in Marx & Engels (1975), p196.
16  Marx (1974), p290.
17  Marx (1970), p197.
18  Marx (1973), pp172-3.
19  Marx (1973), p173.
20  Marx (1970), p33.
21  Marx (1970), p33.
22  Grossman (1948), p83.
23  Marx in Marx & Engels (1975), p196.
24  Rubin (1972), p81.
25  Marx (1974), p47.
26  Marx (1973), p158.
27  Marx (1971), p880.
28  Marx (1973), p113.
29  Marx (1973), p711.
30  Stalin (1972), p19.
31  Cliff (1970), p142.

32  Engels in Marx & Engels (1975), p393.
33  Preobrazhensky (1967), pp59-60.
34  Lenin 'Report on the substitution of a tax in kind for the surplus grain appropriation system, tenth congress of the RCP(B)', *CW32*, pp215, 225.
35  For a useful discussion of this debate see Day (1981).
36  See Lewin (1973), p91.
37  Bukharin (1980), p13.
38  See the discussion in Davies (1980), p35.
39  Preobrazhensky (1967), p38.
40  See the useful review article by Ellman (1975).
41  See *Pravda,* 8 October 1931.
42  Cited in Haslam (1983).
43  *Bandierra Rossa,* July 1965.
44  See *Planovoye khozyaistvo,* No 5, May 1982.
45  Amann (1982).
46  Miller (1964).
47  Granick (1967), p143.
48  Cited in Hutchings (1984), p30.
49  Fal'tsman & Kornev (1984), p44.
50  Kheiman (1984).
51  Zaslavskaya (1984).
52  Zaslavskaya (1984).

# 6. Laws of motion

The failure of economic regulation is widely recognised both inside and outside the Soviet Union. For some years both Soviet and Western economists have pointed to the failure of the system to make a transition from what they refer to as an extensive to an intensive mode of development.

*Extensive* growth means expanding production by mobilising more resources of labour and other inputs. *Intensive* growth on the other hand implies an increase in productivity through improvements in technology. Most experts now agree that the pattern of extensive growth of the period before the war has become obsolete at today's higher level of technological development.

Both Soviet and Western authorities identify the problem of economic regulation in technical terms. For Soviet experts it is a question of bad planning. Zaslavskaya pins the blame on lack of innovation in the apparatus and argues that the methods of economic management 'correspond for the most part to the level of development of the productive forces of Soviet society in the thirties'.[1] The implication is clear: the solution to the problems of Soviet society lies in institutional reform designed to organise the productive forces at the higher level of the eighties.

The Soviet leadership also argues that social development is thwarted by outdated social relations. In 1983 Andropov agreed with the academic diagnosis and conceded the need for restructuring:

> 'Why have we not been as successful as we need to be in improving the efficiency of production and of the economy as a whole? Why are we not getting the proper return on our huge capital investments, and why are scientific and technological achievements not being incorporated in production fast enough? The main reason is that our efforts to improve and restructure the economic mechanism and the forms of management have been lagging behind the demands posed by the present level of Soviet society's development.'[2]

The same message was reiterated by Gorbachev shortly after he took office in 1984.[3]

Stating that the level of the productive forces in the Soviet Union has gone beyond the existing forms of social organisation is an oblique way of admitting that Soviet social relations are a barrier to further development. This recognition of reality is however merely an empirical one. Soviet academics and politicians have avoided drawing out its logical consequence — that the existing social relations are not only a legacy of the thirties, but are continuously re-created in the present.

## The persistence of spontaneity

The centralised command of resources introduced under Stalin was the only way to guarantee the survival of the bureaucratic regime. It has produced considerable, but highly uneven, economic development: impressive technological achievements coexist with backward methods of production. The high percentage of unskilled manual labour in the Soviet workforce today and the continual squandering of raw materials indicate that social development is still retarded. Indeed the uneven advance of technique and the parallel lack of progress in the socialisation of labour reveal a close correspondence between forces and relations of production. The methods of the thirties are not, therefore, just a legacy from the past: they lie at the heart of the Soviet system. Any attempt to overcome the limitations which the old structures still impose on development would require a fundamental social transformation.

Soviet literature blames the persistence of spontaneous elements, not on basic social relations, but on individual failings and institutional conservatism. For example Kurashvii, a severe critic of old-fashioned economic methods, blames 'conservative and inactive elements in the state apparatus'.[4] Gorbachev has also emphasised this theme in numerous speeches and, ironically, many Western specialists make the same point. Granick for example argues that, with more innovative managers and a better system of incentives, the Soviet economy could become dynamic.[5]

Radical critics recognise that the problems facing the Soviet Union are more fundamental. However, there is a general tendency to confuse symptoms with causes. Mandel has often remarked on the tension that exists between the central planning apparatus and the individual enterprises. It is well known that enterprises claim the maximum amount of resources from the centre and give back as little as possible in the form of products. According to Mandel, this contradiction explains the failure to achieve planning targets. 'One of the main conflicts', he contends, is that 'between (1) potential optimisation of economic growth and use of economic resources which flows from planning and expresses the conditions of socialised property, and (2) the actual indifference to such optimisation by the individual bureaucrats, whose aims are only those of maximising their own production.'[6]

As a description Mandel's account may be correct. The conflict between what he calls the 'representatives of the collective interests of the bureaucracy' and individual sections of the bureaucracy seems to influence most aspects of economic life in the Soviet Union. But to reduce the issue to the prevalence of self-interest — individual bureaucrats 'maximising their own production' — is to avoid explaining how the Soviet system has allowed self-interest to flourish. Every social formation that has not overcome the problem of scarcity will experience a contradiction between collective and individual interests. Marx clearly recognised this in his discussion of the lower and the higher stages of communism.[7] However, Marx never argued that self-interest had to be eradicated before communism could be built. On the contrary, he recognised the reality of self-interest and considered it as an important influence on the process of transition to communism.

The self-interest of Soviet enterprise directors explains little about the social formation. Everybody can agree that officials want to maximise their personal consumption; everybody can accept that this may explain why they steal and cheat. But the consumption patterns of the bureaucracy are not the main barrier to social development. Personal greed can explain neither the underlying tendency towards the fragmentation of the division of labour, nor the immanent obstacles to realising its social character. The individual enterprise head is not just a greedy consumer: above all, he is a product of the existing social relations. The tendency towards spontaneity forces even the most ascetic and conscientious enterprise director to behave in the same way as his corrupt colleagues.

Even during the first five year plan managers and directors had to take account of the anarchic tendencies in the division of labour. Unless, at the level of the enterprise, steps were taken to compensate for the lack of coherence in the economy, the manager would meet with failure. As a result, enterprise directors instinctively hoarded resources and labour and tried to make themselves as self-sufficient as possible. Thus a study of metallurgy in 1932, published in the authoritative *Planovoye khozyaistvo*, noted that 'factories which had not aimed at self-sufficiency paid for it with lower construction tempos'.[8]

The inherent defect of the Soviet system is its tendency to push individual enterprises away from co-operation and specialisation. In 1941 Malenkov made the familiar complaint that 'in many enterprises, raw materials, processed materials, tools, things for which our industry has a desperate need, are piled up wherever they happen to fall, spoil, rust, become useless'.[9] Malenkov was little concerned about bureaucratic consumption; but he was very much worried by enterprises which responded to the uncertainty of supply by hoarding resources.

Once the issue of 'self-interest' is posed in a descriptive or ahistorical way, the investigation of social relations will yield meagre results. The subjective desires of bureaucratic consumers are not the driving force of Soviet society and little can be achieved by analysing them. On the contrary it is this subjective outlook that needs to be explained from an analysis of the social relations of Soviet society.

Many radical critics of Soviet society have tried to explain it in terms of conflicting economic laws, generally pursuing the tension between the law of the plan and the law of value identified in the discussions of Preobrazhensky and Trotsky. This dualistic model provided useful insights into developments in the twenties, but it mystifies the tendencies that emerged with the rise of the Soviet social formation in the thirties. Thus while Mandel can maintain that 'conscious distribution of economic resources through the plan is now the decisive characteristic of the new production relations', he is forced to note that in reality not all is conscious.[10] As we have seen, he qualifies his argument by inventing a commodity market in the consumer goods sector.

Instead of discussing Soviet society in terms of conflicting economic laws, it is more useful to begin from its peculiar form of social labour. The Soviet social formation is characterised by the absence of control over the distribution of labour-time; hence the tendency towards spontaneity is the dominant trend. The effects of this trend can be curbed through central control over material resources and the system of priority allocations. But spontaneity itself cannot be suppressed or overcome, and indeed most patterns of social interaction are reproduced through the attempt to curb it. The autarchic patterns of Soviet economic life are themselves created and re-created through the attempt to come to terms with the forces of spontaneity. This can also be seen in the way that the system of priority allocation has come into conflict with the standard institutions of the central bureaucracy.

In recent years the Soviet bureaucracy has used priority projects as short-term expedients to solve a complex range of problems. Special goal-oriented programmes, cutting across existing ministries, have been set up to deal with key problems.[11] The result of this mushrooming of special projects and experiments is that, to respond to immediate pressures, the bureaucracy is forced to cut across its own institutions. Hence what the literature calls 'planning', or 'the economic mechanism', or 'the law of organisation', is really an administrative response to forces which remain outside the bureaucracy's control. Consequently the institutions of the Soviet bureaucracy are often the result of a pragmatic adaptation to the forces of spontaneity rather than the outcome of conscious policy.

The Soviet bureaucracy has managed to live with the element of spontaneity and to institutionalise many of its effects. But it has singularly failed to transform its framework for dealing with the economy into a mechanism for regulating the distribution of labour-time. This is a historic failure which is now widely recognised. The dominant response has been to give up trying to achieve conscious regulation and to allow the spontaneous element to assume the form of a market. This response is based on the assumption that a market would at least regulate the distribution of labour-time and overcome the fragmentary character of the existing relations of production.

In Soviet literature the restoration of the market is given a bizarre justification: the law of value, it is argued, is an essential component of the transition to communism. This view first emerged among the Soviet reformers of the sixties. The failure of the planning mechanism led even former anti-marketeers like Strumilin, a key figure in *Gosplan* in the thirties, to denounce 30 years later those who believed in the directly social character of social labour. The rehabilitation of the law of value was an empirical adjustment to the persistence of unregulated economic relations.

In recent years, and especially since the death of Brezhnev in 1982, there has been a growing tendency to criticise economic managers and enterprise directors for not taking sufficient advantage of the law of value. The economists of the Novosibirsk institute have emphasised this point. Zaslavskaya has called for 'more active use of "automatic" regulators in balancing production, linked to the development of market relations'.[12] Using the June 1983 plenum of the central committee of the Soviet Communist Party to legitimise the revision of Marx's theory of value, top bureaucrats also drew attention to the lack of economic coherence between different sectors and approved the wider operation of the law of value as a means of overcoming it.

Kronrod has since explained that one of the aims of socialist development is to improve the use of the law of value: 'In our view forms of using the law of value in a socialist economy will be improved with the development of the socialisation of production.' He has criticised current restrictions on the law of value, noting that the 'violation of the law of value and laws of monetary circulation is especially costly to society'.[13]

The modern attempt to reinstate the law of value as a superior economic regulator is not designed to restore capitalism in the Soviet Union, though that is its logical conclusion. The real aim is to legitimise the non-directly social character of labour. The market enthusiasts thus make a virtue of a fundamental defect of the Soviet social formation. For Marxists the failure of the Soviet system to make the labour of every individual a part of the labour of society, through a conscious plan and division of labour, is a key index of its failure to develop towards communism. Yet Soviet economists elevate this into a positive feature of what they call 'developed socialist society'. Their approach thus becomes an apology for spontaneous tendencies, expressing a disenchantment with the bureaucracy's attempts to control society's resources and a longing for the market.

The key to understanding Soviet society lies in the unique character of its division of labour. Maintained through central control, the technical division of labour is insufficient to sustain co-operation and a social division of labour on a national scale. There exist no mechanisms through which the process of production can socialise labour. Without these, the social character of labour is realised only in special circumstances and with a great deal of effort. The tendency towards the fragmentation of the division of labour and the atomisation of individual producers dominates Soviet society.

The effectiveness of the Soviet Union's public institutions is proportional to the extent to which they can adapt and curb fragmentary tendencies. This explains both the effectiveness of the system of priority allocations and the irrelevance of the central targets of the plan. As we shall show, the dominant character of this tendency is confirmed by the fact that every policy and every organisational measure simply modifies the working out of this tendency and reproduces it in a different form.

In the absence of both a market and a plan, the distribution of labour-time has the advantages of neither. Instead spontaneity breeds fragmentation and successful state policy is the exception, not the rule. Let us look closer at the social patterns that have emerged on the basis of Soviet social relations.

## Central control and the enterprise

To survive, every society needs to reproduce itself through the creation of a surplus fund. One of the strengths of the Soviet social formation, as it demonstrated in the Second World War, is its ability to mobilise manpower and raw materials for the purposes of investment and the creation of a surplus product. High levels of fixed investment are a longstanding feature of the Soviet Union: its total fixed assets more than quadrupled between 1960 and 1980. Many observers have argued that high investment is a progressive feature of the Soviet Union, but high levels of investment are not necessarily a sign of social development. The criterion for assessing whether investment is progressive is its contribution to the creation of a surplus product.

High rates of investment — what some have described as 'production for its own sake' — are not a matter of choice for the Soviet bureaucracy. High growth in heavy industry and the tendency to overfulfil targets indicate anarchy in the deployment of resources, rather than conscious choice. One useful study of Soviet economic policy in the late forties and early fifties concludes that planning had little direct influence on growth:

**'Heavy industry did grow rapidly after the war. The evidence of this book suggests that it did so in spite of the leadership's wishes and not because of them.'**[14]

The construction sector provides perhaps the clearest example of the lack of control over investment. For decades the Soviet bureaucracy has tried to reduce the investment tied up in construction, but, despite regular declarations of cutbacks, the number of projects has risen inexorably. By 1970 the total of 35 000 sites was three times greater than the construction capacity of the economy.[15] In the seventies unfinished buildings more than doubled — at a total cost equivalent to almost 80 per cent of total fixed investment.[16]

Even a cursory inspection of investment policy shows that high rates are forced on the bureaucracy by the spontaneous character of economic relations. Massive investments are used to compensate for the lack of economic regulation. Because of its difficulty in socialising labour, the Soviet system has major problems in transforming investment into a surplus fund. This problem expresses the contradictions of the social formation in a most acute form. It indicates that the barriers to further development cannot be overcome on the basis of the existing social relations.

The Soviet system's inability to realise the social character of labour condemns it to stagnation. Investment leads to an absolute increase in national income, but yields on investment have a tendency to fall. Declining rates of growth in output and productivity are the result of the lack of a coherent division of labour in the Soviet social formation.

In the absence of an economic regulator the bureaucracy attempts to give coherence to the division of labour through direct central intervention. But, although the centre can pursue certain priority objectives and control the distribution of material resources, it cannot abolish elements of spontaneity. In practice, individual production units must respond both to the demands of the centre and to the spontaneous forces that influence their activities. Spontaneous forces always modify central directives.

Individual production units can only survive if they are able to mitigate the effects of the forces of spontaneity. They can rely on investment funds from the centre — but everything else is unpredictable. The instinct for self-preservation leads individual enterprises to go for maximum self-sufficiency and access to resources and labour. Since in an industrial society there are limits to the degree of self-sufficiency that can be achieved at enterprise level, local managers are compelled to make informal arrangements with other enterprises and industries. All managers are thus forced to engage in barter, theft and black marketeering.

The compensating measures of the individual enterprise and the allocations of the central bureaucracy complement each other to give a degree of coherence to the division of labour. But this means adapting to the forces of spontaneity, forcing producers to engage in activities which inhibit the development of the forces of production and the socialisation of labour. In adapting to the forces of spontaneity, production units become atomised and acquire conservative tendencies. They become more concerned about getting hold of resources than about what they produce. This is because, in general, spontaneous forces have a greater immediacy for the individual enterprise than the dictates of the centre.

Apart from regular exhortations, there is no incentive for producers to fall in line with central directives in anything other than a formal sense. The ultimate welfare of the enterprise depends on the resources and inputs it can obtain, rather than on its achievement of output targets. Hence production units tend to try to meet targets with the minimum of effort. The whole organisation of the enterprise is shaped by this conservative approach. This explains why economic experiments which rely on enterprise initiative do not work.

In the Soviet Union there is simply no drive towards innovation or dynamism at enterprise level. This is particularly evident in the introduction of new technology and new production methods. Ever since the thirties most factory directors have looked upon new technology as a nuisance. As senior bureaucrat Bulganin observed more than 30 years ago, factory directors persist in producing obsolete goods 'apparently because it is easier and simpler to produce obsolete models': switching to the organisation and production of new goods 'calls for hard work and the overcoming of difficulties. One can run into trouble if one is not careful.'[17] Such fears persist to this day. The number of new equipment models in key industries has declined since 1980.[18]

Because there is no real local initiative, virtually all the pressure for change comes from the centre. This means that it is only through the efforts of the central bureaucracy that any new policy or technique can be followed through. Despite all the talk about local initiative, the bureaucracy realises that the reproduction of the system depends on central control. The importance of central organisation is recognised even by an emigré like Kushnirsky, a former research worker at the Ukrainian branch of the scientific research institute for planning and norms: 'If the system cannot work to create some risk for utilising additional resources and nobody takes material responsibility for it, we would say that resources are safer when they are centralised.'[19] The resources may be safer with the centre, but central control cannot be a substitute for local initiative, dynamism and co-operation. Investment is distributed, not regulated; as a result the transformation of labour into a surplus product is fraught with difficulties. Despite the availability of considerable material resources, the existing form of social production provides a narrow basis for surplus extraction.

A significant portion of society's labour-time is used either to reproduce an already existing division of labour at a local level (self-sufficiency), or to expand production without regard to efficiency (hoarding of raw materials and labour, cavalier use of inputs), or to make goods without regard to social need (overproduction of certain items, poor quality goods, particularly consumer durables). As a result labour-time is squandered. Specialisation and co-operation fail to develop and a significant portion of society's products emerge as non-use values. The crisis in the shoe industry in 1985, when thousands of shoes were produced with heels attached to the toes, is only a grotesque example of the tendency towards the production of non-use values.[20]

One important consequence of the difficulty of realising the surplus product is that the basis for the consumption fund becomes restricted. The crisis of the consumer goods industry is well known and its effects go beyond the realm of living standards. More importantly for the reproduction of the social formation as a whole, shoddy consumer goods and widespread shortages prevent the establishment of a system of incentives that could stimulate people to work.

The absence of genuine incentives explains the indifference of the working class to work and thus the difficulty of raising productivity. From time to time the bureaucracy may succeed in forcing people to work harder. But without a system of incentives it cannot make workers really work. And without a fundamental change in social relations there will be insufficient resources to transform existing products into goods and services that workers really want and need. This is one of the unresolvable contradictions of the Soviet social formation.

Given the formidable obstacles to social reproduction, how does the Soviet Union survive? It survives because the central bureaucracy can, for the most part, contain trends towards disintegration; it cannot change the basic social relations, but it can use its control over material resources to hold things together. Priority allocation has sustained an impressive defence sector. While the bureaucracy cannot get local enterprises to innovate, it can import foreign technology to establish new industries and new lines of products. In certain instances it can even provide material incentives to workers, as it does in priority industries. When all else fails the threat of force provides a temporary solution to pressing problems.

Over the past 50 years the Soviet leadership has also skilfully taken advantage of the decline of the capitalist system. Despite Western hostility, rivalries among the imperialist powers have provided Moscow with important opportunities to consolidate its system. The Soviet bureaucracy has even managed to use Western technology to compensate for its own lack of dynamism. Although the arms race forces the Soviet regime to spend an excessive amount of valuable resources on defence, the bureaucracy has in general benefited from its relations with the imperialist world. We now turn to look more closely at the crisis of the Soviet social formation.

## Symptoms of crisis

The Soviet Union has never had an efficient economic regulator. But until the late fifties the Soviet bureaucracy could live with the consequences of this. It could boast of its record of economic growth, as well as point to spectacular achievements, such as the Moscow Underground. Although the 20 per cent growth rate achieved during the fourth five year plan (1946-1950) has never been repeated, growth remained at a respectable seven per cent throughout the fifties.

Towards the end of the decade, however, a new pattern emerged: after 1958-59 the rate of growth of industrial production began to decline. Both the CIA figures and Soviet statistics show the same trend (see tables).[21]

| Soviet industrial output (CIA figures) (1970 = 100) | | | | | |
|---|---|---|---|---|---|
| Year | Output | Growth (%) | Year | Output | Growth (%) |
| 1950 | 20.36 | — | 1965 | 73.65 | 7.0 |
| 1951 | 22.68 | 11.4 | 1966 | 77.98 | 5.9 |
| 1952 | 24.61 | 8.5 | 1967 | 83.82 | 7.5 |
| 1953 | 27.33 | 11.1 | 1968 | 89.59 | 6.9 |
| 1954 | 30.22 | 10.6 | 1969 | 94.03 | 5.0 |
| 1955 | 33.64 | 11.3 | 1970 | 100.00 | 6.4 |
| 1956 | 37.10 | 10.3 | 1971 | 106.87 | 6.9 |
| 1957 | 41.18 | 11.0 | 1972 | 112.03 | 4.8 |
| 1958 | 45.77 | 11.1 | 1973 | 119.02 | 6.2 |
| 1959 | 50.42 | 10.2 | 1974 | 126.46 | 6.3 |
| 1960 | 53.59 | 6.3 | 1975 | 133.49 | 5.6 |
| 1961 | 56.90 | 6.2 | 1976 | 138.45 | 3.7 |
| 1962 | 61.30 | 7.7 | 1977 | 144.12 | 4.1 |
| 1963 | 64.75 | 5.6 | 1978 | 149.46 | 3.7 |
| 1964 | 68.81 | 6.3 | | | |

| Industrial Output (Official Soviet figures) (billion rubles) | | | | | |
|---|---|---|---|---|---|
| Year | Output | Growth (%) | Year | Output | Growth (%) |
| 1950 | 52.0 | — | 1965 | 229.4 | 8.0 |
| 1951 | 60.5 | 16.4 | 1966 | 248.3 | 8.2 |
| 1952 | 67.6 | 11.6 | 1967 | 285.9 | 15.1 |
| 1953 | 75.6 | 11.8 | 1968 | 322.8 | 12.9 |
| 1954 | 85.6 | 13.2 | 1969 | 345.0 | 6.9 |
| 1955 | 96.2 | 12.4 | 1970 | 374.3 | 8.5 |
| 1956 | 106.4 | 10.6 | 1971 | 395.7 | 5.7 |
| 1957 | 117.0 | 10.0 | 1972 | 420.0 | 6.1 |
| 1958 | 129.0 | 10.3 | 1973 | 447.3 | 6.5 |
| 1959 | 143.8 | 11.5 | 1974 | 479.6 | 7.2 |
| 1960 | 157.4 | 9.5 | 1975 | 511.2 | 6.6 |
| 1961 | 172.6 | 9.7 | 1976 | 527.9 | 3.3 |
| 1962 | 188.4 | 9.2 | 1977 | 553.7 | 4.9 |
| 1963 | 201.0 | 6.7 | 1978 | 577.0 | 4.2 |
| 1964 | 212.4 | 5.7 | | | |

In recent years the slowdown in economic growth has become even more pronounced. According to Soviet statistics, the growth in industrial production fell from an annual average of 4.3 per cent in the late seventies to 3.8 per cent in 1981, and to 2.8 per cent in 1982. The falling industrial growth rate has been paralleled by dwindling improvements in the productivity of labour. Productivity grew by 3.5 per cent a year in the sixties, at 2.1 per cent in the early seventies and at 1.4 per cent in the late seventies.[22] The most worrying trend for the bureaucracy has been what Soviet economists term the falling 'dynamics of the efficiency of industrial production': the tendency for output yields on investment to fall. This poses a major problem for a system that relies on the mobilisation of investment resources to compensate for the problem of economic regulation.

It was the crisis of declining efficiency in investment that sparked off the quest for economic reforms in the sixties. Kosygin surveyed the problems in the speech with which he launched the 1965 reforms:

'It should be said that in recent years the volume of the national income and industrial output per ruble of fixed assets has declined somewhat. The rates of growth of productivity in industry, which also represent an important index of the efficiency of social production, have slowed down somewhat in recent years.'[23]

The same message has since been repeated by many prominent representatives of the politburo as the situation has continued to deteriorate. In 1982 the respected Soviet economist Trapeznikov calculated that a one ruble increase in production assets in 1958 yielded 52 kopeks additional income, but that in 1980 such an increase yielded only 16 kopeks.[24]

The inefficiency of investment is shown by the difficulty that the Soviet Union has in reducing the cost of production in terms of either material inputs or labour. According to one estimate the costs of production outlays were reduced by 4.9 per cent during the eighth five year plan, but by only 0.4 per cent in the tenth plan.[25] This was one of the problems discussed by Andropov at the November 1982 plenum of the central committee of the Soviet Communist Party:

'**Labour productivity — the main indicator of the economy's effectiveness — is growing at a rate that cannot satisfy us....There is virtually no decline in the material-output ratio. Plans continue to be fulfilled at the price of high expenditures and production costs.**'

The declining rate of return on investment poses a major problem for the Soviet bureaucracy. It indicates that, as time passes, investments have less and less effect in improving output. Investments are not used to develop productive forces so much as to patch things up. To increase output requires more and more investment. One CIA source summed up the deteriorating situation in the early eighties: 'Whereas in the early seventies each additional ruble's worth of output required three additional rubles of capital, by the end of the decade over six additional rubles of capital were required.'[26]

The declining efficiency of investment stems from the lack of any effective means of regulating society's labour-time. In relation to investment this problem is expressed in the difficulty of maintaining control over the flow of resources. As industry becomes more complex, increases in investment have less and less effect in sustaining growth. More investment can no longer substitute for the absence of an internal dynamic of development. Not only is Soviet investment becoming more inefficient, but the high cost of production threatens to limit the availability of investment resources. The Soviet bureaucracy cannot indefinitely rely on mobilising new resources to invest in industry. Unless industry itself generates more resources for investment, the tendency towards crisis will be exacerbated. There is already considerable discussion of scarcity of natural resources and of labour.

Aware that massive investment could not put off economic problems indefinitely, the Kremlin changed course in the mid-seventies. It recognised that reliance on investment was too costly and thus began to lower the rate of investment in industry. This approach was ratified at the December 1977 plenum of the central committee of the Soviet Communist Party, at which Brezhnev insisted on the need to intensify production.[27] The growth in investment — seven per cent a year in the early seventies — was halved between 1976 and 1980.

The symptoms of the crisis are well known and widely debated in the Soviet Union. The following factors have at one time or another been blamed for the declining efficiency of investment.

1. Lack of 'personal material responsibility'
2. Lack of co-ordination between sectors and regions
3. Long gestation periods for the realisation of investments
4. Scattering of investment over too many projects
5. Low productivity of labour and bad work habits
6. Too many uncompleted construction projects
7. Specific industrial problems in transport, coal and agriculture
8. Lack of control over the use of material and other resources
9. Slow introduction of new technology
10. Ineffectiveness of success indicators and of the system of incentives.

The Soviet discussion of economic problems tends to explain one symptom of the crisis by another. The economist Fil'ev provides a typical illustration of this approach:

**'The effectiveness of production has fallen mainly as a result of the slow rate of introduction of the achievements of scientific and technical progress; the ineffective utilisation of capital investments, labour, and material resources; delays in commissioning and running in new capacities; the limited sanctions towards violators of plan, production, and labour discipline.'[28]**

This sort of superficial explanation stems from a reluctance to probe matters more deeply. Even the more critical studies reduce the causes of the crisis to technical problems, or exhort readers to appreciate the advantages of some new technique.

The technical approach sidesteps the fundamental question of social relations and inevitably transforms the problem from an objective into a subjective one. The Soviet bureaucracy has embraced the familiar methods of Western social science. Zaslavskaya, who purports to offer a devastating critique of the social system, explains the crisis as a result of subjective failures:

**'Nowadays, higher public value is placed not on the activities of the more talented, brave and energetic leaders, but on the performances of the more "obedient" chiefs, even if they cannot boast production successes.'**[29]

Bureaucratic conservatism and the lack of a Protestant work ethic are the villains of this piece.

The emphasis on subjective failures is entirely consistent with the views of the Soviet bureaucracy. Andropov in particular tried to explain the failures of the system as failures of individual responsibility. This is how he put it in a major speech to the November 1982 plenum of the central committee of the Soviet Communist Party:

**'It is necessary to enhance responsibility for observing the interests of the entire state and of all the people and to resolutely eradicate departmentalism and parochialism. We must wage a more resolute struggle against all violations of party, state and labour discipline.'**[30]

This idealist approach reflects an instinctive refusal to get to grips with the problems. The central weakness of the system is that, in the absence of any tendency towards the socialisation of labour, increases in investment cannot guarantee increases in productivity. Thus investment can yield increments of growth, but cannot accelerate it by consistently cheapening material and labour inputs. Intensive growth cannot be achieved through institutional reform or administrative manipulation. It presupposes a system based on continuous advances in the social division of labour, greater specialisation, and the systematic replacement of living labour by new technology. In a non-capitalist society this can only come about through growing co-operation, social participation and workers' democracy.

## The tendency towards fragmentation

The forces of spontaneity in Soviet society undermine co-operation, a critical element in the development of the forces of production. For Marx, co-operation represented a 'new power' which increased the 'productive power of the individual'.[31] He regarded the co-operation carried out through the capitalist social division of labour as limited because it was established *a posteriori*; it was a 'nature-imposed necessity, controlling the lawless caprice of the producers'.[32] Under capitalism co-operation is established indirectly, through the competitive conflict of the market place.

Under a system of workers' democracy, co-operation would be established directly and would form a framework for the conscious pursuit of productive activity. In the Soviet Union the main pressure to co-operate comes from the centre. This leads to the establishment of formal ties between enterprises and the centre, but does not create effective links among different enterprises and industries. Since enterprises are not responsible for what they sell, there is no market or system of incentives with which to stimulate co-operation.

The main pressure the centre puts on enterprises is to meet targets. Enterprises set about reaching these targets by whatever means are available. However, reaching targets imposes no pressure to co-operate — on the contrary, it tends to foster self-reliance. The only competition that exists is competition to secure resources from the centre, but this has no cohesive effect. It puts the emphasis on acquiring and consuming raw materials and resources, rather than on achieving efficiency in production. As a result, the goal of any enterprise manager is to reduce his reliance on the overall division of labour to a minimum, to gain the best chance of reaching centrally-imposed performance targets.

In practice the tendency towards self-sufficiency is curbed both by the centre and by the need for a developed technical division of labour. But while these factors can limit the scale of the problem, they cannot compensate for the lack of drive towards specialisation and co-operation. The way in which the tendency towards fragmentation operates confirms this.

From the outset the bureaucracy recognised that the industrialisation drive would exact a high cost. But the Soviet leadership regarded its lack of control over resources as a temporary problem that would be overcome as industrialisation proceeded. It accepted the difficulty of transforming labour into a surplus product as a price worth paying for industrial development.

In any society industrialisation is a disruptive and traumatic process. In the Soviet Union these difficulties were compounded by lack of economic control — at a time when the abolition of the market made this more important than ever before. Marx predicted that after the removal of market forces, 'the book-keeping' involved in 'the regulation of labour-time and the distribution of social labour among the various production groups' would ultimately become 'more essential than ever'.[33] In the Soviet Union the absence of proper planning—what Marx called 'book-keeping'—made even the basic control of resources difficult.

In the thirties the bureaucracy's emphasis was on production rather than on the cost of production. It knew that the cost of modernising the Soviet Union was high, but took comfort from the fact that new industries were built and new products produced. The widely debated Soviet obsession with gross output targets stems from this period. The ready availability of resources meant that the bureaucracy could ignore costs and reckon progress only through increases in production.

From a materialist point of view, however, progress is measured not by increased production, but by the increased productivity of labour. Progress means reducing the amount of labour-time necessary to produce a certain product. Efficiency in the deployment of labour-time, leading to an increase in society's surplus labour-time, comprises the Marxist criterion for progress.

For many years the Soviet bureaucracy was obliged to turn a blind eye to the question of costs. The only problems it recognised were those arising from defects in production: shoddy goods, poor quality and shortages. The bureaucracy also drew constant attention to the problems of waste and hoarding, but took no effective steps to force enterprises to produce more efficiently. Exhortation was its only response to lack of restraint in the deployment of resources. Indeed it was not until after the slowdown in economic growth became apparent that any steps were taken to reduce production costs. In 1959 cost-cutting became for the first time one of the explicit goals of the enterprise bonus system.[34]

Today, everybody agrees on the need to cut production costs. In 1983 leading bureaucrats such as Andropov even took to quoting Marx on the subject: 'The economic law that Marx considered the first law of collective production, the law of economising labour-time, is still not fully operative in our country.'[35] While Andropov understates the problem, Soviet economists are more candid. They openly admit that there is no tendency whatsoever towards economising labour-time.

The belated recognition of the problem of economising labour-time obscures something more fundamental: that the central bureaucracy has little control over the distribution of society's labour-time. Without any mechanism for regulating this, individual enterprises find it relatively easy to get around the rough guidelines controlling the allocation of resources. The centre has difficulty in evaluating output performance; but it has even less power to assess whether the inputs that go into the final product have been used effectively — whether indeed they have been used at all. Thus the bureaucracy is saddled with a high-cost strategy which can no longer even achieve its stated objective: growth. In his first major speech on the economy, Andropov complained: 'The materials-intensiveness of output shows virtually no decrease. Plans continue to be fulfilled at the cost of large outlays.'[36]

Lack of control over costs means that a significant portion of society's labour never realises its social character — or that it does so in a limited way. According to Kushnirsky, one of the central objectives of reform was 'to encourage managers and workers to operate with the feeling that the inputs they manage and use belong to them when indeed it is not so'.[37] Lack of control over resources manifests itself in three main ways: overbidding for investment funds, irrational use of resources and hoarding.

Individual enterprises and industries tend to claim from the centre as many resources as they can. Managers exaggerate estimates for new projects and production costs to gain leeway to meet performance criteria. In July 1982, for instance, *Pravda* noted caustically that the ministry of farm machinery had overstated the amount of metal needed to build tractors at its Cheboksarky plant by more than 16 tons per vehicle![38] One result of this process is 'over-investment' and the consequent immobilisation of massive resources; the widespread phenomenon of unfinished capital construction projects is another result. According to one estimate in 1970 there were three times as many investment projects under way as the economy could handle.[39]

There is no mechanism for ensuring that resources are used either efficiently or to produce the goods that society requires: inputs are used with little regard to costs. The Soviet press is full of illustrations — the waste of metal is probably the most notorious. In 1950, for example, one pig-iron casting shop in Moscow spoiled three and a half as many castings as it turned over to the other shops of the Kolomna plant.[40] More than 30 years later the problem persisted: in 1982, a survey of the electrical equipment industry showed that it wasted one third of all the rolled metal it used.

Inflated claims for resources inevitably lead to hoarding, particularly of inputs that are in short supply. According to one Western writer 'the propensity to accumulate large stocks is one of the oldest and most firmly rooted propensities in Soviet industrial practice'.[41] Hoarded resources are euphemistically referred to as 'reserves' in Soviet economic literature. One of the objectives of central planners is to find out where these 'reserves' are located, so that they can make better use of them.

Enterprises not only hoard material resources but also living labour. To guarantee a stable labour supply, many enterprises cook the books and employ more workers than are necessary. This inefficient deployment of labour restricts the scope for raising productivity. *Izvestia's* sarcastic attack on a factory director in 1952 would not be out of place in the Soviet press today:

**'In order to conceal the unlawful size of his staff he decided to change their appearance. Thus, the accountant was listed as a mechanic and the book-keeper as a driver. He made men out of two women — a cashier and a typist, listing them as a loader and a machine-worker, respectively.'**[42]

Because of the chicanery of enterprises, lack of control over resources leads to a tremendous squandering of labour-time. It not only immobilises considerable resources and labour, but also deploys labour-time with little regard to efficiency. This puts pressure on resources, helps foster shortages and disproportions and exacerbates the general problem of material supplies. Uncertainties with supplies reproduce the same pattern and strengthen the tendency towards fragmentation. In the end the central bureaucracy does not even know what is happening to the resources of society.

## The question of quality

Production is not only carried out at a high cost, but also with little regard to the quality of the final product. The aim of the individual enterprise is to meet formal targets — it has no responsibility for selling its products. The enterprise produces not for a market or for social need, but for a set of targets. Achieving target norms is much more important than the quality of the product.

Systematic intervention by the centre, through the system of priority allocations, is the only guarantee of quality. The state ensures that key sectors, such as defence, are provided with inputs of an adequate standard. But further down the hierarchy of priorities the problem of quality becomes more and more acute. Enterprises have no inhibitions about skipping a stage in the production process as long as this is not apparent in the end result. There is no way that enterprises producing spare parts or other inputs can be held to account for the goods they produce.

A high priority enterprise may have the leverage to demand that goods and spare parts meet the desired specifications. But less significant enterprises have no choice but to accept what is sent them. This explains the permanent problem of defective goods in the consumer goods sector. Individual consumers have no power or influence over the quality of goods. Producers of consumer goods face even less pressure than their colleagues in other sectors.

While the central bureaucracy can keep an eye on the quantitative aspects of production, it has no mechanism for ensuring precision and attention to detail. Soviet enterprises pay attention only to quantitative factors and regard demands for quality as obstacles to the attainment of output quotas. This leads to a preference for producing goods which require a high input of material and labour. It is easier to meet plan targets in these areas than in production processes that demand meticulous work. Production in bulk in heavy industry thus triumphs over the production of sophisticated manufactured goods.

The fact that the products of industry do not automatically become objects of use has long been acknowledged in the Soviet Union. Public discussion of the problem of 'planning for spoilage' took place as early as the thirties.[43] Spoilage, waste and the production of non-use values are permanent features of Soviet production. Random examples from Soviet literature illustrate the scale of the problem:

'These "self-bending" nails and forks lie on the shelves and evoke the consumers' just indignation. This is the same cartel that introduced into the retail network a large quantity of luggage locks which neither open nor close.'[44]

'Our factory produces footwear — over 3 million pairs annually. Our products do not attract people but repel them: they are crammed on shelves in a grey pile, and buyers' glances slip past them indifferently. And we ourselves never buy the footwear we produce. It's embarrassing to wear it even on a weekday. And add to its unappealing appearance its poor quality. Nearly two per cent of the total volume is defective, and moreover, 10 per cent fails to meet state standards. And these are the official figures, as they say. In reality, the quantity of such footwear is far greater.'[45]

The production of non-use values is particularly evident in the consumer goods sector. Between 1950 and 1965 stocks of unsold goods multiplied by a factor of 3.5 each year.[46] The uselessness of many consumer goods is apparent because of the public outcry it provokes: but other types of goods suffer from similar problems. For example, in 1981 nearly 44 per cent of the Soviet Union's pool of farm machinery was made up of obsolete and inefficient tractors.[47] Goods which are obsolete and of no use to society continue to be manufactured because there is no mechanism for stopping established production processes. Gorbachev's rhetorical question sums up the widespread sense of frustration: 'Why does it happen that an enterprise produces outdated output on a low technical level or consumer goods for which there is no demand, but lives normally and sometimes even prospers?'[48]

Useless and defective goods are a symptom of the problem of the production of use values in the Soviet Union. There is a wide spectrum of final products, from those which are totally useless, through goods of various degrees of defectiveness, to products which are not defective but do not correspond to what people need:

'Between the perfect product and the useless product is a broad latitude within which changes of various kinds may be made. The difference is usually not between a product which will work and one which will not, but rather between a product which will work better and one which will work worse.'[49]

The usefulness of products is often restricted by structural faults, malfunctioning, or a tendency to wear out rapidly. The towns recently built around the new trans-Siberian railway are already disintegrating, leading to the exodus of railworkers. The station manager of Mogot describes the state of affairs in striking terms:

'The town, which is just slightly over five years old, looks pitiful today. The concrete sidewalk slabs have jutted up here and caved in there. Collapsed windows gape from the...midwife's station and the administration and consumer services building. The doors of the railroad terminal are boarded up tight. The other half of the same building, meant to serve as a signal control centre and communications office, is also in a state of emergency; the mis-shapen roof leaks.'[50]

The direct production of non-use values, to which Ticktin in particular has drawn attention, is only the most extreme manifestation of the problem.[51] Waste is not unique to the Soviet Union — the experience of the people of Mogot is familiar to many residents of Western inner-city housing estates. However, only in the Soviet Union is there absolutely no way of ensuring that the products of industry are useful to others. There is no mechanism to enforce the needs of individual or industrial consumers upon producers. One group of producers cannot rely on inputs from another group of producers. Managers are obliged to operate on the assumption that, somewhere along the line, there will be a problem with supplies.

Receiving supplies is better than not receiving them, but they often still require attention before they can serve a useful function in the production process. Soviet economist Trapeznikov outlines the lack of responsibility of producers for the quality of their products:

**'A situation has come about in which the producer, in effect, has no responsibility for the operational efficiency of his output. After officially turning over the product, the producer walks away, and the customer is forced to correct any defects on his own, in a makeshift fashion.'[52]**

A significant portion of the products of the labour of society become use values only through their conversion by the buyer.

The need to convert non-use values into use values indicates the obstacles to the realisation of the social character of labour. It reveals the absence of any general law that ensures that the products of labour become use values. As a result the Soviet bureaucracy cannot eliminate the problem. It can only act to limit the proportion of useless products and try to ensure that standards are maintained in a number of key sectors.

The need to devote considerable resources to the conversion of useless products into usable goods is evident in the mushrooming of the repair sector and of activities designed to make plants more self-sufficient. A Soviet economist's report on his visit to 30 foreign machine-building plants in 1982 brought out some interesting comparisons:

'I didn't see repair, construction or tool shops at a single foreign plant. This is borne out by statistics. The proportion of repair workers, toolmakers and transport and warehouse workers in our machinery industry has risen to 38 per cent, whereas it is only 11 per cent in that industry in the United States.'[53]

The problem of realising the social character of labour, which is expressed through the production of goods that are not yet use values, also has a corrosive effect on the division of labour. It forces enterprises to modify inputs, strengthens the tendency towards self-reliance, and works against any attempt to achieve greater specialisation. The problems of supply provide the strongest impetus towards the fragmentation of production relations.

## The disintegrating division of labour

The restricted scope for the further development of the Soviet social formation is shown by its inability to extend the division of labour. Because it works within the confines of a single country, the Soviet division of labour is already severely limited in comparison to the international division of labour available to capitalist countries. But in addition to the limits imposed by national boundaries, the Soviet Union also suffers from the problem that every attempt to increase specialisation promotes tendencies which counteract its positive effects.

In the Soviet Union the development of the division of labour is generally discussed from a technical point of view. Economic experts often complain of conservatism, of reluctance to introduce new technology and new products. These factors have a negative effect, but the real problem is more fundamental. Soviet social relations lead to the prevalence of spontaneous forces, to lack of co-operation and to uncertainty of inputs. These factors encourage a tendency towards a division of labour that is more responsive to the demands of local enterprises than to the needs of the national economy. By fostering autarchic methods of production, this tendency contributes to the further dissolution of the social division of labour.

The tendency towards fragmentation is apparent in the replication of the national division of labour within enterprise, industry and region. Ever since the thirties this problem has become more and more serious. In the post-war period the main concern was supply shortages. According to Dunmore, different industrial ministries responded by establishing the framework for the maximum degree of self-sufficiency: 'They sought to provide as many of their own services as they could, from consumer goods to construction work, labour, and transport, to reduce their reliance on outside suppliers.'[54] This sort of ministerial 'empire building' led Khrushchev to complain in 1955 that every minister wanted 'to carry on production in seclusion'.[55]

Khrushchev's famous 1957 *sovnarkhoz* reform sought to abolish industrial ministries and ministerial authority through the establishment of a regionally based organisation of production. The result was that some of the autarchic tendencies that previously operated within ministerial departments were now reproduced at the level of regional organisation, as each region tried to become more self-sufficient.

A persistent striving for self-sufficiency leads to declining productivity, as industries and enterprises set up their own repair shops, transport systems and construction facilities. It also undermines the cohesion of the division of labour. According to Dyker, in some cases 'one particular ministry may be practically "annihilated" by the autarchical tendencies of others. More than 70 ministries and departments produce timber products...and the forestry ministry accounts for only 37 per cent of total timber output.'[56]

Although the centre has attempted to moderate tendencies towards autarchy, officials have no inhibitions about using it for their own ends. To compensate for the inefficiency of the consumer goods sector, the bureaucracy has tried to use the more efficient defence sector to produce consumer goods as a sideline.[57] In the seventies Brezhnev repeatedly urged this: the aviation ministry was told to give a lead in producing baby-prams.[58] By 1979 the proliferation of sideline consumer goods production led to a situation in which 40 different models of refrigerators were being produced in 20 plants under eight ministries.[59]

The bureaucracy lavishes praise on those enterprises in which the drive towards self-sufficiency contributes to food production and thus helps ease the crisis of agriculture. Enterprises which run auxiliary farms to attract workers are often singled out for approval in the press. A leading bureaucrat in the power machinery ministry has noted that, for enterprises in remote areas, 'reliance on one's own food resources, on one's "garden", is simply essential'.[60] In reality the provision of auxiliary farms, while attractive to workers who cannot get fresh food in any other way, is irrational from the point of view of the national economy. The diversification of industry into agriculture is the very antithesis of specialisation.

A similar process operates in the sphere of housing. The same official who has praised factory gardens applauds enterprises which provide houses for employees. With such encouragement it is not surprising that 60 per cent of housing remains outside the control of municipalities.[61] Local initiatives fulfil a useful purpose in taking pressure off the central bureaucracy.

The adaptation of the centre to autarchic tendencies in consumer goods, food and housing shows that a full national division of labour does not exist in the Soviet Union. In the end the bureaucracy has to rely on the centrifugal forces of autarchy to provide essential services for the population; and even the fundamental distinction between industry and agriculture is dissolved.

The limited social character of labour, as revealed through the tendency towards the dissolution of the social division of labour, is the central barrier to the development of the Soviet social formation. This tendency has acquired the character of a law which restricts the socialisation of labour. Thus while the Soviet Union widens its technical division of labour, it cannot do the same for the socialisation of labour. Indeed even the technical division of labour is in practice modified by the tendency towards autarchy. The erosion of the national division of labour by autarchic tendencies highlights the privatised character of social production. Ironically, despite the elimination of the market, production relations in the Soviet Union have become more privatised than under capitalism.

## The atomisation of society

In the Soviet Union, local or individual self-sufficiency is preferred to social co-operation. There is no incentive for co-operation, since material rewards depend on the pursuit of narrow self-interest. In 1983 Andropov reflected on the difficulties this causes for the Soviet bureaucracy:

> 'One of the most important tasks in improving our economic mechanism is to give precise consideration to individual and local interests and the specific requirements of various social groups, and then to find the best way of combining these interests with those of society as a whole, thereby turning them into a motive force of economic development.'[62]

But there is neither a system of material incentives nor a system of political participation that could foster social co-operation in the Soviet Union.

Local and departmental interests have been consolidated because this is the way to gain access to society's resources. Individual greed or ambition or incompetence are irrelevant: all the significant trends within Soviet society correspond to a much more basic fragmentation of economic and social activity. While Soviet experts are reluctant to admit the depth of the problem, they are aware of its systematic character. Zaslavskaya is on the right track when she notes that the Soviet economic mechanism 'is "tuned" not to stimulate, but to thwart the population's useful economic activity. Similarly it "punishes" or simply cuts short initiatives by the chiefs of enterprises, in the sphere of production organisation, aiming at the improvement of economic links.'[63]

Reforms or incentive schemes cannot compensate for an incoherent social division of labour. Any improvements within an enterprise, or within a specific industry, are offset by the spontaneous forces that subvert the wider division of labour. The tendency towards fragmentation imposes a tremendous penalty on Soviet society. The potential for setting up new industries and using new technology to assist the socialisation of labour is frustrated by the existing social relations. The lack of social links among different sectors provides endless scope for the operation of autarchic forces.

The dispersal of society's labour-time through the fragmentation of productive activity further strengthens the tendency towards the atomisation of economic and social life. The squandering of labour-time reduces the resources available to society, creates shortages and so further encourages the struggle for self-sufficiency. It also prevents the establishment of a system of incentives that could stimulate work and higher productivity.

The tendency towards fragmentation affects social life and individual consumption as well as productive activity. The working class cannot depend on the mechanism of distribution for its own survival. In the modern Soviet Union the average family spends nearly two hours a day queuing in shops.[64] Working class families are also forced to find more informal ways of obtaining the use values they need for their survival. This creates a quest for self-sufficiency even at the level of the household.

The forces that push enterprises to adopt autarchic practices also influence the individual consumer. From growing food on small plots of land to converting goods into useful products, the individual is forced to compensate for the defects of the social system. This imposes a private character on social life in the Soviet Union which goes beyond anything experienced in capitalist societies. The atomisation of social life is the most tangible index of the limited social character of labour in the Soviet Union.

## Notes

1 Zaslavskaya (1984), p89.
2 *Kommunist*, No 3, February 1983.
3 See *Pravda*, 11 December 1984.
4 Cited in Brown (1985), p19.
5 Granick (1983).
6 Mandel (1974), p17.
7 Marx (1968).
8 Hutchings (1982), p59.
9 *Izvestia*, 16 February 1941.
10 Mandel (1974), p9.
11 See Cocks (1983), pp46-62.
12 Zaslavskaya (1984), p91.
13 See Kronrod (1984), p76.
14 Dunmore (1980), p147.
15 Kushnirsky (1982), p33.
16 See Leggett (1983), p142.
17 *Pravda*, 17 July 1955.
18 See *Ekonomicheskaya gazeta*, No 6, 1984.
19 Kushnirsky (1982), p35.
20 *Izvestia*, 5 April 1985.
21 Cited in Weitzman (1983).
22 See Bond & Levine (1982).
23 *Izvestia*, 28 September 1965.
24 *Pravda*, 7 May 1982.
25 *Pravda*, 28 June 1983.
26 Leggett (1983), p139.
27 *Pravda*, 18 December 1977.
28 Fil'ev (1983), p13.
29 Zaslavskaya (1984), p107.
30 *Pravda*, 23 November 1982.
31 Marx (1974), p309.
32 Marx (1974), p336.
33 Marx (1971), p851.

34  See Dyker (1983), p32.
35  *Kommunist,* February 1983.
36  *Pravda,* 22 November 1982.
37  Kushnirsky (1982), p43.
38  *Pravda,* 28 June 1982.
39  Dyker (1983), p37.
40  *Izvestia,* 18 February 1950.
41  Hutchings (1984), p77.
42  *Izvestia,* 10 July 1952.
43  Berliner (1957), p146.
44  *Pravda,* 14 January 1949.
45  *Izvestia,* April 1984, abstracted in *CDSP,* 14 May 1984.
46  See Lewin (1973), p143.
47  *Pravda,* 16 October 1982.
48  *Pravda,* 12 April 1985.
49  Berliner (1957), p144.
50  *Gudok,* 15 March 1985, abstracted in *CDSP,* 10 April 1985.
51  See Ticktin (1973).
52  *Pravda,* 7 May 1982.
53  *Pravda,* 8 December 1983.
54  Dunmore (1980), p17.
55  *Pravda,* 19 May 1955.
56  Dyker (1983), p40.
57  *Pravda,* 1 June 1980.
58  *Pravda,* 14 November 1978.
59  See Schroeder (1983c), p327.
60  *Pravda,* 1 November 1982.
61  See Dyker (1983), p93.
62  *Kommunist,* February 1983.
63  Zaslavskaya (1984).
64  Schroeder (1983c), p326.

# 7. Counteracting chaos

The stagnation of the Soviet economy has been a subject of widespread debate for some time. It is evident that the Soviet social formation has not succeeded in generating any internal dynamic of development: change has always resulted from the intervention of the centre. A consensus has emerged among Soviet and Western experts that economic mechanisms which worked reasonably well in the thirties are no longer efficient and now require reform. While there are differences of emphasis, most authorities agree that a return to the market and decentralisation could provide the answer. Dyker's call for the radical reform of planning is typical.[1] Few modern Soviet economists would disagree.

The present debate on the Soviet economy does at least address the real issues. But discussion is restricted to the technical aspects of the problem. Indeed all participants, especially those inside the Soviet Union, display a marked indifference to the underlying relations of production. A 'no entry' sign bars the way to the analysis of social laws. It is not surprising that Soviet writers recoil from pursuing a materialist inquiry, for that would reveal the real nature of the system, and in particular its unresponsiveness to reform.

The bureaucracy has two objectives in sponsoring academic investigation of Soviet society. First, it seeks to show that the Soviet system is free of any fundamental contradictions. Second, it wants to show that the economic problems of the system are episodic, superficial and thus susceptible to reform. This framework gives even the most critical Soviet studies a fundamentally apologetic character. Even the more radical Soviet writers always end inconclusively, with the qualification that 'more work needs to be done on this subject'.

## The reform debate

Andropov provided many examples of the bureaucracy's inconclusive approach. Many Western observers regarded his open style as a healthy shift away from Stalinist dogma. Thus Kux, a Western anti-communist writer, characterised the following statement by Andropov as a 'frank and sensational admission': 'We have not yet studied properly the society in which we live and work, and have not yet fully revealed the laws governing its development, particularly economic ones.'[2] What Kux took to be sensational was simply an attempt to shift the debate on to new administrative and economic techniques. Andropov had no wish to discuss the basic social relations of the Soviet Union.[3]

Many writers use Marxist terminology to give the search for economic solutions an air of theoretical rigour. The lack of correspondence between Soviet reality and communism as envisaged by Marx, Engels and the Bolsheviks has forced the Soviet bureaucracy to develop a 'theory' that reconciles the two. The bureaucracy does not want investigation of its society to go too far. Hence the central committee of the Soviet Communist Party has restricted the scope for future research by confining it to 'the non-antagonistic contradictions that are characteristic of mature socialism'. With the chaos of Soviet society defined in advance as 'non-antagonistic', the results of official research can easily be predicted: they will portray the Soviet Union as a healthy society — with minor deviations.

For all practical purposes 'non-antagonistic contradictions' mean symptoms of the problem, not causes. This is why there is such freedom in the discussion and why top bureaucrats and experts are at liberty to admit that they do not understand Soviet society. Most of the debate is about which of the symptoms of the Soviet crisis should be defined as the basic contradiction. The only significant aspect of the debate is the fact that everybody readily admits that nobody really understands Soviet society.

The disjunction between Soviet theory and Soviet reality is both the starting point and the conclusion of discussion in the influential journal *Voprosy filosofii*. An editorial in October 1984 noted that 'one area of particular weakness is the study of dialectics of social development in light of the real experience of the socialist social system'. Indeed this area of weakness is considered so critical that, despite having 'offered its pages for the exposition of various scholarly views on the question', *Voprosy filosofii* bemoans that 'there is as yet no consensus' on 'what constitutes the basic contradiction of socialism'.[4]

The enthusiasm of Soviet social scientists for conceding their collective ignorance of their own system has the appearance of a process of honest soul-searching and is widely welcomed as a breath of fresh air in Soviet intellectual life. In reality, this discussion is merely a device for taking a distance from earlier orthodoxies of the academic world which have long been discredited. It also has another purpose: by admitting to the existence of a range of social problems specific to the Soviet Union, the experts can argue that these problems are inherent in socialist society. In this way the Marxist conception of socialism as the lower stage of communism is used to legitimise a society that is in every respect antithetical to communism.

Gorbachev and his colleagues are quite prepared to tolerate a free debate, as long as it does not touch upon the historically transient character of the Soviet social formation. If the debate did go this far it would show that the only alternatives in the present situation are either a real workers' state or capitalism.

In fact there is not much new in the current criticisms of the Soviet economy. In a major speech in April 1985, Gorbachev justified his call for the usual range of reforms on the grounds that the 'concept of the restructuring of the economic mechanism has now become clearer to us'.[5] It is not clear what aspect of the 'concept' had become clearer in 1985 compared with 1970 or 1950. Every issue raised by Gorbachev has been discussed at one time or another in the post-war period.

Take a typical statement by Gorbachev on what he considers to be the 'fundamental question of the party's economic policy':

**'Today a large part of our production assets has become obsolete, and as a result the sphere of capital repair has swollen inordinately. The return on assets is declining, the number of new workplaces is growing, and at the same time mechanisation is not being introduced very well.'[6]**

Much the same points were made repeatedly by leading bureaucrats in the fifties and sixties.

Malenkov's report on industry to the nineteenth congress of the Soviet Communist Party in October 1952 is indistinguishable from the exhortations of present day bureaucrats:

'The mechanisation of production of any enterprise must inevitably be accompanied by redeploying some of the workers so that they may be employed at the enterprise concerned or for work at new enterprises. However, some managers of enterprises, instead of seeing to the proper use of mechanical equipment and thus raising the productivity of labour, not infrequently employ outdated organisation of work with extensive use of manual labour.

'Instead of increasing production through better utilisation of the enterprises' internal resources, the ministries quite often demand state capital investments for the construction of new enterprises.'[7]

The only difference between Malenkov and Gorbachev is that the latter now finds himself having to talk about declining returns on investment — a phenomenon which was not in evidence in 1952.

Of course the problems confronting the Kremlin today are not exactly the same as they were 30 years ago. The parallel between the rhetoric of Gorbachev and Malenkov merely underlines the need to put the current discussion on reforms in its proper historical context. The symptoms of the problem have been recognised in one form or another by the Soviet leadership throughout the post-war period. The premise of all discussion has been the Soviet Union's essentially healthy character, its durability, stability and basic integrity. Although certain Soviet institutions — ministries, regional government, enterprise management — have been legitimate targets of criticism, the role of the central bureaucracy has always been beyond question. However, the emphasis of the bureaucracy's approach has shifted as it has tried to tackle different symptoms of the problem.

In the latter stages of Stalin's rule there was little scope for experimentation: particular planning failures could be criticised, but no major reforms could be tolerated. The bureaucrats generally confined themselves to exhortations and exemplary punishment of enterprise directors and officials. After Stalin's death, however, bureaucratic concern shifted to what was perceived as the overcentralisation of the system. The bureaucracy blamed ministries for ignoring local conditions and for stifling initiative. This discussion culminated in Khrushchev's 1957 territorial reorganisation. The failure of this reform coincided with the bureaucracy's awareness of the slowdown of the Soviet economy. The ensuing debate focused on the problem of success indicators: what was required was a system of incentives to stimulate higher productivity and technological innovation. The result was the

Kosygin reforms of 1965.

The failure in turn of the Kosygin reforms was followed by a brief reaction against experimentation. Rises in raw material and energy prices in the West after 1973 gave the Soviet bureaucracy a windfall in hard currency. It sought to compensate for the demise of its reform programmes by purchasing foreign technology, hoping that this external boost to productivity would serve as an acceptable alternative to successful structural reforms. By the mid-seventies it was evident that the Soviet economy had reached an impasse. The bureaucracy was preoccupied with dwindling returns on investment and also with a new problem — the shrinking base of easily available natural resources. It had become clear that the traditional strategy of massive investment no longer obtained results.

The Soviet bureaucracy began to try to come to terms with the problem of productivity. The emphasis was now on cheapening material and labour inputs and on technological change. The new productivity-conscious approach was evident in the 1979 planning decree and in experiments announced in July 1983. It was reasserted in the August 1985 joint party and council of ministers resolution 'On the broad dissemination of the new methods of economic management and increasing their influence on the acceleration of scientific and technical progress'.

The changing emphasis of the bureaucracy's reforms reflects the different ways in which it has sought to counteract the effects of the laws of motion of the Soviet Union. The reforms have failed because the forces of spontaneity cannot be curbed simply by modifying institutions. Every reform simply provokes an adaptation to new circumstances, rather than real change. In the Soviet Union reforms inevitably mean no more than changes in administrative techniques or in the distribution of resources. As such, they do not alter the existing social relations and are doomed to failure. In the absence of a genuine social regulator, no artificial 'economic mechanism' can organise the efficient distribution of labour-time. In practice the bureaucracy has gradually abandoned its dreams of reform and opted instead just to minimise the effects of the forces of spontaneity.

## The failure of decentralisation

The objective of the first serious attempt to reform the Soviet economy was to curb the effects of what was seen as overcentralisation. In the late forties there was much public discussion of the incoherence of regional planning. Critics particularly centred on transport and the wasteful character of cross-shipment. After Stalin's death, criticism became more systematic and cohered around the problem of the industrial ministries' lack of responsiveness to local conditions. The ministries were fairly accused of stifling local enterprises through bureaucratic demands for petty detail. For example the oil industry ministry was ridiculed for attempting to plan the production of window frames for local enterprises.[8] Khrushchev himself gave the example of the Ryazan farm machine-building plant, which received 2580 directives from the ministry of machine building in one year alone — 1953.[9] Not to be outdone, Khrushchev's rival, Malenkov, accused planning agencies of being ignorant of local conditions.[10]

It is now known that one of the main motives behind the campaign against overcentralisation was Khrushchev's desire to shake up the party and establish a power base for himself. But Khrushchev was also responding to what was widely identified as one of the most acute symptoms of the ineffectiveness of the planning mechanism — ministerial departmentalism. Ministries adapted to the tendency towards autarchy and diverted resources into auxiliary sources and repair facilities. Within a particular region ministries seldom co-operated with each other: instead they relied on their own internal supplies. Officials sometimes transported raw materials and plant from thousands of miles away rather than use inputs which, though local, were only available from another ministry.

Regional development was one of the main victims of departmentalism. Ministries simply pursued their own objectives regardless of whether it made sense for the development of the region in which they operated. According to one authoritative study, departmentalism thwarted regional development plans drawn up for the Urals, Siberia and Far Eastern regions. Ministries 'generally chose to maximise the output of the branch to fulfil their own plans rather than those of particular regions, to help fulfil the plan for which some other organisation (a party organ or a *Gosplan* department) was responsible'.[11]

Departmentalism led to the underutilisation of existing capacity and the squandering of labour-time. Numerous examples were quoted where enterprise A, with excess stocks, refused to assist nearby enterprise B, with desperate stock shortages, because it 'belonged to a different ministry'. Departmentalism meant that industrial ministries pursuing their own plan indicators might do well according to official criteria — but at the expense of society as a whole.

Khrushchev's 1957 *sovnarkhoz* reform sought to eradicate the autarchic tendencies undermining the economy: it abolished 25 major economic ministries at a stroke. The ministries that survived were primarily involved in production for the defence sector. A network of 105 regional economic units was established: it was to operate under the direction of councils of the national economy *(sovnarkhozy)*. Each province was given a *sovnarkhoz* to guide local economic policy. The fate of the 1957 territorial reorganisation provided the model for all subsequent reforms. The ministerial departmentalism which the reform aimed to suppress was in essence the expression of autarchic tendencies as they affected the existing chain of command. Abolishing the ministries could not eliminate the laws which pushed them into the quest for self-sufficiency. These laws simply reasserted their influence in a new form.

Now the regions, rather than the ministries, tried to win a degree of self-sufficiency regardless of the consequences. Khrushchev's reform probably worsened the existing social division of labour, for every region now sought to establish its own capacity to produce steel and other industrial inputs. By April 1958, only 11 months after the introduction of the reform, the new term 'localism' was on every planner's lips. Localism — the diversion of resources to a local region at the expense of the Soviet Union's overall social division of labour — reproduced all the problems that had prevailed under the old ministries. Horror stories about local barons lining their pockets filled the newspapers. As the laws of Soviet society asserted themselves, the reform was quietly shelved. In the middle of 1958, the bureaucracy took discreet steps to recentralise economic activity under ministerial control.

The failure of the 1957 reforms demonstrated that the forces of spontaneity could not be curbed through administrative measures. It is ironic that most observers at the time — and many since — shared Khrushchev's assumption that the Soviet Union was too centralised. The chaos of regional development appeared to confirm the view that the system was overcentralised. From a Marxist point of view this is a superficial assessment.

The central bureaucracy was and remains overloaded with petty detail. However, this reveals not the centralisation of social and economic life, but rather its opposite. The Soviet Union's lack of conscious control over its resources means that there is no effective force to counteract the tendency towards fragmentation. Hence the evasion of central directives becomes a part of everyday life, and the centre is forced to adopt an all-pervasive role in society in an attempt to counteract the resulting chaos. This is not centralisation, but a desperate attempt to retain a grip on the basic levers of society.

The 'centralisation-decentralisation' couple is a technical way of looking at the problems of Soviet society. As long as the present social relations persist, they will reproduce the laws of the Soviet Union at every level. Without a regime of workers' democracy, the decentralisation of the Soviet Union will simply breed bureaucratism in miniature. Given more authority, the local bureaucrat will simply assume the habits and customs of his superiors in Moscow.

## The search for a success indicator

The 1957 reforms attempted to overcome the defects of the planning mechanism by changing the line of authority. But the more the economic slowdown became apparent, the more the bureaucracy had to shift its attention towards the basic institutions of the economy. As early as August 1958 Khrushchev remarked that the issue was not simply more growth but the efficient and rational use of investment.[12] Khrushchev made this speech at a ceremony to open a hydro-electricity station at Kuybyshev on the Volga, implying that in future such giant schemes would be assessed from the point of view of the efficient use of labour-time. His observation that 'time is worth more...than any immediate material outlays' has a distinctly contemporary ring.[13] But how was the question of efficiency to be tackled?

After 1957 the emphasis shifted away from ministries to enterprises. The bureaucracy attempted to raise efficiency by limiting the ability of enterprises to make decisions which contradicted the national plan. The discussion soon turned to the obvious problem of how to measure efficiency. It has been recognised since the thirties that plan targets are an inadequate indicator of enterprise performance. The *val* (gross value of output) indicator relied on measuring enterprise output in terms of physical units. But enterprises could meet these physical targets without regard for quality, and crude indicators of physical output were no guide to productivity or the cheapening of material inputs. Indeed use of the *val* actively encouraged profligacy in labour and materials.

Plan targets forced enterprises to meet production quotas, but not to produce efficiently: large, crude, uniformly-designed products which met formal criteria at the expense of precision, detail and variety became characteristic of Soviet industry. In 1949 the council of ministers 'condemned the practice of fulfilling the plan for gross output through producing secondary items while not fulfilling the plan for the most important types of product and variety'.[14] These criticisms were repeated throughout the fifties. An editorial in *Izvestia* in 1954 provides a typical example: 'In their drive to meet the gross output, plan heads of certain enterprises flout the public interest and prefer to produce goods which are more expensive or easier to produce.'[15]

The failure of plan targets to force enterprises to produce efficiently sparked off the next reform debate, as Soviet economists embarked on a search for a more realistic indicator. From the late fifties a consensus grew that enterprises had to be allowed to take more initiative and be given more incentives if they were to produce efficiently. Senior bureaucrats emphasised the need to make enterprises responsible for cost accounting by taking sales revenues and profits as the new indicators of success. Many economists recommended allowing market forces more freedom to force enterprises to compete, arguing that this would help overcome the conflict between enterprise self-interest and the public good.

In an influential article published in 1962, Liberman captured the prevailing desire for harmony through enterprise autonomy, initiative and general flexibility. According to Liberman, if enterprises were given more freedoms and more rewards, then resources would not be squandered in producing useless goods. The quest for profit would ensure that everything worked smoothly:

**'The system proposed proceeds from this principle: what is profitable for society should be profitable for every enterprise. And, on the contrary, what is unprofitable for society should be extremely unprofitable for the staff of any enterprise.'**[16]

Liberman's phrase 'the flexible economic management of society' became fashionable among top bureaucrats. Trapeznikov, a well-known establishment economist, reiterated Liberman's thesis: 'Control must be patterned so that the personnel of an enterprise find it economically profitable to organise their work along the lines that are profitable to the national economy as well.'[17] Profit was promoted as a success indicator that would solve the problem of enterprise inefficiency. This new indicator was justified on the grounds that there were clearly no administrative solutions to the problem of inefficient production. Experience had shown that dictates from the centre provoked an enterprise response which, though it could meet administrative criteria, could not improve efficiency. The reformers believed that, as part of a package of material incentives, profit would change all this. Leont'ev provided a typical example of the argument in 1964:

**'Economic methods of planned management have the advantage of putting into action the power of material incentive: what is good for society is good for the enterprise. There is no such coinciding of interest with administrative management methods, when the enterprises quite often prove to be interested not in enlarging production, but in getting an "easier" plan.'**[18]

The Soviet bureaucracy had become once again receptive to proposals for reform and experimentation. In 1963 an experiment was launched in the Bolshevichka and Mayak textile enterprises. This pilot scheme relied on profit as a main indicator and allowed the enterprises a degree of autonomy in fixing prices and in working out deliveries on the basis of orders from specified retail outlets. Liberman considered the experiment a success, but worried that incentives had to be maintained if they were to have a long-term effect.[19] After the removal of Khrushchev in October 1964, the Soviet bureaucracy felt obliged to go beyond experimentation and initiate a full-scale reform. Brezhnev and Kosygin moved cautiously, at first extending the Bolshevichka experiment to other regions. Then, in a September 1965 decree, the Kremlin launched a comprehensive package of reforms.

The Kosygin reforms of 1965 were the most ambitious attempt so far to confront the consequences of the lack of economic regulation in Soviet society. The decree reorganised industry along pre-1958 lines, on a sectoral rather than a regional basis. The centre conceded greater independence to the enterprise and, most importantly, the number of plan indicators was reduced from 30 to 9. Sales, total profits and rate of profit (defined as a percentage of fixed and circulating capital) were designated as key indicators. The reforms attached special importance to the enterprise incentive fund. The decree also promoted 'direct' relations among enterprises — horizontal, enterprise-to-enterprise links as opposed to the existing vertical, centre-to-enterprise connections. In addition, the state promised an overhaul of the price system, to bring in prices that were more realistic and profit-related.

The overall objective of the 1965 reforms was to institutionalise a system of material incentives that would make for the efficient deployment of investment resources. Although the decree announced a whole series of changes, pride of place was given to market-related success indicators. After the decree was passed, four good harvests helped create the impression that the Soviet economy was doing well and that the reforms were working. But by the early seventies, the failure of the Kosygin reforms could no longer be denied: nothing of substance had changed. What went wrong?

Most Western observers blamed the conservatism of the bureaucracy for thwarting the reforms. Some writers reckon that the instability created by economic reforms in Czechoslovakia in 1968 forced a pull-back from reform; others point to the opposition of regional party secretaries and conservative elements in the state machine.[20] There can be no doubt that the Soviet bureaucracy is highly resistant to change. But conservatism cannot explain the failure of the 1965 reforms.

The bureaucracy was genuinely committed to the reforms, but it soon became clear that they were unworkable. A system of material incentives may lead to a short-term burst of higher efficiency. However, the enterprise still has to meet centrally determined targets, and the fulfilment of these targets must still determine enterprise activity. Enterprise independence becomes formal if it is reliant on centrally allocated supplies at fixed prices and if plan targets still hold sway. The failure of the Kosygin strategy highlights the point that, in the Soviet Union, the market mechanism cannot be introduced piecemeal.

Even with the most comprehensive package of incentives and bonuses, enterprise performance is still measured in relation to plan targets. Hence enterprises have a strong incentive to negotiate easily realisable targets rather than increase their efficiency. Even if they have a degree of autonomy, the ministry that is responsible for them does not. It is still responsible for the production of a specified quantity of physical units: one way or another it will ensure that, when it comes to enterprise decisions, physical quotas continue to prevail.[21]

Even the best thought-out reforms will flounder if they are implemented in an environment which remains unaltered. For example, no system of material incentives at the level of the enterprise can provide a solution to the perennial problem of supply. Enterprises will continue to worry more about obtaining supplies than about what they produce. The inevitable result — the re-emergence of autarchic tendencies — followed soon after the 1965 reforms. If anything, modifying the system of central allocation of supplies in the direction of making it even more unpredictable had the effect of strengthening autarchic tendencies, not weakening them.[22] An opinion survey of enterprise managers in 1970 showed that 80 per cent of those questioned felt that the reform had not improved the supply situation; all but two per cent of the remainder claimed that such improvements as it had made were negligible.[23]

The limited scope of the reforms was revealed above all in their narrow focus on enterprise performance. The central planning and economic institutions were left essentially intact. This meant that enterprises were supposed to make adjustments while the most powerful institutions carried on in the same old way. It is not surprising that reforms at enterprise level were limited by the actions of the central economic institutions. This was not simply a case of bureaucratic inertia. The central institutions still maintained responsibility for giving coherence to the system — they still had to intervene to limit the effects of the tendencies towards fragmentation. Under these circumstances the reforms were implemented in such a way that one measure cancelled out the effect of another. Frequent changes of plan targets, for example, made a mockery of the system of bonuses and incentives.

Both Soviet and Western academics attribute the failure of the reform programme to the inconsistency and conservatism of Soviet officials. But the prevalence of these traits in the Soviet Union is the result of the specific laws that govern it as a social formation. The forces of spontaneity cannot be reformed out of existence. Reforms can change only the forms in which social laws work themselves out.

Soviet and Western economists consistently overestimate the scope for the introduction of market forces in the Soviet Union. Prices and profits in the capitalist sense presuppose capitalist market relations. The operation of the law of value establishes prices and profit rates automatically, through competitive interaction among capitalists. Through competition, the rate of profit is equalised and the labour-time of society distributed among different branches of production. The efficiency of the profit mechanism lies in its capacity to regulate the distribution of the productive forces. The drive for profits leads to the elimination of unprofitable activities and encourages the concentration of resources in sectors that are efficient from the capitalist point of view.

In the twenties, Preobrazhensky explained that, in the absence of the market, the category of profit can have only a formal character.

When prices are fixed centrally and the enterprise has no direct responsibility for selling its products, it ceases to act according to the criterion of profitability. For the enterprise, profits can at best act as a notional ratio — as the percentage increase in output over invested input. This ratio may be of some use as a plan indicator, but it cannot operate as an incentive mechanism. Preobrazhensky showed that without the market 'the category profit not only vanishes, as a distribution-relation of bourgeois society...but also...almost completely ceases to operate as the regulator, on the basis of the law of value, of the distribution of the productive forces between the different branches of the collective state economy'.[24] Since the Soviet bureaucracy cannot reintroduce the capitalist market without destroying its own position in society, all its attempts to modify prices and use profit as a success indicator are destined to fail.

The failure of profit as a success indicator soon became apparent to the Soviet bureaucracy. Enterprises sought to improve their profit position by saving on inputs at the expense of quality. In addition enterprise managers directed activities towards lines which carried the highest profit margins. Any enterprise could improve its profit position by skimping on inputs, or by using shoddy materials for products whose only virtue was that they carried high profit margins.[25]

The use of sales revenues as a success indicator also had predictable consequences. Because sales still had a formal character, suppliers could more or less force customers to accept deliveries regardless of the quality of supplies. The success indicator for sales could best be met by producing material-intensive goods at high prices. Sales contracts could thus be met without regard for demand. The Soviet economist Lokshin explained how the system worked in practice:

> 'Experience in planning the production of enamelled steel cookware demonstrates the shortcomings of any general plan index that fails to take into account all the factors that determine the quality of items and their value to consumers. Prior to 1978 the production of such cookware was planned in tons, which gave enterprises an incentive to produce large, heavy and uncomplicated items. But the shift to planning production in rubles prompted some enterprises to start producing more expensive deluxe models and cookware to be sold in sets.'[26]

The new success indicators simply shifted the emphasis of plan fulfilment. The enterprise responded by meeting the main plan targets, but at the expense of other aspects of production. In essence, relationships between enterprise and centre remained unaltered. Enterprises still sought to improve their position by hoarding resources, relying on self-sufficiency and on product lines which required the minimum amount of effort and resources. The success indicators could do nothing to improve efficiency, raise productivity or stimulate technological innovation. Enterprise managers still regarded new technology as a disruptive factor that threatened the production cycle and hence the attainment of plan targets.

Inevitably, enthusiasm for profit as a success indicator waned. By the early seventies it was more or less abandoned. Nevertheless, despite the disappointing outcome of the 1965 reforms, the search for a panacea continued. The bureaucracy placed particular emphasis on developing an indicator that would enhance efficiency through cutting back on the labour and material inputs into the final product. In the early seventies discussion centred around a new success indicator based on net output. The object of using 'normed net output' (NNO) as an indicator was to discourage the profligate use of investment resources by granting rewards only in proportion to the 'value added' in the enterprise.

Schroeder explained how NNO was supposed to work:

> **'The primary purpose of the adoption of net output to measure plan fulfilment is to eliminate the revealed preference of managers for producing material-intensive output; the weightier and more expensive the inputs, the higher was the value of total output and the easier it was to meet the plan. With plan fulfilment evaluated by net output, the argument goes, enterprises no longer will have an incentive to favour material-intensive products, or, in the case of machinery, to goldplate them. If they do so, costs will increase and profits, a major element of the net output, will be reduced.'**[27]

Soviet bureaucrats looked upon NNO as a solution to the low growth rate of labour productivity. The 1979 planning decree emphasised cost reduction and promised that NNO would be extended throughout Soviet industry. Since 1979 it has become fashionable in Soviet literature to praise the virtues of NNO. Most party and government economic statements recommend the application of NNO to new branches of industry.

But NNO has already suffered the fate of preceding success indicators. Enterprise managers have responded to NNO's emphasis on 'value added' by producing labour-intensive products.

In some cases enterprise managers overstate labour inputs, a practice which is difficult for the centre to detect.[28] As a result, enterprises meet NNO targets at the expense of reinforcing all the familiar distortions. According to one report a rise in NNO in a whole number of sectors has led to a stagnation, or even a decrease, in physical output. This remarkable result was achieved by relying less on outside components and subcontracting, and more on the enterprises' own labour.[29]

In other cases NNO has had different effects. Because it is only one of a number of indicators, the material-saving potential of NNO is rarely realised. In construction in 1982, NNO targets made no positive impact because output targets still retained a primary position.[30] Case histories in the Soviet press show that NNO has not overcome the inevitable distortions that emerge when enterprises are forced to meet formal plan targets. The influence of the *val* continues to prevail, since sales targets are still a feature of the system of indicators. As Schroeder argues, sales targets are 'the sum contractual obligations broken down into physical units and their corresponding prices. Managers' bonuses depend on meeting plans for contractual obligations and for the key products in physical units.'[31]

This point is well illustrated in the case of pipeline construction in the Urengoi gas fields. *Pravda* reports:

> 'Each metre of large-diameter pipe contributes more than 700 rubles to the "gross output" of construction work. That's the cost of the metal itself. On the other hand, in the laying of thin pipes, which construction workers call "straw", the amount of money put to use is much smaller, since the cost per metre of thin pipe is about 86 per cent less than that of trench-line pipe.'[32]

Because 'straw' pipes contain little metal and little 'value added', there can be little surprise when the quotas for the laying of large pipes are, under NNO, generally over-fulfilled and those for thin ones under-fulfilled.

Soviet bureaucrats and economists have still not given up on success indicators. Although indicators are no longer the main focus of discussion, the bureaucracy still feels it necessary to emphasise the virtues of NNO and other measures. Indicators are necessary to provide the centre with some rough yardstick of enterprise performance. At the same time centrally established norms are administrative devices, targets that are met all too often without regard to efficiency or quality. Any attempt to introduce norms to cover a wide range of enterprises will prove impossible to monitor.

Tracking performance through indicators is a particularly unsuitable means of promoting technological innovation. Meeting plan targets depends on smooth production lines and keeping disruption to a minimum. Enterprise managers inevitably regard all attempts to introduce new machinery as irritating and disruptive. The NNO indicator has singularly failed to counteract the conservatism of enterprises towards new technology. The prevalence of obsolete plant and equipment is now widely recognised as a monument to this failure.

Soviet economists are increasingly prepared to face up to the failure of administrative indicators. They now place growing emphasis on 'automatic regulators' related to the development of market relations.[33] Unlike in 1965 there is now a limited recognition of the limitations of success indicators in a non-market environment.

## Organising around the forces of spontaneity

The failure of past reforms has forced the Soviet bureaucracy to look for new solutions. Since the seventies, falling returns on investment have been accompanied by the drying up of resources available for investment. The bureaucracy has become sensitive to the need to use resources efficiently and has attempted to reduce the costs of production. This has been the main theme of most of the past decade of discussion on 'intensive development'.

The bureaucracy has set about trying to counteract the effects of fragmentation by organising around the anarchic development of the different sectors of the economy. In practice this amounts to an attempt to institutionalise many of the informal practices that enterprises have adopted. A 1973 decree promoted the establishment of production associations — small numbers of enterprises grouped together to ensure a coherent division of labour at least among themselves. The bureaucracy considered that the autarchic tendencies that prevailed at the enterprise level could now be put to good use at the level of the production association.

Some economists argued that, if production associations had their own research and development facilities, then this would go some way to solve the problem of technological innovation. The

July 1979 reform decree took this argument a step further and promoted production associations as the basic production units of industry. By the end of 1980 it was reported that there were 4083 production and science-production associations, accounting for 48.2 per cent of total industrial output.[34]

It soon became apparent that production associations mainly existed on paper; that in practice most enterprises carried on as before. Nevertheless the reorganisation indicated the direction of the bureaucracy's thinking. Official encouragement of production associations, reiterated again in the 1983 reforms, led to a wider reorganisation of administrative institutions. However, the economic effects have been marginal because nothing has been done to establish coherent links among production associations.

The most significant development within the production association scheme was the move towards specialised projects organised on an inter-departmental basis. This was an attempt to apply the priority sector principle to specific projects in an attempt to overcome the incoherence of the planning mechanism. In 1980 and 1981 special commissions were set up to supervise the development of the West Siberian oil and gas projects. Several inter-departmental commissions were established to deal with priority projects, such as the trans-Siberian railway, and new ministries were created to overcome the longstanding difficulties of the ministry for fruit, vegetables and canning. This approach may produce beneficial effects in the short term. However, as the number of projects increases, it becomes more and more difficult to give each 'priority' the attention it deserves.

The emphasis on special projects indicated that the Soviet bureaucracy had given up trying to reform the economic mechanism in favour of trying to minimise its disruptive effects. Gorbachev has promoted special projects which have the effect of extending the framework within which autarchic tendencies prevail. Instead of operating at the level of the enterprise, autarchic tendencies now unite several enterprises within one association. This widens the effective division of labour and extends the scale of co-operation. Gorbachev encouraged this trend in a major speech in summer 1985:

> 'The basic reserves for achieving the highest efficiency are to be found at the points where branches overlap. All this puts on the agenda the question of creating agencies for the management of major national-economic complexes.'[35]

Gorbachev's approach amounts to an attempt to establish projects that fill the gap in the existing division of labour. This can only be done through cutting across the lines of the existing division of labour between branches and ministries. The long-term effect will be either to undermine further the existing division of labour, or to foster yet another administrative reorganisation of the economy. Either way the relationships among the special complexes will be no different from the relationships among existing ministries.

The recent establishment of a new super-ministry, the co-ordinating bureau for machine tools, undermines the power of existing ministries.[36] This measure is justified on the grounds that it sweeps away the bureaucratic interests of the ministries that have undermined co-operation and reform. But since such an administrative reorganisation must still operate within the existing social relations, all that will happen is that the super-ministry will simply adopt the autarchic methods of the old institutions.

The super-ministry will offer increased scope for the development of autarchic tendencies. It may or may not be able to use these tendencies to improve the division of labour within its confines. But it will certainly heighten the contradictions within the national division of labour as autarchic tendencies spread. Gorbachev's reforms can only work at the expense of the national economy as a whole. Organising around the forces of spontaneity is a stop-gap measure that can only really work if market forces are fully restored.

## The case of agriculture

The incoherence of the Soviet social division of labour is particularly striking in agriculture. However, most studies tend to look at agriculture in isolation, rather than as part of a broader division of labour. In reality, the problem does not lie in agriculture as such, but in the wider difficulties that stand in the way of the realisation of the social character of labour in Soviet society.

There are many problems that are specific to the farming sector. But the critical obstacles to agrarian development are not dissimilar to those facing industry. Agricultural enterprises operate in a climate of incessant conflict with the rest of the economy. Supply difficulties force agricultural units to operate in an autarchic manner, and there is no incentive to deploy resources efficiently. As a result, the diminishing rate of return on investment has had an even more devastating effect in agriculture than in industry. According to one calculation the value of gross output per 1000 rubles of fixed assets in 1965 was 839. By 1970 it had fallen to 705, in 1975 to 458 and in 1980 it was down to 388, less than half the 1965 level.[37]

Despite the growing cost of agricultural production, the Soviet bureaucracy has been diverting more and more resources into it. The Kremlin is desperately concerned to maintain food supplies to avert dissatisfaction and unrest. Investment in the agro-industrial complex increased threefold between 1965 and 1980; its share in total Soviet investment rose from 28 to 38 per cent.[38] With so many resources tied up in agriculture, the Soviet bureaucracy is naturally concerned about the inefficient use of its investment.

Since the days of Khrushchev there have been numerous attempts to reform agriculture. According to Rumer, in the Brezhnev era alone about 250 different resolutions on agricultural problems were passed by the central committee of the Soviet Communist Party and the council of ministers.[39] The failure of each wave of reform was followed by an increase in investment, culminating in the latest major reform, the 1982 food programme. This programme was drawn up to minimise the effects of the agrarian crisis by a huge expenditure of investment resources. At the same time the bureaucracy hoped to use tendencies towards self-sufficiency to improve output. The food programme instructed every industrial enterprise to set up its own auxiliary farm.[40] Payment in kind was extended to agricultural workers and to those who volunteered for harvest work.[41]

Both Soviet bureaucrats and Western specialists identify similar causes for the stagnation of agriculture. Both believe that the problem is the stagnation of agricultural prices. Rumer writes of the 'economically irrational failure of the Soviet leadership to raise retail prices for simple foods'.[42] The Soviet bureaucracy blames the problem on too much consumption. An article in *Pravda* announcing the decision to implement the food programme singled out excessive demand as the cause of the problem:

> **'What's the problem? Firstly, the demand for foodstuffs is still running ahead of food production — although the latter is increasing year by year. This is caused by the growth of the population's cash, which with stable retail prices for basic foods, leads to an increased consumption of food.'**[43]

High subsidies for food production, a prerequisite for social stability, may explain the strain on investment resources. However, they explain little about the problem of production. The real question that must be asked is: why does investment make little impact on productivity and efficiency in agriculture? The answer is that, in agriculture as in industry, there is little incentive to produce efficiently.

It is obvious that the Russian climate — the subject of intense debate all round — explains little about the Soviet Union's agricultural problems. The fact that Soviet people can grow food in the prevailing climatic conditions is shown by the performance and the multiplicity of private plots. In 1979, the total private plots of collective farm members totalled 3.86 million hectares while other private plots totalled 3.70 million hectares. Altogether this amounted to 1.4 per cent of all Soviet farming land. But these private plots accounted for between 25 and 27 per cent of all agricultural output — including 30 per cent of meat, milk and eggs, more than 50 per cent of fruit and selected vegetables, and 60 per cent of potatoes.[44] The reason for the success of private agriculture is clear: producers have an incentive to produce efficiently, since every aspect of their work on the land is motivated by direct material gain.

After the passing of Brezhnev, the bureaucracy recognised the potential for increasing agricultural output through private farming. In recent years the Soviet leadership has taken a number of cautious steps to create more scope for private farming. In contrast to industry, there is considerable scope for privatising agricultural production. Allowing the market to operate in agriculture need not represent a direct threat to a bureaucracy still in control of industry and foreign trade. Lenin's New Economic Policy was an attempt to rely on private farming to boost production, and other countries in the Eastern bloc — notably Hungary — have followed this course with some success. There is no doubt that the privatisation of Soviet agriculture would lead to a major increase in output. Yet the bureaucracy has been very reluctant to give private farming a real boost. Why?

The reluctance of the Soviet bureaucracy to privatise farming has nothing to do with any considerations about agriculture as such. Private agriculture could work, but the Soviet system could not handle the consequences. Private farming would raise agricultural producers' incomes, but what would the farmers buy with their money? Much of the existing investment fund in agriculture is not used because industry cannot supply agriculture with the equipment it needs.

Small-scale machinery is always in short supply. In 1977 *Izvestia* showed that between 10 000 and 12 000 small tractors could be sold in Belorussia alone.[45] According to a study in 1981, nearly 44 per cent of the Soviet Union's pool of farm machinery was made up of obsolete and inefficient tractors. This meant that 131 of the 272 models manufactured by the ministry of tractors and farm machinery were in need of 'thoroughgoing modernisation' and that 40 models ought to have been scrapped. However the ministry planned to replace only 12 obsolete models by 1983 and a further five by 1984.[46] Fertilizers, spare parts and other machines are allocated on paper, but do not arrive.

Soviet manufacturing is simply not geared up to equip an efficient agrarian sector. Nor is it in a position to provide the consumer goods which would be demanded by a prosperous group of private farmers. The implications of this state of affairs can be seen from an experiment carried out in a near-bankrupt farm in the Altai region of Siberia. A system of incentives was introduced by the Siberian institute of economics and industrial organisation. The incentives met with immediate success — production increased and within two years the farmers were making a profit of 1.3 million rubles. At the same time the wages of farm workers trebled.

The problem was what to do with the money. Although villagers had 1.2 million rubles in the bank, there were only goods worth 288 000 rubles in the village shops, of which products worth 200 000 rubles were unsaleable.[47] The incentives that worked in this village might be easily introduced elsewhere. However, the problem of unfulfilled consumer demand could precipitate a rural upheaval on the scale of the late twenties.

The inability of the Soviet system to overcome the problems of producing use values means that it cannot come up with incentives that make sense to private farmers. Given the inadequacies of industrial goods, private farmers are forced to choose between stuffing themselves with their produce, holding on to rubles or dealing on the black market. The privatisation of agriculture could only work if the market extended to industry. One leading Western specialist regards this as the unavoidable outcome of the reform process: 'The conclusion is inescapable that a positive approach to the agricultural planning problems must ultimately imply the marketisation of large areas of Soviet light industry, engineering and chemicals.'[48] This 'positive' approach — the restoration of capitalism — is a step that the Soviet leadership is not prepared to countenance.

Although by its very nature agriculture has problems that are distinct from those of industry, the failure of reform has little to do with the peculiarities of this sector. Even within the present framework there seem to be plenty of opportunities for increasing agricultural output. But the inability of the system to produce what farmers want to purchase prevents these opportunities being grasped. In turn, agrarian stagnation strengthens the trends towards autarchy, leading to a bizarre situation in which industrial workers become more concerned with their plots on the enterprise auxiliary farm than with their full-time employment.

## Making them work

The failure of reforms in both industry and agriculture has forced the bureaucracy to look to ways of making workers work harder. Measures designed to make more efficient use of manpower are necessitated by key developments in Soviet society. One is the perennial problem of productivity; another is the emergence of serious labour shortages. The recent preoccupation with the Soviet Union's declining birth rate indicates official concern about the supply of labour. The old reserves of rural labour are fast disappearing, and the hoarding of labour in industry means that technological development is not freeing workers for other activities. The result is a chronic labour shortage which appears to be the result of a slowdown in population growth.

Virtually all the relevant studies agree that the Soviet Union's labour supply will decrease sharply in the eighties. The civilian workforce grew at a rate of 2.3 per cent a year in the sixties, 1.4 per cent in the seventies, but it will expand by only 0.4 per cent by the end of this decade.[49] For Soviet industry, which has traditionally relied on the absorption of large quantities of new labour, this is a major blow. While the bureaucracy has made some attempts to devise a demographic strategy, it recognises that the only answer lies in raising the productivity of labour and reducing the existing levels of manning in industry. Much attention is now given to the high proportion of workers engaged in manual work as opposed to working with machines: nearly half the workers in industry and more than half in construction are employed in unmechanised physical labour.[50]

Since the late fifties there have been numerous attempts to create a system of incentives to encourage the efficient allocation of labour and higher productivity. The most well known and still widely acclaimed reform is the so-called Shchekino experiment. The vice-chair of the Soviet state committee on labour and social questions enthused about the scheme in 1983:

> **'The method devised by the Shchekino chemical workers has been adopted widely....This method and its basic elements were used in industry in 1982 by enterprises that account for 70 per cent of all industrial-production employees. In just the past year alone, existing factories of these enterprises economised on labour resources by almost a quarter of a million workers and saved over 400 million rubles in wages.'**[51]

The 'saving' of 250 000 workers seems a considerable achievement. Has the bureaucracy finally hit upon a reform that works? Let us look at the record of this experiment.[52]

The experiment at the Shchekino Chemical Combine in Tula province was started in October 1967. The project was straightforward: enterprise management was given the right to fire workers, while the wage fund remained fixed — hence the managers and the remaining workers would benefit directly from savings in the wages fund. Within a year 900 workers were sacked, leading to wage increases for those workers who remained. Between 1967 and 1974 the volume of production grew 2.5 times, the number of employees fell by 1500, labour productivity increased 3.1 times and average wages grew by 44 per cent.[53] These were impressive figures: in 1969 they prompted a decree recommending the extension of the experiment to other sectors of industry. The experiment was in operation in 630 enterprises in 1972; by 1982 it covered 3300 enterprises fully, and a further 8000 were partially involved. More than 20 million workers were, to varying extents, affected.[54]

Yet the Shchekino model's early promise was not fulfilled. In the Soviet Union it was, and remains, politically unacceptable to make large numbers of workers redundant. There is inevitably resistance from managers to giving up their hoards of labour; and there is also the problem of working class hostility to job losses.

There were also inherent defects in the Shchekino experiment itself. After 10 years, the plant began to lag behind its targets. The reasons were obvious: after an initial burst of higher productivity, the momentum could be sustained only through technological change and the expansion of capacity. In the overall division of labour, the Shchekino plant faced the usual supply problems, delays in deliveries of essentials, plus delays in design and construction.[55] By 1982, the first secretary of the Shchekino city party committee was complaining that the experiment was 'not being used even at the enterprises where it was born'.[56] He noted that the experiment could not overcome the difficulties posed by an unreformed economic environment: 'The method is effective only if the entire complex of work is implemented.'[57]

It is worth noting that even many of the short-term gains of the experiment could not be generalised to all sectors of industry; in many sectors, it is not easy to save on labour. For example, a survey of engineering plants in Leningrad showed that what kept labour productivity down in machine-building was the spread of non-specialised units running labour-intensive auxiliary services.[58] Elsewhere, over-manning based on a low level of mechanisation cannot be eliminated through cutting down on labour without also reducing output.

The fate of the Shchekino experiment indicates the difficulty the Soviet system has in replacing labour with machinery. Although the bureaucracy still swears by the experiment, most of its hopes are now placed on the simpler strategy of finding new sources of labour and increasing the intensity of work. At different times attempts have been made to involve more women and pensioners in the labour market. But since participation in the labour force is already very high — in fact higher than in any other industrialised country in the world — it is unlikely that this approach can have much effect. Attempts have also been made to create a system of incentives to reward hard work. As with most systems of incentives, these make little impact. Workers are reluctant to work harder for wages with which it is often impossible to buy basic necessities.

In the eighties, the bureaucracy has put much effort into disciplining the working class. The August 1983 decree 'On stepping up work to strengthen socialist labour discipline' provided a model for subsequent crackdowns on the working class. Gorbachev has attempted to tighten up on discipline through an anti-alcohol drive. In a situation of labour shortages, these campaigns have little effect.

The bureaucracy is still reluctant to concede defeat in the sphere of economic reforms. In 1985 *Pravda* was still calling for 'the all round development of socialist competition and brigade forms of the organisation of labour and incentives'.[59] It singled out the Shchekino method as 'a specific and realistic form of achieving high work results'. But such exhortations simply obscure the impasse of work-related reforms. Only the creation of a free labour market could generate the incentive for higher levels of labour productivity. The fact that many Soviet observers — notably the Novosibirsk social scientists — are now discussing this very possibility indicates the dimensions of the problem. Lack of control over the working class is symptomatic of the bureaucracy's overall inability to regulate the labour-time of Soviet society.

## Notes

1 Dyker (1985).
2 *Pravda*, 23 November 1982.
3 This banal interpretation of the discussion on 'socialist contradictions' can be found in Kux (1984).
4 *Voprosy filosofii*, No 10, October 1984.
5 *Pravda*, 24 April 1985.
6 *Pravda*, 12 June 1985.
7 *Pravda*, 6 October 1952.
8 *Pravda*, 22 March 1954.
9 *Pravda*, 27 April 1954.
10 *Pravda*, 27 April 1954.
11 Dunmore (1980), p71.
12 See Schwartz (1965), pp95-6.
13 *Pravda*, 11 August 1958.
14 *Pravda*, 11 March 1949.
15 *Izvestia*, 8 September 1954.
16 *Pravda*, 9 September 1962.
17 *Pravda*, 17 August 1964.
18 *Pravda*, 7 September 1964.
19 *Pravda*, 20 September 1964.
20 See Kelley (1980), p41.
21 Berliner (1983), p355.
22 See Dyker (1985), p53.
23 Schroeder (1972).
24 Preobrazhensky (1967), p199.
25 See Dyker (1985), pp55-6.
26 *Planovoye khozyaistvo*, No 8, August 1981, abstracted in *CDSP*, 25 November 1981.
27 Schroeder (1983a), p72.
28 See discussion in *Ekonomicheskaya gazeta*, No 28, July 1983.
29 See Selyunin 'Paradoxes in the new index' in *Sotsialisticheskaya industria*, 1 March 1983, abstracted in *CDSP*, 13 April 1983.

30  *Pravda*, 30 June 1982.
31  Schroeder (1983a), p87.
32  *Pravda*, 6 July 1982, abstracted in *CDSP*, No 23, 1982.
33  See Zaslavskaya (1984), p91.
34  Schroeder (1983a), p81.
35  *Pravda*, 12 June 1985.
36  See *The Guardian*, 19 October 1985.
37  Hedlund (1984), p11.
38  Rumer (1984), p29.
39  Rumer (1984), p29.
40  *Pravda*, 25 May 1982.
41  *Pravda*, 25 May 1982.
42  Rumer (1984).
43  *Pravda*, 25 May 1982.
44  Malish (1983), p52.
45  Hedlund (1984), p177.
46  *Pravda*, 18 October 1982.
47  See *Financial Times*, 24 October 1985.
48  Dyker (1985), p138.
49  See Campbell (1983), p69.
50  See *EKO*, No 5, 1981, p13.
51  See *Ekonomicheskaya gazeta*, No 49, 1983.
52  For an excellent discussion of this experiment, see Arnot (1981).
53  See Arnot (1981), p45.
54  See Rutland (1984), p348.
55  See Arnot (1981), p49.
56  *Pravda*, 14 June 1982.
57  *Pravda*, 14 June 1982.
58  See Dyker (1985), p67.
59  *Pravda*, 1 February 1985.

# PART III
# Class and international relations

The next three chapters extend the analysis of the Soviet social formation by incorporating a study of the main social forces in Soviet society and its relationship with the outside world. The previous discussion of the laws governing the movement of Soviet society provides the framework for examining the interaction of different social groupings in the Soviet Union. The problems of economic regulation act as a barrier to the Soviet bureaucracy transforming itself into a class. The bureaucracy's lack of control over the distribution of the labour-time of society in turn weakens its capacity to control the working class.

One of the central themes of this book is that the survival of the Soviet Union has depended on developments in the West. Through looking at the external relations of the Soviet Union, we can see how it has succeeded in taking advantage of the difficulties of the capitalist world. By linking this discussion to the earlier study of the Soviet social formation, it is possible to explain the peculiarities of Soviet foreign policy.

# PART III
# Class and international relations

# 8. The bureaucracy

The study of relations among different social groups in the Soviet Union remains a subject of controversy. While Soviet writers preface their comments with assurances about 'non-antagonistic contradictions', they cannot ignore the existence of social conflict in Soviet society. They often draw attention to the clash of interests between workers and foremen, workers and enterprise directors and other 'vertically aligned' groups. Soviet commentators appear to have become influenced by the approach of Western sociology. Hence there is a tendency to survey attitudes or cultural values, or to analyse social groups in terms of occupational structure. Such methods, even if rigorously pursued, yield meagre results. Without an analysis of developmental tendencies, it is not clear what is being classified, or which distinctions are of primary or secondary significance.[1]

By limiting the investigation to the external characteristics of social groups, Soviet writers avoid confronting the basic antagonistic forces of Soviet society. Hence each social problem is given more or less equal weight, be it alcoholism, the breakdown of the family, or labour indiscipline. This concern to gloss over social conflicts is also apparent in the statements of the leaders of the Soviet bureaucracy. Thus, according to the Soviet Communist Party's new draft programme, the Soviet Union is in the process of becoming a socially homogeneous society: 'An important law of development of social relations at the present stage is the *drawing closer together* of the working class, the collective-farm peasantry and the intelligentsia, and the establishment of a classless structure of society with the working class playing the decisive role in that process.'[2] To go beyond this essentially apologetic approach, it is necessary to reconstruct the Marxist theory of class relations.[3]

## The Marxist theory of class

'The history of all hitherto existing society is the history of class struggles,' wrote Marx in the *Communist Manifesto,* indicating the pivotal place of the class struggle in his theory of social development. Many, including both supporters and opponents of Marxism, regard this theory as virtually synonymous with recognition of the class struggle. Indeed, the term 'Marxist' is often applied to any analysis of social forces in terms of class. However, the equation of Marxism with class analysis violates the procedures of historical materialism. Class as such is only one aspect of Marxist theory. Moreover, the recognition of the role of the class struggle is in no way exclusive to Marxism.

In a famous letter written in 1852, Marx insisted that the distinctive feature of his theory was not its recognition of the class struggle, but the way it established the connection between social classes and the changing conditions of social production:

**'Now as for myself, I do not claim to have discovered either the existence of classes in modern society or the struggle between them. Long before me, bourgeois historians had described the historical development of this struggle between the classes, as had bourgeois economists their economic anatomy. My own contribution was...to show that the existence of classes is merely bound up with certain historical phases in the development of production.'**[4]

For Marx, classes evolved in specific historical circumstances and changed as new social relations emerged. It follows that class relations cannot be understood in their own terms, but must be derived from an analysis of material circumstances. The positions occupied by individuals in the process of production determine their class relations. Engels summed up the Marxist conception of class in his famous defence of the theory against its early critics:

**'The materialist conception of history starts from the proposition that the production of the means to support human life and, next to production, the exchange of things produced is the basis of all social structure; that in every society that has appeared in history, the manner in which wealth is distributed and society divided into classes or orders is dependent upon what is produced, how it is produced, and how the products are exchanged.'**[5]

A materialist analysis of the class relations of a particular society presupposes an investigation of its production relations and its basic tendencies of development. Marx held that it was the 'specific economic form in which unpaid surplus-labour is pumped out of direct producers' that determined 'the relationship of rulers and ruled' and revealed 'the innermost secret, the hidden basis of the entire social structure'.[6] Classes as such cannot be deduced directly from a study of material conditions; they have to be derived through what Marx called the 'analysis of the empirically given circumstances'.[7] These 'empirically given circumstances' must be analysed as part of the totality of social relations.

Marx's theory of class is an integral part of the theory of historical materialism — it cannot be mechanically separated from this wider perspective or made into a purely sociological model. According to Grossman's useful conceptual breakdown, Marx's theory of history contains three distinct elements:

'**(1) a doctrine of a "universal social dynamic" of structural changes in society, valid for all "antagonistic" societies; (2) the theory of the objective developmental tendency of capitalism; and (3) the theory of the subjective bearer of change, that is, the class struggle theory.**'[8]

Marx's theory combines evolutionary and revolutionary aspects. The potential for change is given by the evolving social organisation and the contradictions arising from the restricted basis for the further development of the productive forces under the existing relations of production. The realisation of the potential for change requires the intervention of a human agency. The status of the class struggle in Marxist theory is that it is the subjective bearer of change, the mechanism through which historical change is achieved. However, as Grossman recognised, the class struggle is not just an arbitrary form of human interaction:

'**In Marx the class struggle is not merely a description of actual facts but a part of an elaborated historical theory: he explains genetically the necessary emergence of class conflicts in various historical epochs and explains their origin, form, and intensity by the development of the productive forces in each period and by the position individuals and classes occupy in the production process.**'[9]

Given the widespread practice of examining class relations in isolation, we need to situate class within the wider framework of

Marxist analysis. It is understandable that non-Marxists should adopt an abstract sociological approach; but this method also prevails among writers who purport to offer a Marxist analysis.[10] Much radical analysis begins with a ready-made set of concepts, instead of deriving these from the study of Soviet social relations. When this approach is applied to the Soviet Union, the distinctive features of the Soviet social formation are lost.

For example, Cliff's attempt to prove that the Soviet bureaucracy is a capitalist class proceeds from the statement that 'an examination of the definitions of a social class given by different Marxist theoreticians will show that, according to all of them, the Stalinist bureaucracy qualifies as a class'.[11] Mandel, who holds the view that the bureaucracy is not a class, but a caste, also relies on the method of definition to substantiate his argument. He notes that the bureaucracy 'is not a class rooted in the production process but a social layer growing out of the proletariat. This definition is not a question of a play on words: it is of crucial importance in formulating the correct strategy for the international working class movement'.[12]

The definitional approach not only violates the method of historical materialism, but also ignores the process of class formation. Classes are not formed ready-made: they are constituted through the process of social development. Marx acclaimed the work of the French historian Thierry because he demonstrated how the capitalist class arose through a 'sequence of metamorphoses leading up to the domination' of this class.[13] In the Soviet Union today, just as in eighteenth century France, it is only by examining the process of social development that any insights into class relations can be gained.

## Class power in history

Left-wing debates have long focused on the nature of the Soviet bureaucracy. They have suffered from a narrow preoccupation with whether the bureaucracy owns or controls society's resources.[14] The controversy over ownership and control is misplaced, because the best that can be achieved by analysis along these lines is a description of the mechanisms through which the bureaucracy exercises power.[15] But describing the *mechanisms* through which the bureaucracy rules does not explain the *nature* of its power. By reducing power to ownership or control, the radical critics assume what has yet to be explained.

A close reading of Marx and Engels shows that the historical study of classes must be used with care. The significance of classes varies from society to society, depending on the level of social development. The cohesion and power of classes is different in varying social circumstances. While the class struggle is the bearer of change, it assumes a distinct form only in certain circumstances. Marx and Engels emphasised that the theory of the class struggle could only be elaborated at an advanced stage of historical development. Engels argued that it was only with the development of capitalism that class antagonism acquired a clearly perceptible pattern:

'But while in all earlier periods the investigation of these driving causes of history was almost impossible — on account of the complicated and concealed interconnections between them and their effects — our present period has so far simplified these interconnections that the riddle could be solved.'[16]

The low level of development of the productive forces in pre-capitalist societies meant that the emergence of distinct social strata was retarded. Individuals appeared to occupy different positions in society according to their family or kinship connections, or because of particular local circumstances. Social status seemed to have no clear relationship to the role people played in the economic life of the community, in producing society's needs: social differentiation appeared unrelated to production relations. Individuals appeared to form allegiances and antagonisms according to diverse and arbitrary factors. They did not stick together or form clear rivalries according to their positions in the process of production. Social groups defined in this way lacked cohesion.

The development of the productive forces under capitalism was paralleled by the consolidation of class relations. In capitalist society the link between social status and economic position became clear and unmistakable. Engels noted the marked contrast between feudal and capitalist society in this respect:

'If it was possible at first glance still to ascribe the origin of the great, formerly feudal landed property — at least in the first instance — to political causes, to taking possession by force, this could not be done in regard to the bourgeoisie and the proletariat. Here the origin and development of two great classes was seen to lie clearly and palpably in purely economic causes.'[17]

Under capitalism, people were clearly identifiable as capitalists or workers according to their role in social production. The development of capitalist society led to the crystallisation of distinct classes, their internal consolidation and their growing antagonism to one another. It is not only the social weight of classes, but the nature and exercise of class power that changes with historical development. The power of the absolute monarch, the capitalist entrepreneur and the Soviet bureaucrat are the products of specific social circumstances and must be analysed in their own terms.

In pre-capitalist societies the relations between exploiter and exploited were direct and undisguised. In societies based on slavery, or various forms of serfdom, there was no mechanism of exploitation distinct from the wider process of social domination. There was no separation of the sphere of production (economics) from the world of social conflict (politics). The ruling class lorded over production, as over every other aspect of society, by the exercise of force. Social relations were reproduced by direct duress.

In capitalist society the wage-labour/capital relation provides a mechanism for exploitation which is separate from the wider process of class rule.[18] As a result, the economic sphere is separated from the political sphere. The ruling class is no longer obliged to enforce exploitation by force and social relations are reproduced automatically. The automatic reproduction of social relations in capitalist society is made possible by the development of the forces of production and the productivity of labour through the influence of the market mechanism. Occasionally, when the system breaks down and heads for crisis, the capitalist class is forced to resort to coercion. But political intervention is always a supplement to the functioning of the capitalist market, not a substitute for it. In general there is no need to force the working class to produce surplus value — the discipline of the market is sufficient.

Marx emphasised the way that capital itself enforces the basic relations of society:

**'Capital comes more and more to the fore as a social power, whose agent is the capitalist. This social power no longer stands in any possible relation to that which the labour of a single individual can create. It becomes an alienated, independent social power.'**[19]

Capital as a social power confronts and dominates the working class. It also compels each individual capitalist to produce surplus value on an extended scale.

The accumulation of capital is at the same time a process of social domination, mediated through the market.[20] Class structure is governed and regulated through the automatic reproduction of capitalist social relations. The emergence of capital as a social power is the secret of the strength of the ruling class in capitalist society. As Marx observed, the manner in which class power is exercised in capitalist society is quite different from previous societies:

'On the basis of capitalist production, the mass of direct producers is confronted by the social character of this production in the form of strictly regulating authority and a social mechanism of the labour process organised as a complete hierarchy—this authority reaching its bearers, however, only as the personification of the conditions of labour in contrast to labour, and not as political or theocratic rulers as under earlier modes of production.'[21]

Under capitalism domination is no longer based on the exercise of political authority. The ruling class is merely the social representative of economic relations: the capitalist is the personification of capital.

The recognition of classes as the social expression of production relations is central to Marx's analysis of capitalist society:

'In view of what has already been said, it is superfluous to demonstrate anew that the relation between capital and wage-labour determines the entire character of the mode of production. The principal agents of this mode of production itself, the capitalist and the wage-labourer, are as such, mere embodiments, personifications of capital and wage-labour.'[22]

Exploitation itself creates and re-creates capitalist class relations and endows capitalist class power with its strength and coherence.

The development of classes as the personification of production relations is dependent on the dynamism of the accumulation of wealth. This is clear even within capitalism. Among the backward capitalist countries of the third world, the narrow base for accumulation limits the scope for the development of a bourgeoisie. In these circumstances the capitalist class does not personify production relations and its domination has to be exercised politically, through coercion. Social relations can only be enforced by capitalists acting as political agents, relying primarily on state intervention rather than upon the market.

How then is social power exercised in the Soviet Union? Cliff argues that the Soviet bureaucracy is 'the personification of capital in its purest form' because it is interested in accumulation for its own sake and pursues this objective single-mindedly through its control of the state.[23] This use of the term 'personification' is either a play on words or the result of a misreading of Marx. The personification of capital presupposes the automatic reproduction of social relations — that is, a context in which class agents merely execute the dynamics of social relations. But classes can only act in this way in capitalist society, because the process of surplus extraction goes on independently of political events.

The Soviet bureaucracy cannot rely on any automatic mechanism to reproduce social relations and enforce surplus creation. On the contrary, it is forced to intervene in every aspect of social life; its domination is dependent to a considerable degree on the exercise of political power. Insofar as spontaneous forces can be detected, they work directly against the bureaucracy, which is forced to try to counteract their effects. To give a semblance of coherence to his argument, Cliff suggests that it was Soviet economic growth that transformed the bureaucracy into a class:

**'A caste is the outcome of the relative immobility of the economy — a rigid division of labour and immobility of the productive forces — whereas the Stalinist bureaucracy was transformed into a ruling class on the crest of the dynamism of the economy.'**[24]

But it is the *lack* of a developmental dynamic that dictates the actions of the bureaucracy. Even critical Soviet writers would not go as far as to claim that their economic system possesses a developmental dynamic.

Although the thesis that the Soviet bureaucracy is a capitalist class does not stand up to elementary Marxist analysis, in principle we cannot exclude the possibility that the Kremlin may represent some other class. We cannot follow Mandel in dismissing this possibility simply because those who subscribe to it have drawn right-wing conclusions from their analysis.[25] However, if the thesis that the bureaucracy has become a class is to be sustained, it is necessary to point out the relations of production and the developmental tendencies that have made this transformation possible.

## The power of the Kremlin

The historical origins of the bureaucracy are central to its subsequent development. The bureaucrats did not set out to create a new social formation: the Stalinist system was the outcome of the operation of general laws of development rather than a consciously-determined objective. In the twenties the bureaucracy sought only to consolidate its own position through a series of short-term responses to threats to its survival. Hence it was prepared for a time to experiment with the market and, when that experiment created new problems, to adopt a different tack.

By the late twenties, the bureaucracy had consolidated its position, but its power was limited and threatened by its lack of control over the economy. The tendency of market forces towards the restoration of capitalist relations was inconsistent with the survival of the Kremlin's authority. The bureaucracy was therefore forced to destroy the market and take over direct control of society's resources. But was this a necessary stage of historical development?

The collectivisation of agriculture and industrialisation cannot be regarded as rational responses to underlying economic laws. Both the capitalist market and workers' democracy are means by which the tendency towards the socialisation of labour can be developed. The new social formation of the thirties cannot be regarded as a viable expression of this tendency. The primary impulse behind the new system was not economic development, but political control.

The panic-stricken manner in which the new policies were implemented reveals how narrow the Kremlin's ambitions were. Collectivisation in particular was a measure for which there was no economic rationale: it was designed solely to crush the political threat from the countryside. The bureaucracy's take-over of power from the working class and its destruction of the market provided the starting-point of the new social formation. It is ironic that the new order was founded on the elimination of two workable forms of economic regulation — workers' democracy and the capitalist market. Like any influential social force, the Soviet bureaucracy would have had no inhibitions about transforming itself into a class. But without a viable form of economic regulation, the basis for surplus extraction remained too narrow to make this transformation possible.

The emergence and survival of a new social formation, one without any developmental dynamic, was a result of special historical circumstances. The worldwide defeats of the working class made the consolidation of the bureaucracy possible. At the same time the weakness of the world capitalist system throughout the inter-war period, which led to persistent economic depression and imperialist rivalry, provided a breathing space for the new system. A tremendous reservoir of resources and labour also supplied the material prerequisites for the development of the Soviet Union. If any one of these accidental factors had been missing, the survival of the new social formation would have been jeopardised.

Marxist writers are often horrified by the prospect of historical accidents. To many they appear to contradict the convenient schema of feudalism, capitalism and communism. But there is no place for schemas in the scientific study of social relations: the path of human development is not a straight one. In his own day, Marx commented sarcastically on how one of his critics had transformed his 'historical sketch of the genesis of capitalism in Western Europe into an historico-philosophic theory of the general path of development prescribed by fate to all nations, whatever the historical circumstances in which they find themselves'.[26] The emergence of the new social formation transformed the Soviet bureaucracy. In the twenties its power lay primarily in its control of the state machine; in the thirties massive resource mobilisation and the establishment of new industries created a new bureaucracy whose position rested on the growth of the new forces of production.

However, the peculiar growth of the productive forces in the Soviet Union has prevented the transformation of the bureaucracy into a class. This growth is not the result of laws immanent to the Soviet social formation, for there is no internal drive towards technological innovation or higher productivity. Rather, it relies on factors external to the economic sphere. In the Soviet Union, growth does not take place through the development and transformation of existing industry, but by building industries from scratch — often with the aid of foreign technology. This form of growth, which has little organic relationship with the previous stage of development, is not at all self-generating. Growth can only be sustained through the systematic intervention of the bureaucracy and a high-cost investment programme.

What passes for planning in the Soviet Union is more an ad-hoc response to economic conditions than real central direction. The forces of spontaneity continually undermine bureaucratic control. State intervention can limit the damage caused by the tendency towards fragmentation, but cannot initiate a new phase of social development. The potential for bureaucratic action is further restricted by the capitalist world market and the hostile international environment. The higher productivity of the capitalist international division of labour is a constant source of pressure on the Soviet Union. The arms race is only the most striking example of the way the deployment of Soviet resources is circumscribed by the capitalist world.

In the absence of a developmental dynamic, the material basis for the emergence of a new bureaucratic class in the Soviet Union does not exist. The obstacles to the reproduction of society's wealth limit the scope for surplus extraction. The forces of spontaneity restrict the extent to which the bureaucracy can expand its surplus through investment. The bureaucracy's insecure grip on the surplus fund militates against its transformation into a class.

Given the low level of the development of the productive forces in the Soviet Union, political intervention is not enough to give the bureaucracy a secure grip over society's surplus. The only mechanisms that could achieve this are the automatic process of surplus extraction through the market, or a system of workers' democracy. Lacking either of these, the bureaucracy resorts to political interference or coercion. The artificial character of the bureaucracy's relationship to the process of production is confirmed by its need to keep reorganising economic activity.

The bureaucracy plays a key role in the Soviet economy. Yet it does this, not as the personification of production relations, but through its monopoly over political power. This power is based ultimately on its control over society's resources; but using these resources depends on consistent political intervention. This indicates the difficulty of extracting and deploying a surplus in Soviet society. From a historical perspective, the Soviet social formation has transcended the division between the economic and political spheres characteristic of capitalist society, but without achieving the integration of economics into politics which would be characteristic of a communist society.

Under capitalism, automatic economic regulation is primary and politics and the use of force are secondary, compensating mechanisms. In the Soviet Union, the political sphere is primary and production relations are highly politicised. It is true that, in a society subject to workers' management, automatic economic regulation would also be abolished. But instead of economic relations being politicised, politics would come to embody economic relations. In such a society, the sphere of economics would be reduced to the administration of purely technical matters. The distribution and regulation of labour-time would be the central concern of political life.

Whether the Soviet bureaucracy owns or controls the means of production or the state is of secondary importance. For Marx, discussion of property or legal forms revealed little about real social relations.[27] Our starting point must be the material basis for class formation; from this perspective it becomes clear that there is no underlying logic propelling the bureaucracy to transform itself into a class.

In the Soviet Union production relations do not reproduce the bureaucracy. It has to take steps to reproduce itself: its power is maintained through political control — it functions as a political order. But the transformation of this political order into a class is fraught with difficulties. Because individual bureaucrats have no power other than that endowed on them by their peers, the exercise of political power is necessarily a collective process. Individual bureaucrats exercise power by virtue of their appointment, and a system of centralised appointments serves as a mechanism for the exercise of collective power. Even the most powerful bureaucrat functions as an appointee and understands that power depends, not on independent influence or wealth, but on appointment.

The Soviet appointments system has developed into a hierarchy termed the *nomenklatura*. Position within the *nomenklatura* determines a bureaucrat's access to power: because appointments can be made or taken away, the hierarchical system limits the scope for the individualisation of power. For the purposes of this discussion, we identify the bureaucracy as including those in charge of state administration and their associates — in practice this group is coterminous with the *nomenklatura*. The intelligentsia is a wider category, including all those who have received a higher education and receive a salary.

Most discussion of the *nomenklatura* views it largely as a system of privileges.[28] However, it plays a more important role as the regulator of bureaucratic power. The fact that the bureaucracy needs such an artificial device illustrates how far it is from transforming itself into a social class. As a political order the bureaucracy cannot but try to counteract the individualisation of power. This does not mean that it is a harmonious collective unit. On the contrary, because political power and influence are arbitrary, individual bureaucrats can never feel confident of their position. Even today, when the secret police have receded into the background and *nomenklatura* appointees often maintain their privileges after demotion, no bureaucrat is ever truly safe. The bureaucracy is continually wracked with internal tensions.

Soviet bureaucrats do not function merely as representatives of defined social groups, but as individuals pursuing their own private interests. Since there is no mechanism for reconciling the individual interests of the bureaucrat with those of the collectivity — other than an artificial regulator — the Soviet bureaucracy lacks internal coherence. Not only do bureaucrats promote their interests at each other's expense, but also in defiance of the objectives of the bureaucracy as a whole.

In capitalist society there is bitter competition within the ruling class. But whatever the subjective motives of individual capitalists, the market ensures that they are all forced to act as the agents of the system. The Soviet bureaucracy has no such mechanism for keeping its agents in line. Repression and a system of appointments are inadequate instruments for enforcing the general interests of the bureaucracy. The continual conflict between the central bureaucracy and enterprise management illustrates the scale of the problem. Managers are forced by tendencies towards fragmentation to pursue goals which contradict central directives. The reproduction of this conflict through the action of the laws of the Soviet social formation prevents the bureaucracy from becoming a class.

Many writers have stressed the parasitic nature of the Soviet bureaucracy and in particular its urge for personal consumption. But such writers end up explaining the behaviour of the bureaucracy as a manifestation of human greed. Thus Voslensky explains that 'nomenklaturists are fanatics, not of industrialisation or even of profit, but of power'.[29] This approach is not only subjective, but also ahistorical. In conditions of scarcity, all ruling groups strive for power; but the pursuit of self-interest or self-gratification by a particular ruling stratum tells us nothing about its specific social situation.

Mandel attempts to explain the aims of individual bureaucrats as 'only those of maximising their own consumption'.[30] Yet the urge to consume is not peculiar to the Soviet bureaucracy, nor is it its characteristic feature. In any circumstances such expressions of self-interest are not an independent variable, but the effect of social laws on the actions of individuals. The bureaucracy is the product of the Soviet social formation: its privileged place in the division of labour is determined by the necessity for detailed political intervention. As a privileged political order, the bureaucracy's life depends on the maintenance of the Soviet social formation. The actions of individual bureaucrats which contradict the development of this social formation are not a sign of greed, but a response to the forces of spontaneity.

Over the years the Soviet bureaucracy has taken steps to guarantee its own stability. The climate of fear created by the purges of the thirties has been substantially modified, and the excesses of the security police have been curbed. Bureaucratic positions have become much more secure and the rate of turnover of personnel in key posts has declined.[31] However, there are limits to the extent to which the bureaucracy can succeed in consolidating its collective interests. The Soviet Communist Party is supposed to represent the overall interests of bureaucracy and state. On paper it is committed to fighting departmentalism and the pursuit of special interests. But, in reality, the party reflects wider social forces and splinters along lines similar to the bureaucracy. As one Western writer notes:

'One of the more significant effects of the party's active role in the local economy is the enhancement of the tendency towards local self-sufficiency.'[32]

The central state bureaucracy tries to pursue a rational course of action according to its perception of its collective interests. But if it had to rely simply on its subjective will and on its monopoly of force, the bureaucracy would soon succumb to the forces of fragmentation. There are however two important factors which impose a sense of collective responsibility on the bureaucracy. These are the pressures of the capitalist world, and the problems of managing the Soviet working class.

The Soviet bureaucracy rightly regards the superior development of the capitalist world as a threat. Hence it is prepared to unite at every level in a common commitment to defend the Soviet social formation against both military and economic pressures from abroad (see Chapter 10). The working class at home is an even greater stimulus to bureaucratic unity. The working class is a creation of the bureaucracy, and its exploitation is essential for the reproduction of the system. Maintaining the power and privilege of the bureaucracy depends on excluding the working class from political life. Every Soviet bureaucrat knows that the survival of the system depends on the domination of the working class, and this awareness helps to pull the bureaucracy as a whole together. Paradoxically, it is in relation to the working class that its collective weakness becomes most apparent.

## Bureaucrats and workers

From a Marxist point of view, the bureaucracy has more of the attributes of a *caste* than of a *class*. Whereas individuals are united in a class by virtue of their common role in the process of production, members of a caste are united by their common position in a legal order of society. The nobility and the church in mediaeval society are typical examples of castes. A caste is a legal-political concept, in contrast to that of a class, which is a broader social one. The *nomenklatura* provides the bureaucracy with a hierarchical internal system characteristic of a caste.

However, characterising the bureaucracy as a caste is problematic. The bureaucracy has no legal existence: the *nomenklatura* is not recognised in law — indeed the bureaucracy is keen to shield its hierarchy and its system of privileges from public view. More importantly, the power of the bureaucracy goes beyond the legal-political sphere. It plays an essential role in the maintenance of economic and social relations. Its power is more pervasive than that of traditional castes. The bureaucracy is similar to a caste in that it can only exercise its power politically; it is different in that it has much wider functions in society.

The bureaucracy is more than a caste, but not yet a class. The bureaucrats would like to become a class, but the obstacles thrown up by the Soviet social formation have prevented this metamorphosis from taking place. Because of the political nature of its power, we can provisionally characterise the Soviet bureaucracy as a *political order*; more precisely, it is a political order which dominates society. By contrast with the bureaucracy, the working class has a real social existence as a class. The Soviet working class is certainly unique, and its experience is quite different from that of the working class under capitalism. Soviet workers do not sell their labour power — labour power is not a commodity, and there is no market in labour. Nor do Soviet workers earn wages in the same way as workers in the West: the relationship between wages and living standards that prevails under capitalism has been substantially modified in the Soviet Union.

To be precise, we should designate Soviet workers as a *proletariat*. In common with the proletariat in other societies, Soviet workers own nothing but their capacity to work. In contrast to capitalist society, however, the capacity to work in the Soviet Union does not assume a commodity form. Nevertheless, despite this crucial difference, we can still loosely refer to this section of Soviet society as the working class. This unusual procedure is justified because, from a Marxist point of view, history has assigned the workers of the Soviet Union a role parallel to that of workers in capitalist society: that of the revolutionary class.

A study of the relationship between the Soviet bureaucracy and the working class reveals much about the nature of the ruling political order. The consolidation of bureaucratic power in the thirties depended on drawing millions of peasants into industry. The working class, formed by industrialisation, was the direct product of the bureaucracy. In turn, the mobilisation of millions of workers and the creation of a new working class provided the foundations for the new Soviet social formation. In a modified form, the terms of the relationship established between bureaucrats and workers in the thirties persist today.

The relationship between the bureaucracy and the working class was founded on the use of force. Millions of peasants were driven from the countryside into factories, where they were forced to work on terms dictated by the bureaucracy. Workers were deprived of all rights and severe penalties were imposed for refusal to work, absenteeism and lateness. Force was needed to discipline the working class into accepting consumption levels barely sufficient for physical survival. To ensure the subordination of the working class, the bureaucracy could not restrict force to the workplace. Every aspect of working class life was ruled by an extensive apparatus of repression.

The virtual enslavement of the working class was not the result of some totalitarian streak in the psychology of the Stalinist bureaucrats. Soviet industrialisation required the deployment of labour without restraint on an unprecedented scale. This was the only way the bureaucracy could compensate for the absence of a mechanism for regulating labour-time. A steady flow of labour counteracted the inefficiency of the system through sheer weight of numbers. The new relations of exploitation were based on force rather than incentives. The bureaucracy's drive to free itself as far as possible from the constraints of consumption allowed it to disregard the production of consumer goods, and also to increase the surplus fund by enforcing low living standards.

The new system of exploitation succeeded in consolidating the Soviet system. The labour of millions created new industries and a new infrastructure. However, force is of limited use for extracting surplus in a modern industrial society. It is always possible to compel people to go to work, and, in certain circumstances, it is possible to make them work hard. But force alone cannot make people work efficiently today: under conditions of coercion, workers are interested only in minimising their effort and have little regard for the use of machinery or material inputs. Workers go through the motions and produce the physical quantities demanded, but with little regard to quality.

Even in the thirties it became evident that the bureaucracy could dominate, but not control, the process of work. It soon realised that force had to be supplemented by incentives if economic growth was to be sustained. At the time, there was not much scope for a system of incentives based on access to consumer goods. Instead the main form of incentive lay in the prospect of promotion and upward social mobility. The industrialisation drive created new employment opportunities and hundreds of thousands of workers were elevated into administrative and managerial posts. The prospect of promotion tended to limit the erosion of the will to work.

The system of forced labour remained substantially unaltered until the fifties. By this time coercive exploitation had become irrational from every point of view. The inefficient results of this system now outweighed any advantages it might once have offered. A new way of getting people to work efficiently had to be found. In 1956, repressive labour laws were repealed and workers were for the first time allowed to change their jobs. Conditions gradually improved as working hours were reduced and living standards raised.

Yet modifying the relationship between the bureaucracy and the working class failed to solve the problem of inefficient working. All attempts to introduce incentive schemes failed, because higher wages did not necessarily mean more consumer goods or better services. As long as shop shelves were empty, there was little incentive to work hard and efficiently. Moreover, the grip of the bureaucracy on the working class was further weakened by the decline in the labour supply. Despite economic growth, the system still relied on massive inputs of labour. Growing shortages of labour forced enterprises to compete against each other to attract workers. This obviously strengthened the position of the working class against the bureaucracy. Workers became increasingly aware of their power, and aware too that management could do little to make them work.

It is still illegal to refuse to work in the Soviet Union and the bureaucracy has the power to force people to get jobs. But the growing demand for labour has weakened central control over the workplace and the bureaucracy faces increasing difficulty in deploying labour according to economic priorities. The central allocation of labour is now minimal and competition between enterprises has strengthened the forces of spontaneity in the distribution of labour. According to Soviet statistics, institutions associated with the state committee for labour and social problems control directly or indirectly less than 15 per cent of all job placements.[33] The table below shows that enterprise recruitment is now the most important factor in the distribution of labour.

**The structure of organised forms of manpower distribution in the Soviet Union in 1980; in %:**[34]

| | |
|---|---|
| Organised recruitment of workers | 0.7 |
| Agricultural resettlement | 0.2 |
| Youth employment | 2.8 |
| Distribution of graduates of vocational-technical training schools | 9.3 |
| Personal distribution of graduates of higher educational institutions | 1.9 |
| Personal distribution of graduates of secondary specialised educational institutions | 3.0 |
| Transfers | 3.8 |
| Public appeals | 0.5 |
| Hiring by enterprises themselves | 77.8 |
| — of which, through the job placement service | 9.7 |
| **Total** | **100.0** |

The disorganised distribution of labour illustrates the problem the bureaucracy has in controlling the working class. This problem will continue as long as there is a shortage of labour — a phenomenon which is not the result of falling birth rates, but the inevitable outcome of the Soviet system of production. Even the advent of new technology provides no answer to the shortage of labour. Fil'ev's study of the iron and steel and mineral fertiliser plants in Cherepovets shows that, despite the introduction of new technology, the ratio between output and assets declined between 1976 and 1980, necessitating the employment of 15.7 per cent more workers.[35]

Labour shortages are a result of the tendencies of Soviet society which force production units to try to become self-sufficient. Even the most modern plants hoard labour and engage in auxiliary activities, such as repairs and transport. As a result, in recent years the rate of growth in the employment of repair workers in industry has been nearly three times that in overall employment.[36] Even in enterprises created in the eighties, one in every three workers carries out manual labour.

The Soviet bureaucracy's lack of control over the working class is a major obstacle to the system's development and a serious threat to its stability. Without an efficient workforce, the growth of the surplus fund remains restricted and the domination of the bureaucracy is weakened. It is significant that the problem of control over the working class has emerged as a major focus of discussion in the bureaucracy over the past decade. Experts have blamed the poor performance of the economy on the unorganised character of work. This is the key problem identified by Zaslavskaya:

**'Motivated by individual and group interests, the socio-economic behaviour of workers has a substantial influence on practically all aspects of the economy and is therefore one of the sources of spontaneity in its development. The role of the spontaneous, that is not regulated, behaviour of the workers in the development of the socialist economy has many ramifications. Several aspects of it often infringe upon its planned character, cause disproportions and lower the rate of production development.'**[37]

In her attitude towards the working class, Zaslavskaya is typical of the bureaucracy. The inclination to blame the workers for the performance of the Soviet economy is not simply an attempt to shift responsibility. It also reveals an instinctive recognition that, for the bureaucracy, the working class is a barrier to be overcome.

The anti-working class attitude of the bureaucracy is a familiar part of everyday life in the Soviet Union. The bureaucrats' prejudice is shared by the Soviet intelligentsia, which resents the way the strength of the working class has led to the narrowing of differentials in living standards. Since Andropov took over in 1982, cracking down on the working class has been a central element of the bureaucracy's strategy. We now turn to examine this strategy and its chances of success.

## Notes

1. See 'Social stratification and class' in Lane (1985a) for an illustration of the limitations of this narrow approach.
2. CPSU (1985), p59.
3. The Soviet ideologue Kosolapov provides an eloquent example of apologetic sociology in *Pravda*, 4 March 1983. He attempts to depict social contradictions in the Soviet Union as merely conflicts between individuals. According to him 'the transformation of all social contradictions into non-antagonistic ones and the lowering of residual antagonism to the individual level is an enormous achievement of socialist society'. With a sleight of hand, he declares: 'Inaccuracies in interpreting this question are in large part due to the fact that non-antagonistic contradictions, like antagonistic ones, may take the *form* of a conflict.'
4. Marx in Marx & Engels (1983), p62.
5. Engels (1968b), p411.
6. Marx (1971), p791.
7. See Marx (1971), p792.
8. Grossman (1943), p518.
9. Grossman (1943), p522.
10. See for example the works of Wright (1978) and Poulantzas (1973).
11. Cliff (1970), p116.
12. Mandel (1984), p87.
13. See Marx & Engels (1983), p474.
14. An honourable exception is Ticktin's attempt to explain the emergence of what he calls the 'Soviet elite' through an analysis of the relations of production. See Ticktin (1978a).
15. For a review of this controversy see Lane (1985a), pp83-100.
16. Engels (1968a), p614.
17. Engels (1968a), p614.
18. Richards (1979), pp4-14.
19. Marx (1971), p264.
20. See Marx (1974), p542.
21. Marx (1971), p881.
22. Marx (1971), p879-80.
23. Cliff (1970), p118.
24. Cliff (1970), p117.
25. Mandel (1984), p89.
26. Marx & Engels (1975), p293.
27. 'To try to give a definition of property as of an independent relation, a category apart, an abstract and eternal idea, can be nothing but an illusion of metaphysics or jurisprudence.' Marx (1976b), p197.
28. See for example Voslensky (1984). The system of party appointments to key positions was initially organised under a special department of the central committee in 1920. In the thirties this became the modern *nomenklatura* system.

29 Voslensky (1984), pp124-5.
30 Mandel (1974), p17.
31 See Hough (1979) and Bunce & Echols (1980).
32 Grossman (1983).
33 Kotliar (1984), p21.
34 Kotliar (1984), p21.
35 Fil'ev (1983).
36 Goodman & Schleifer (1983), p335.
37 Zaslavskaya (1984), p94.

**MIKHAIL GORBACHEV:** *a younger face at the top – but the same old policies*

**CHURCHILL, TRUMAN, STALIN:** *shaking hands on the carve-up of the post-war world*

**NIKITA KHRUSHCHEV:** *revelations and reforms at the end of the Stalin era*

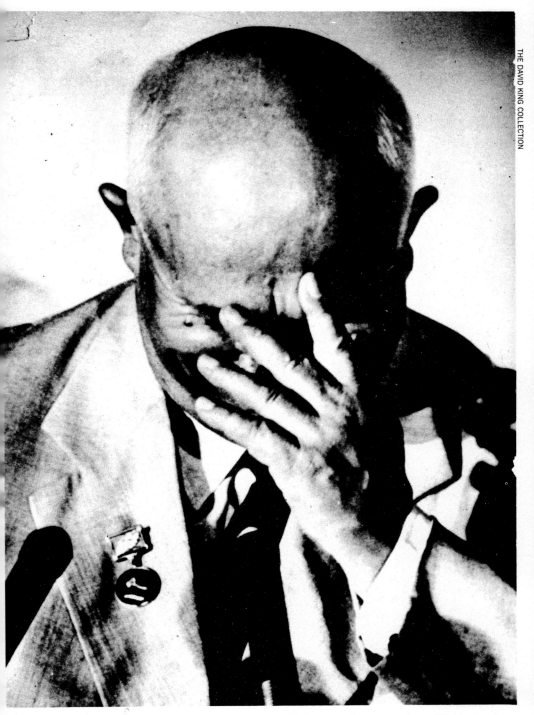

**KHRUSHCHEV HIDES HIS FACE:** *but nothing could disguise the stagnation of Soviet society*

**ALEXEI KOSYGIN:** *launched the drive to raise productivity in the seventies*

**LEONID BREZHNEV:** *reaching out to the West – with West German premier Willy Brandt in 1971; and looking forward to meeting a Hollywood actress at Richard Nixon's California home in 1973*

**OP BRASS ON PARADE:** *grim-faced bureaucrats in uniform stare blankly into the future*

**YURI ANDROPOV:** *tried to modernise, bu[t] still had to chain down public telephones to stop the vandals*

**GORBACHEV:** *advertising commercial deals with Western firms*

**YEGOR LIGACHOV:** *Gorbachev's staunch lieutenant in the Kremlin*

# 9. The working class

Many Western commentators depict the Soviet working class as a passive mass which lives in fear. Liberals and Soviet dissidents condescendingly dismiss Soviet workers as an uneducated and backward force, preoccupied with securing material comforts and indifferent to questions of civil rights and political reform. For Stalinist apologists, by contrast, there is nothing to discuss — the working class rules and enjoys the fruits of its labour.

Yet, far from being an inert mass, the working class has become the most important political problem facing the Soviet bureaucracy — especially over the last decade. Unable either to admit or confront the inherent limitations of its system, the bureaucracy looks upon the working class as the main barrier to further development. As labour shortages become more acute, bureaucrats are forced to reorganise the terms of exploitation to ensure that workers produce a higher level of output.

When Andropov took over from Brezhnev in 1982, he opened an era of direct confrontation with the working class. Andropov set about the task of getting people to work harder and more efficiently. For years public debate had raged over the problem of 'labour discipline'. Three aspects of this problem were singled out for special attention: absenteeism, labour turnover and drunkenness. The usual explanations favoured by Western sociologists and industrial relations experts were put forward to account for the lack of motivation of Soviet workers. Some argued that life had become too soft; others blamed the decline of family values for eroding the work ethic. Others still drew attention to a growing lack of respect for foremen and those in authority.[1]

Pseudo-scientific studies suggested that workers were either too stupid or too well educated to perform their jobs adequately. Gordon and Nazimova complain that because most workers have only recently arrived in the city from the country, they lack the 'ethical components of the culture of industrial labour'.[2] Other sociologists, such as Zaslavskaya, looked back nostalgically to the thirties, when an uneducated and brutalised workforce presented few problems for the bureaucracy:

'An overwhelming number of workers in industry had only recently left their villages and had a weakly developed sense of their rights, and no claims to participation in management. For the majority of them material incentives predominated at work over social and spiritual ones. Being relatively undeveloped, they were a convenient object of management.'[3]

The golden age of Soviet industrial relations has now passed. Workers now expect more from life: for Zaslavskaya, they have become 'a much more complex object of management than previously'.

Taking advantage of the consensus on tackling labour indiscipline, as the only way to get the economy moving, Andropov launched an offensive against the working class. It is striking that, of all the areas of reform discussed in the early eighties, the sphere of labour discipline was the one in which the bureaucracy took the most tangible initiatives. This issue was the starting-point and central focus of Andropov's reform programme, as he emphasised in his first major speech after assuming power:

'It is necessary to create conditions...that will stimulate good quality, productive work, initiative and enterprise. Conversely, poor work, laziness and irresponsibility should have an immediate and unavoidable effect on the remuneration, job status and moral prestige of personnel....We must wage a more resolute struggle against all violators of party, state and labour discipline.'[4]

Within weeks Andropov launched a law and order campaign.

In the spring and summer of 1983 the authorities made a series of highly publicised raids on bars, swimming pools and other public places — to discourage loafing. The media promoted an atmosphere of vigilance against idleness and malingering. In August 1983, the politburo promulgated a new law, 'On stepping up work to strengthen socialist labour discipline'. The law threatened to penalise managers who failed to maintain discipline: absenteeism would now be punished by loss of holidays, drunkenness at work would lead to temporary demotion, and workers would be liable for damage to materials and machinery.[5]

The campaign for labour discipline continued after Andropov's death in 1983, though it lost momentum during the Chernenko interregnum. However, within days of Gorbachev's succession in 1984, it was relaunched with renewed vigour. Gorbachev's main contribution was to shift the emphasis of the campaign: in May 1985 a new law restricting the consumption of alcohol was introduced. Gorbachev has made alcoholism the number one social issue, using exemplary punishments as a warning to others. In August 1985, officials in the city of Perm were pilloried for not tackling alcoholism in their region.[6]

Alcoholism is a serious problem in the Soviet Union. According to a study cited by Arnot, 90 per cent of absenteeism is caused by alcohol, and productivity could rise by as much as 10 per cent if drunkenness in the workplace could be controlled.[7] Alcoholism, a symptom of the deeper malaise of Soviet society, is now treated as the cause of all its social problems. The campaign against alcohol has gone to almost ludicrous extremes: drink has been blamed for everything from mentally retarded children to the rise of crime. Yet the campaign has a rational purpose — to strengthen the grip of the bureaucracy over the working class. To assess its value as a solution to the difficulties facing the bureaucracy, we need to look more closely at the question of labour discipline itself.

## The drive for labour discipline

The drive behind the campaign for labour discipline arises from the bureaucracy's awareness that it can no longer compensate for economic inefficiency by drawing more people into employment. The demographic patterns are clear. The number of people employed in Soviet industry increased from 15 million in 1950 to more than 34 million in 1975, but the rate of growth has steadily declined. Industrial employment grew by 3.9 per cent each year between 1950 and 1959; however, between 1971 and 1975 the annual increase dropped to 1.5 per cent.[8] In 1983 the number of workers in industry grew by only 0.6 per cent. The growth of the labour force in the eighties is expected to be less than half that of the seventies.[9]

As the countryside has become more sparsely populated, the old reserves of labour have dried up. Attempts to draw more women into employment have had little effect, for 90 per cent of Soviet women are already either working or studying full-time. The scheme for putting more old people back to work can also have only a marginal impact — too many are already working. The recent attempt to 'reform' education by giving school students 'annual labour experience' is more a gesture of desperation than a rational strategy.[10] To make matters worse, since the sixties there has been a sharp fall in the birth rate, plus a rising mortality rate among men aged between 24 and 44.[11]

Although demographic factors have contributed to the labour shortage, it is essentially a symptom of the low productivity of labour in the Soviet Union. The laws of Soviet society counteract the replacement of living labour with machinery. There are conflicting estimates of the proportion of the workforce engaged in non-mechanical manual labour. In 1982 Aganbegyan reckoned that 40 per cent of all workers in industry were involved mainly in loading and unloading, and in repair work.[12] A survey conducted in 1984 estimated that 36 per cent of those employed in industry worked with their hands.[13] It is generally conceded that in sectors such as construction and agriculture, the proportion varies between 55 and 70 per cent.

The profligate use of labour in the Soviet Union is the main cause of shortages. Investment plans between 1976 and 1980 projected more than one million jobs for which no workers could be found. This has had devastating consequences in certain sectors of industry. For example, the number of machine tools in the machine building industry is 50 per cent greater than the number of operators.[14]

The shortage of labour has greatly weakened the hold of the bureaucracy over the working class. Workers can take advantage of this situation to take it easy and set their own conditions on the job. When workers are in short supply, the scope for the exercise of managerial authority is seriously restricted. Dismissal ceases to be a real sanction — in fact workers can put pressure on managers by threatening to quit. Every year more than 20 per cent of all workers and employees change jobs.[15]

Competition for labour among enterprises ensures that workers can get jobs no matter how poor their work record. Laskavsky explains how the disciplinary effect of dismissal has been undermined:

'The management of an enterprise is authorised to fire a worker for regular breach of discipline. This right is often exercised. However, the measure does not always yield perceptible results....To be frank, those fired at one enterprise for breach of discipline are greeted at another with open arms....They find themselves no worse off than they were before, both socially and in terms of wages.'[16]

In fact getting sacked often opens the way to a better paid job. According to Kotliar, workers fired for disciplinary reasons and those who quit jobs 'without proper grounds' receive on average 30 per cent higher pay at their new place of work.[17]

While the authorities have tried to tighten up on labour discipline over the past few years, competition for workers, especially those with skills, has intensified. Managers now have to go out of their way to attract workers: given the uncertainty of supplies, they still have every incentive to hoard labour. Wage rates are often set with a view to attracting and holding on to workers rather than in relation to the potential productivity of the employee.[18] It is not surprising that in these circumstances the much-publicised campaigns against violations of discipline have achieved very meagre results.

Competition for labour has rendered the new laws ineffective. Public exhortations, police raids and the occasional showcase crackdown have not succeeded in restoring labour discipline. The persistence of absenteeism is regularly reported in the Soviet press:

> **'Crowds can be seen in the city's shops when various scarce items are offered on sale. One wonders how people find it possible to queue for hours on end during the working day. Where are their bosses? It cannot be that they have totally failed to notice how their employees are wasting time — not minutes but days.'**[19]

Under pressure from their workforces, managers sign and stamp the official documents that workers need to justify their absence from work: hence, a bad work record no longer has much deterrent effect.[20] Workers can now lose their work records with impunity, since enterprises desperate for labour will willingly provide replacements.

The failure of the campaign to improve labour discipline illustrates the Kremlin's difficulty in imposing its will over the working class. Workers can take advantage of the system's chronic labour shortage to restrict the terms of their exploitation.

## Skilled and unskilled

The working class is the most substantial section of Soviet society. In 1982, manual workers and their families made up 60.9 per cent of the population.[21] There are many different ways of classifying the Soviet working class, but, for our purposes, it is sufficient to emphasise the distinction between skilled and unskilled workers.

According to Zaslavsky, relatively unskilled workers mainly engaged in manual labour made up 79 per cent of the workforce in the mid-seventies, while highly skilled workers who performed both manual and intellectual labour made up the rest.[22] Though this classification is fairly crude — truly skilled and privileged workers, for example, represent less than 10 per cent of the total — it highlights the most important division within the working class.

There are considerable differences in pay and working conditions between skilled and unskilled workers. A skilled machine tool operator can earn three times as much as an office cleaner. Over the past decade the income gap between skilled workers and the intelligentsia has narrowed, as Pravda has noted:

**'Many skilled workers earn more than teachers and technicians and as much as doctors, and the earnings of the most highly skilled manual workers overlap with the salaries of middle-ranking engineers and managers.'**[23]

Some experts, including Pravda and Zaslavsky, argue that skilled workers are more likely to support economic experiments and reforms than unskilled workers. This assumes that, while unskilled and semi-skilled workers have a stake in the status quo, the skilled aspire to material advances through market-related experiments. It is certainly true that these two sections of the working class have different standards of living and different aspirations for the future. However, it is simplistic to draw such far-reaching conclusions from these differences.

Although levels of income are important, other factors enter into the determination of the structure of the working class. Access to food, consumer goods and services is one such factor. Hence regional differences have a significant effect on working class life. A system of internal passports regulates residence in 'closed' cities like Leningrad and Moscow, where access to goods is better than in provincial towns. The steady flow of illegal migrants into the closed cities shows the advantages of living in these centres.[24]

Another important factor that affects the character of the Soviet working class is the phenomenon of 'closed enterprises'. Closed enterprises are located in priority sectors, particularly those related to defence and export, and offer special privileges to their workforce.[25] Workers in closed enterprises receive higher pay than they would elsewhere. More importantly, they have special access to services, housing and consumer goods. Workers in one high technology plant linked to the defence sector have direct access to fresh fruit and vegetables from the plant's auxiliary farm. The largest aircraft factory in the Soviet Union in Kuybyshev runs its own poultry farms to feed its workers.[26] The system of incentives in closed enterprises allows the bureaucracy to exercise a considerable degree of control over a key section of the working class.

There is a significant division between men and women in Soviet society. Women are relegated to unskilled and semi-skilled jobs in industry and the service sector. According to McAuley, women's earnings are between 60 and 70 per cent of those of men.[27] The differential in wages is only one aspect of women's inferior role in social production. Women are clustered in non-priority areas and in general have less access to services and goods through their place of work than men. Women with traditionally recognised skills do not fare much better. There may be a high proportion of female teachers and doctors, but their pay is often below that of skilled male manual workers. The monthly wage of a miner, for example, is double that of a school teacher. Although equal pay for equal work is established by law, sectors dominated by women, such as textiles, clothing and food, are run by men.

Women make up a significant section of the unskilled manual working class. As manual workers, women face conditions of employment which are worse than those experienced by men. Laws designed to protect the health of women are simply ignored: for example, the law barring women from work involving lifting loads of more than 20 kilos is routinely broken.[28] A report on health conditions in the province of Astrakhan revealed that women were working in 'deep-freeze' conditions. In one plant where noise levels were described as 'excruciating', women workers were not provided with ear plugs.[29]

## Changing living standards

The prolonged quiescence of the Soviet working class is not the product of coercion alone. In the thirties and forties force played an important role in disciplining the working class. But, as the bureaucracy soon realised, no society can survive indefinitely through force alone. Since the fifties the Soviet bureaucracy has sought to reach a compromise with the working class. In 1956 repressive labour laws were repealed and workers won the right to leave their jobs and move their homes. Thus, although force retains an important role, it is no longer the bureaucracy's sole means of neutralising the working class. In recent years the Soviet leadership has tried to preserve social stability by raising living standards and extending the availability of consumer goods. Despite the shortage of investment resources, the Kremlin has continued to subsidise food prices.

Living standards have risen substantially in the Soviet Union. Since 1950, consumption per head has risen at an average of 3.4 per cent a year. According to one American expert, this has resulted in 'a near-tripling of the level of living of the average citizen'.[30] An expanding range of consumer goods has been made available to the public and the quality of the Soviet diet has improved significantly. Social services, including housing and public transport, have also improved. The Soviet bureaucracy has been sensitive to the need to maintain living standards and, over the past decade, has diverted considerable resources towards importing food and raw materials. Since he came to power, Gorbachev has declared his determination to tackle the problem of shortages of consumer goods.

The wage reforms of the late fifties dramatically improved the position of the working class. In 1959, a new minimum wage of 40 rubles per month was introduced; in 1968 it was boosted to 60 rubles. Over the same period the proportion of workers' wages determined by the basic wage rate increased from 57.4 per cent to 76.6 per cent, so decreasing workers' reliance on bonuses and piece work earnings.[31] These changes improved the position of manual workers relative to other social groups. Before the Second World War, office workers earned more than manual workers, but since 1960 their earnings have been between 15 and 20 per cent lower.[32] Since 1945 workers have also substantially narrowed the earnings gap between themselves and the *izhenerno-tekhnicheskiye rabotniki* (ITRs) — managerial and technical personnel. Indeed the wages of some skilled workers are comparable to those of ITRs.

Wage levels do not directly determine living standards. According to Zaslavsky the ratio between lowest and highest Soviet pay rates is 1:20 or 1:30; but if services available to the *nomenklatura* are considered, the ratio would be 1:50, or in certain cases even 1:100.[33] Thus twice as many managers and professionals live in self-contained flats as do workers, and ITRs receive preferential access to houses.[34] Nevertheless, despite differential access to services, the relative position of the working class has improved steadily over the last 35 years.

Rising living standards have been paralleled by a degree of upward mobility. Universal education has allowed sections of the working class to rise through the social hierarchy. The education system played a particularly important role in the thirties in absorbing workers into supervisory, managerial and bureaucratic positions. The subsequent growth of white collar and technical occupations has provided opportunities for the children of the working class.[35]

A number of other factors have improved the position of the working class. Price stability is no guarantee of the availability of goods, but does ensure that, when basics are available, they come fairly cheap. Retail prices of bread, milk, meat and vegetables have been frozen for more than 20 years. The Soviet bureaucracy has observed the problems caused by rises in food prices in Poland and has taken care not to provoke the working class at home in the same way. Full employment and job security have also helped the working class to push living standards upwards.

Since the mid-seventies, however, many of the gains which have stabilised the position of the working class have been put in jeopardy. Access to education has become more restricted: the examination system favours the offspring of the intelligentsia and the bureaucracy, and it is increasingly difficult for workers' children to gain access to higher education.[36] A general tendency towards social stratification means that, for most workers, improvement in social status can only come by moving either to a closed city or to a developing region where wages are higher.

The Soviet working class has also experienced stagnating living standards. Growth in consumption per head began to fall in the seventies: at 2.6 per cent a year, it was only half the rate of the previous decade.[37] Schroeder's table below illustrates the underlying trend:

| Average annual rates of growth in consumption per head in the Soviet Union, 1965-81[38] | | | | |
|---|---|---|---|---|
| | 1966-70 | 1971-75 | 1976-80 | 1981 |
| Total consumption | 5.1 | 2.9 | 2.2 | 1.8 |
| Goods | 5.4 | 2.8 | 2.1 | 1.8 |
| Food | 4.3 | 1.6 | 1.0 | 1.4 |
| Soft goods | 7.1 | 3.0 | 3.1 | 2.1 |
| Durables | 9.1 | 10.0 | 5.4 | 2.7 |
| Services | 4.3 | 3.0 | 2.5 | 1.9 |
| Personal | 5.8 | 4.6 | 3.4 | 2.1 |
| Education | 2.9 | 1.5 | 1.6 | 1.3 |
| Health | 3.2 | 1.4 | 1.4 | -0.2 |

Since 1980 shortages of food and basic consumer goods have become commonplace. In 1984 the sharpest drop in output took place in the consumer goods sector. As a result workers, especially those living outside the key centres, today find that they cannot spend their wages to buy what they need. In Siberia and the Soviet Far East, families are thus forced to spend more than 50 per cent of their wages on food and drink. The lack of spending outlets is revealed by the fact that, in 1979, cash deposits in banks exceeded half of total disposable money income.[39]

Shortages of consumer goods do not just mean stagnating living standards: they also put in question the value of wage increases. Workers are forced to queue for essentials and women in particular are forced to spend more time in the home preparing food, mending clothes and generally compensating for the absence of quality consumer durables. As Shatlin notes, money wages are becoming increasingly irrelevant in the Soviet Union:

**'The imbalance between effective demand and the availability of goods and services has a number of negative consequences: it interferes with the application of the principle of pay according to work...it leads to an irrational redistribution of income through speculation, unjustifiably high prices on the unorganised market, the provision of services by private individuals....This imbalance hits people with fixed incomes especially hard.'**[40]

The stagnation of living standards affects not just those with fixed incomes, but the working class as a whole.

The foundations of social stability in the Soviet Union are being eroded. Soviet sources show both a growing awareness of low living standards and higher expectations than ever before. A survey of workers in their twenties, published by the sociological institute of the Soviet academy of sciences in 1984, showed that only 34 per cent believed that their standard of living was good.[41] Other reports indicate a growing tension between working class aspirations and the realities of life. The growth of dissatisfaction among Soviet workers gives rise to the question — why is there no workers' movement in the Soviet Union?

## Passivity and protest

The Soviet bureaucracy has never had to face a coherent working class opposition. There have been no political upheavals of the sort experienced in East Germany (1953), Hungary (1956), Poland (1956, 1970 and 1981-3) and Czechoslovakia (1968). Western and Soviet authorities try to explain the passivity of the Soviet working class on the grounds that Soviet workers have a highly developed respect for authority. Some Soviet dissidents suggest that workers support the government because they have not been educated in the values of democracy and pluralism. Unfortunately such one-sided interpretations influence more scholarly studies. Thus Pravda portrays the Soviet working class as backward:

**'To a greater degree than even other groups in Soviet society, workers seem resigned to the status quo and see little point in trying to change the immutable.'**[42]

Even Zaslavsky links working class passivity to support for the system. He argues that unskilled workers and the bureaucracy have forged an informal alliance to sabotage economic reforms. Hence the regime appears to some workers as their defender against the arbitrary exercise of authority by local managers.[43] These views are propounded by intellectual dissidents and emigrés who regard the working class with contempt. They look upon workers as the lazy beneficiaries of the system, people who are always ready to link up with the bureaucracy to thwart the enlightened and creative impulse of the intelligentsia.

Lane and O'Dell put forward another variant of the view that workers are resigned to the rule of the bureaucracy. They argue that Soviet workers have been 'incorporated' and 'socialised' into the values of the system.[44] They stress the way Soviet education has socialised the working class. This approach exaggerates the effect of education — a point well recognised by Soviet writers. It also attempts to answer all the questions about the Soviet working class without analysing its basic relationship to the bureaucracy. Hence it inevitably remains impressionistic.

The Soviet working class cannot be understood without taking into account the role of coercion. It is essential to recall that the scale and intensity of terror in the Soviet Union in the thirties and the forties went far beyond anything that occurred in other parts of Eastern Europe. The difference was not merely one of degree. In the Soviet Union the working class itself was created through force, whereas in other East European countries working class movements with traditions of struggle existed before the Soviet bureaucracy took over. Soviet workers did not merely experience systematic violence: their whole life was regimented. The system of internal passports and other controls on movement never developed to the same extent in Eastern Europe as it did in the Soviet Union. Even today, the working class is more tightly supervised in the Soviet Union than elsewhere in Eastern Europe.

Despite state terror, Soviet workers have engaged in strikes, demonstrations and riots. Some of these eruptions of the class struggle — such as the mass riots in Novocherkassk in June 1962 — are well known. But even in recent years there have been protests in Tol'yatti and other parts of the country.[45] Yet the most significant feature of the record of collective working class action is its infrequency. The role of the repressive apparatus can provide only a part of the explanation. It explains why many workers are afraid of taking action, but not why action is not taken more often. It explains the difficulty of sustaining even informal workers' organisations, but not why workers have made only minimal attempts at collective organisation. Repression can constrain and shape workers' resistance, but does not explain its apparent absence.

In fact the repressive apparatus has not succeeded in eliminating working class action. The issue is not whether or not workers take action, but what form their action takes. There is considerable evidence that the main focus of working class action is the workplace. Even the more elitist studies concede this:

**'What emigré testimony and Soviet data on industrial conflict point to, then, is the existence at shop-floor level of a widespread assertiveness that contrasts sharply with public, and particularly working-class-group, silence and quiescence at all other levels.'[46]**

The assertion of working class interests in the workplace stems not from the influence of any trade union ideas on Soviet workers, but rather from the fact that the workplace is the one area where the exercise of force can play only a minimal role. Workers can be coerced into the factory, but cannot be made to work: in any modern factory the use of force is inevitably counterproductive. Because of the shortage of labour, workers can assert themselves in the workplace and even demonstrate their alienation from the system. The Soviet bureaucracy is well aware of the limited value of coercion in dealing with an industrial workforce. As Zaslavskaya explains, as far as 'the subjective relationship of the workers to their socio-economic activity' goes, 'administrative methods of management are powerless'.[47]

Working class action in the workplace takes different forms. The most basic is simple lack of co-operation with management over the introduction of 'reforms', new procedures and work practices. Workers often display a reluctance to work, or an unwillingness to work efficiently, or a refusal to go for higher work norms. Workers also protest silently by changing their jobs, and negatively through sabotage and drinking on the job.

Most forms of working class action are individual rather than collective. Although the workplace brings workers together, their actions are more personal protests than organised manifestations of discontent. This is most apparent in absenteeism and job switches. In these ways workers assert their interests, not through mutual organisation and effort, but through a personal retreat from the workplace. The individualised character of workplace action goes a long way towards explaining the lack of mass working class protest in the Soviet Union. Indeed the working class that was formed through the emergence of the Soviet social formation is the most individuated proletariat yet created.

## A class of individuals

Many studies have drawn attention to the atomisation of the Soviet working class.[48] This phenomenon is the result not only of repression but of the way Soviet society works. It is not immediately obvious to Soviet workers that collective activity is the way to overcome their difficulties. Not only is such activity illegal; it often appears irrelevant to the struggle to achieve higher living standards. Workers are concerned about what goes on at their workplace. But they are often even more concerned about obtaining what they need in terms of food, goods and services — matters over which the struggle in the workplace has little, if any, influence.

Because workers have little incentive to work, they tend to protest negatively rather than positively about workplace conditions. Workers' main objective is to get through the day with as little effort as possible, for in the Soviet Union the real struggle for survival takes place outside the workplace. The key challenge facing every worker is not in the sphere of production but in consumption. Workers who put little effort into their jobs are ready to put enormous energy into garden plots or into other enterprises necessary to obtain the goods they need for themselves and their families.

The actions of the working class are not entirely individualised. In most workplaces conditions are governed by an unwritten agreement which is informally enforced by collective action. When higher norms are introduced, workers inevitably respond collectively — slowdowns, working to rule and even sabotage can occur with little organisation. But these measures aim to defend existing conditions. Measures designed to advance the position of workers take on a more individuated form. Quitting a job or moving to another region, preferably a closed city, are all actions relying on the skill and effort of the worker as an individual. Under these circumstances the right to quit and the right to move are more important than the right to work. As Zaslavsky suggests, 'it is difficult to expect workers to resort to collective initiatives when individual action proves at least partially effective'.[49]

The individuation evident in the workplace stems from the basic structure of Soviet society. The Soviet proletariat lives an existence in which the struggle for survival puts a premium on individual initiative and private action. Since the public sphere can provide only the bare essentials, workers are forced to secure all their other needs through informal contacts and individual effort.

The same pressures which force every enterprise to acquire a degree of self-sufficiency also dominate the life of the individual worker. Shortages of goods and services make industrial workers into part-time farmers or gardeners. More than 10 million working class families cultivate private plots.[50] The widespread character of this activity is well illustrated in a report on Khrakov in 1985. Every morning two streams of people cross: villagers coming into Khrakov to sell fruit and vegetables, and workers and technicians on their way to the fields to collect radishes.[51]

The morning scene in Khrakov, an indictment of the incoherent division of labour in the Soviet Union, also throws light on its impact on the life of the working class. It is a measure of the historic bankruptcy of the Soviet social formation that, as a result of its inability to socialise labour, it has encouraged the most privatised forms of work. Whereas Marx wrote of abolishing the distinction between town and country through the industrialisation of agriculture, the Soviet bureaucracy abolishes it through a bizarre ruralisation of towns.

The private production of food is only one aspect of the individuated character of working class life. Shortages and low quality products force the working class family to spend considerable energy converting various raw materials and defective goods into useful objects. Workers also spend hours searching for things they can use, recycling waste products and repairing goods.

The inability of the system to provide the necessary goods and services provides the basis for an informal system of privatised production. Moonlighting and the black market do not merely fulfil demands for exotic and luxury goods, but often supply the very essentials of life. A recent widely acclaimed Soviet survey of moonlighting appeals for it to be legalised. According to Gukasov and Tolstov between 17 and 20 million people are in one way or another involved in moonlighting. In their survey of the city of Talinn, they estimate that independent 'handymen' play a major role in carrying out repair work: on shoes 50 per cent, on housing 45 per cent, on cars 40 per cent, on appliances 30 per cent. In rural areas, as much as 80 per cent of repairs are performed in this informal way.[52] Some Soviet experts and many Western observers reckon that a legalised system of moonlighting could make a major contribution to the economy. This fascination with the market ignores the fact that moonlighting forces workers to fend for themselves in the most degrading way.

The individuation of the working class is reinforced at every level of society. Consumption and living standards are determined through individual efforts which are generally exerted outside the place of work. As consumers searching for a limited range of goods and services, workers are forced to compete with one another. Workers' quality of life depends on individual and ultimately family connections.

The privatised character of working class life has a corrosive effect on collective action. Workers' energies are harnessed to individual survival — the only strategy that appears to make sense. Zaslavsky is wrong to suggest that workers, especially unskilled workers, 'resign themselves voluntarily' to social atomisation.[53] There is nothing voluntary about Soviet working class life. Privatisation is reproduced through productive relations which force workers to engage in individual enterprise and turn the family into an important economic unit. The barriers to the realisation of the social character of labour force workers to pursue individual solutions.

State policy enhances the individuation of the Soviet working class. The system of closed cities and closed enterprises divides workers and puts a premium on individual initiative. The authorities promote a hierarchy among workers with predictable results in further fragmenting the working class. The individuation of the Soviet working class limits opportunities for collective action. However, working class discontent remains widespread. Soviet sociologists regularly report the phenomenon of 'alienation' —

especially among younger workers. At present this discontent is marked by its privatised, essentially anti-social manifestations. Alcoholism is only the most extreme sign of the personal disaffection of the Soviet proletariat.

## The role of the family

In the Soviet Union the family plays an even more extensive role than it does in capitalist society. Under capitalism the central function of the family is the reproduction of labour power.[54] The Soviet family too is responsible for the reproduction of the working class, but it has to undertake a much wider range of activities to keep the working class going. The role of the family unit in growing food and in converting defective products into useful things gives it a considerable economic significance. The absence of class organisations that can promote working class interests through collective activity in the public sphere encourages workers to seek individual fulfilment in the private sphere of the family.

The Soviet bureaucracy is an enthusiastic advocate of the virtues of family life. The 1985 draft programme of the Soviet Communist Party argues for the 'policy of strengthening the family' and promotes as one of its objectives increasing the 'responsibility of parents for the upbringing of children'.[55] The bureaucracy recognises both the essential economic function and the wider socially conservative role of the family.

The traditional Marxist objective of socialising domestic work has become anathema to the Kremlin. Soviet society needs work carried out within the family, and it also needs more new workers to compensate for its chronic labour shortage. In its promotion of the family, the bureaucracy is prepared to stir up the most atavistic prejudices. The Soviet press directs a constant stream of abuse against irresponsible parents, singling out women for special treatment.

'Experts' try to frighten women into having more children with scares about risks of cancer or other 'grave disorders' attending the use of contraception and having small families:

> **'Women's risk of contracting cancer of the mammary glands or reproductive organs increases. Induced abortions threaten them with a whole series of illnesses. Men who do not wish to have children often employ the method of coitus interruptus. This is fraught with grave disorders of the nervous system and the sexual sphere, something that is often a psychological source of drunkenness and alcoholism.'**[56]

Such spurious arguments are backed up with a barrage of publicity about the dangers of sexual licence, aiming to discourage any separation of sexual activity from procreation.

Despite the bureaucracy's propaganda, Soviet families are getting smaller and smaller, especially in urban areas. Large families create economic pressures and family life itself is undermined by the difficulties of making ends meet. Tensions within the family are the inescapable consequence of restricted consumer goods and overcrowded housing. High rates of divorce and the growth of single-parent families indicate the difficulties of family life.

The Soviet family maintains women's subordinate position in society. Women not only perform a full week's work, but are also responsible for an average of 28 hours of drudgery in the home. One Soviet critic claims that 'women spend as much time on domestic chores as in the twenties'.[57] The intolerable burden placed on women in the family is shown by the fact that the vast majority of divorces are initiated by women.

The enslavement of women does not end with the bringing up of children. The state expects grandmothers to look after children so that mothers can continue to work. An article in *Izvestia* in 1985 was typical — it complained that grandmothers were doing everything possible to avoid staying at home with their grandchildren. The writer regretted that mothers and grandmothers look upon childcare 'with a sense of disappointment and annoyance, with heavy hearts and a feeling of being tied down'.[58] The Soviet media constantly celebrates motherhood and women's role as domestic slaves.

The signs that the Soviet family is under strain are clear to see in the statistics on divorce, alcoholism and voluntary single parenthood. Nevertheless, the family is an essential prop for the Soviet bureaucracy; hence it must be constantly promoted. Women more than any other section of Soviet society pay the price for the inability of the system to provide for the reproduction and care of its own citizens. In the Soviet Union, the family influences working class life to an even greater degree than it does in the West.

## The role of ideology

Ideology plays only a limited role in legitimising the authority of the Soviet bureaucracy. In contrast to capitalist societies, where the establishment point of view is often shared by significant sections of the working class, the apologetic character of the bureaucracy's propaganda is immediately apparent to most Soviet workers. The bureaucracy's official ideology, mistakenly referred to as Marxism-Leninism, is more of an embarrassing legacy than a functional ideology. Neither the bureaucracy nor the working class can muster much enthusiasm for the party line. The Soviet leadership is neither popular nor credible — its statements are received with scepticism at best.

In the West the notion that the state serves the interests of the whole of society is still influential in the labour movement; Soviet workers, by contrast, harbour no such illusions. It is obvious to them that the state serves the interests of a bureaucracy which is in no way accountable to the vast majority of society. But if the relationship between the bureaucracy and the working class is clearly perceived, what then is the obstacle to the development of proletarian class consciousness?

It is obvious that the experience of the last 60 years has discredited Marxism in the eyes of Soviet workers. Official 'Marxism' is in general taken to be the real thing, and, on the basis of workers' experience, spontaneously rejected. Thus for Soviet workers Marxism is the butt of jokes. However, this rejection of official Marxism does not exhaust the problem of class consciousness. The individuation of working class life itself fosters an outlook which is in many ways antithetical to proletarian consciousness.

The atomisation of life and the compulsion to pursue individual interests enhance the importance of the private sphere. The fragmentary tendencies that render the social division of labour incoherent endow privatised activity with special importance. This experience inevitably strengthens individual consciousness at the expense of class consciousness. Workers achieve their objectives through individual rather than class struggle. Consumption rather than production preoccupies the energies of Soviet workers. In the realm of consumption the common relationship of workers to the relations of production is far from apparent.

The individuation of the Soviet worker encourages a strong sense of themselves as private isolated individuals. Relying on their own initiative to get by, Soviet workers are susceptible to many of the attitudes traditionally associated with the petit bourgeoisie. The exigencies of self-sufficiency strengthen individualistic attitudes. This is most obvious in the prevalence of backward attitudes towards family life. The heightened sense of individuality among Soviet workers means that the bureaucracy does find a resonance for those aspects of its ideology which relate to privatised consciousness. One indication of this is the popularity of nationalism — particularly the Russian variant — among wide sections of the working class. Indeed the cult of nationalism and the elevation of the national interest are the most effective propaganda weapons at the disposal of the bureaucracy. The growth of ethnic consciousness and of anti-semitism (although this is much more virulent among the intelligentsia) also flows from the individuation of the working class. As a result, episodic expressions of working class protest often take on an ethnic dimension. This has been particularly evident in the disturbances that have taken place in Estonia since 1981.

The bureaucracy has learned from experience and prefers to treat workers as a collection of individuals or families rather than as a class. Hence it pays special attention to the promotion of nationalism, family life and individualistic values. The only component of traditional petit-bourgeois ideology that is missing is religion — even the Kremlin can only go so far in contradicting its official ideology.

Soviet workers' highly developed sense of individuality allows the bureaucracy to promote a degree of consensus around issues of foreign policy, the national interest, family values, morality, and — in limited instances — law and order. Soviet workers have an ambivalent attitude to law and order. Law enforcement agencies are deeply distrusted and universally hated. Nevertheless, workers' sense of isolation and insecurity makes them receptive to bureaucratic campaigns against local arbitrariness and anti-social actions. Individualistic ideology acts more as a barrier to the development of class consciousness than as a positive source of support for the Soviet bureaucracy and its system. Ideology is ultimately a supplement rather than an alternative to the exercise of bureaucratic domination by force.

## Future trends

Though it lacks a heritage of collective action, the working class is a major force in Soviet society. The stagnation of Soviet society has undermined many of the factors, such as rising living standards and upwards mobility, that made for social stability in the past. This has not yet provoked an explosion of protest and resistance because of the individuated character of working class life. In the short term, indeed, the growing labour shortage has had the effect of reinforcing the pursuit of individual solutions.

The social equilibrium which has long been established on the basis of rising living standards, full employment and the right to work is now threatened by economic stagnation. The shortage of labour has weakened the control of the bureaucracy and has led to greater working class assertiveness at the workplace. The failure of the campaign for labour discipline reveals the potential power of the working class. The silent class struggle has not so far assumed a political form, but represents an objective threat to the power of the bureaucracy.

The equilibrium between the bureaucracy and the working class has many of the features of a stalemate. The bureaucracy's dominant position is unchallenged, but its exercise of power is limited by the power of the working class. The proletariat is a barrier to the preservation and advancement of the bureaucracy. The Kremlin well understands that its future depends on eliminating this barrier and forging a new relationship with the working class. The weapons closest to hand are direct repression and market forces.

While the Soviet bureaucracy has no inhibitions about resorting to terror, it recognises that it is of limited use. Many academics and managers have floated the idea of establishing a labour market and using the fear of unemployment to discipline the working class. Kronrod has suggested a strategy which would amount to allowing inefficient firms go bankrupt, adding the rider that 'naturally, the ruination of enterprises is inherently alien to a socialist economy'.[59] However, the introduction of a free labour market is fraught with so much political danger that it is not a realistic option for the bureaucracy. Under present conditions a market in labour could not be introduced without a whole network of market relations. As neither force nor the introduction of a labour market can resolve the problem of labour, the bureaucracy is forced to rely on piecemeal measures.

Most of those currently under discussion aim to introduce greater material incentives. Yet as long as consumer goods continue to be restricted, such measures will have an artificial character. Leading Soviet sociologist Rogovin has proposed the effective privatisation of social services. He considers that this would end the situation in which 'people find it impossible to spend honestly earned income to full effect through socially organised channels to meet their real needs for comfortable housing, organised recreation, medical assistance'.[60]

The privatisation of social services might soak up workers' savings, but in practice would only institutionalise the process by which they are compelled to obtain scarce services through individual enterprise. Rogovin is forced to concede that in the five years preceding his survey Soviet families spent eight billion rubles on private tuition — a sum equivalent to the annual budget for the country's secondary education system.[61] Research would reveal that tips in medical care play a similar role, and that bribes are common practice in the acquisition of housing and of places in holiday resorts.

Another form of privatisation now under review is the extension of private plots and the legalisation of black market services. Following the Hungarian example, Talinn's Elektron radio and television repair association has leased one of its repair shops to a brigade of mechanics. Today a television repair job which previously took two weeks is now completed in three days.[62] Similar experiments on a small scale have been introduced elsewhere in the consumer services sector, and have made a limited contribution to increasing its efficiency. But because of their piecemeal character, they are unlikely to have a major impact on the motivation of the working class. They amount merely to an official endorsement of the expenditure of working class energy on privatised labour.

Limited privatisation measures cannot alter the balance of social forces. The advantages of absorbing the creative energies of the working class are real but, in a climate of labour shortages, are insufficient to undermine the strength of the proletariat. Everything points to the further erosion of the bureaucracy's control over the working class. In the end, only its monopoly over the instruments of coercion can prevent the power of the working class from making itself felt. History has shown that the forward march of the working class cannot be held back for long simply by force of arms.

## Notes

1   A survey conducted by the journal *EKO* summarises this discussion. See *EKO*, No 9, September 1981, pp18-45.
2   Gordon & Nazimova (1980).
3   Zaslavskaya (1984), pp90, 91.
4   *Pravda*, 23 November 1982.

5   *Pravda,* 7 August 1983.
6   *Pravda,* 6 August 1985.
7   Arnot (1981), p39.
8   See Feshbach (1979), p7.
9   Goodman & Schleifer (1983), p324.
10  *Pravda,* 14 April 1984.
11  See Goodman & Schleifer (1983), p326.
12  *Pravda,* 24 February 1982.
13  *Pravda,* 9 March 1984.
14  *Pravda,* 21 January 1985.
15  Kotliar (1984), p28.
16  *Pravda,* 25 October 1981. Also abstracted in *CDSP,* Vol 33, No 43.
17  Kotliar (1984), p34.
18  *Pravda,* 9 March 1984.
19  *Pravda,* 22 January 1985.
20  See the complaint of the deputy personnel director of an Irkutsk aircraft plant in *Izvestia,* 12 January 1984.
21  Lane (1985a), p156.
22  Zaslavsky (1982), p46.
23  Pravda (1982), p7.
24  See Zaslavsky (1982), pp144-5.
25  Zaslavsky's study is particularly useful. See Zaslavsky (1982), chapters 1 & 2.
26  Rumer (1981), p567.
27  McAuley (1981), p21.
28  *Izvestia,* 15 September 1985.
29  *Meditsinskaya gazeta,* 10 February 1982, abstracted in *CDSP,* Vol 34, No 10.
30  Schroeder (1983b), p367.
31  See Chapman (1979), pp161-2.
32  Chapman (1979), p169.
33  Zaslavsky (1982), p69.
34  Pravda (1982), p8.
35  See Lapidus (1983), p189.
36  See Zaslavsky (1982), p57; Lane (1985a), pp188-194 and Pravda (1982), p13.
37  Schroeder (1983b), p369.
38  Schroeder (1983b), p370.
39  Lapidus (1983), pp196-7.
40  Shatlin. See *EKO,* No 1, January 1982, English abstract in *CDSP,* Vol 34, No 10, 1982.
41  *Sunday Times,* 10 June 1984.
42  Pravda (1982), p22.
43  Zaslavsky (1982), p51.
44  Lane & O'Dell (1981), p50.
45  See Gidwitz (1982), pp32-5.
46  Pravda (1982), p22.
47  Zaslavskaya (1984), pp95-6.
48  See Zaslavsky (1982), especially chapter 3.

49  Zaslavsky (1982), p51.
50  *Voprosy ekonomiki,* No 5, 1981.
51  *Pravda,* 7 July 1985.
52  *Izvestia,* 19 August 1985.
53  Zaslavsky (1982), p63.
54  See Marshall (1983).
55  CPSU (1985), p57.
56  *Meditsinskaya gazeta,* 27 September 1985, abstracted in *CDSP,* Vol 37, No 39.
57  Cited in Lane (1985a), p129.
58  *Izvestia,* 31 October 1985.
59  Kronrod (1984), p81.
60  *Sotsiologicheskiye issledovania,* No 1, 1982.
61  *Sotsiologicheskiye issledovania,* No 1, 1982.
62  *Izvestia,* 19 August 1985.

# 10. Foreign policy

The retrograde features of the Soviet social formation are evident in the sphere of foreign policy. The system's lack of an internal dynamic also affects its external relations. Thus, despite its military strength, the Soviet Union's foreign policy is reactive and defensive. The global influence of the Soviet Union is more a result of the decline of Western capitalism than the outcome of Moscow's foreign policy. The Soviet Union's involvement in global conflicts has little to do with the machinations of the Kremlin. The Soviet bureaucracy yearns for stability and the preservation of the status quo.

President Reagan's portrayal of the Soviet Union as the 'evil empire' is part of an enduring Western strategy of reducing all international problems to Soviet subversion. Western discussion of international issues has long been permeated with deep-seated anti-Soviet and anti-communist prejudices. The term 'Soviet expansionism', which figures prominently in the vocabulary of the right and has increasingly been taken up by the left, conveys a sense of primordial and irrational impulses which threaten the whole of humanity. One right-wing French politician describes the Soviets as 'real Martians. Their system could never have been devised by human beings.'[1] It is impossible to conduct a serious discussion of Soviet affairs in these terms.

The comments of the Western media and politicians on the Soviet Union often verge on the hysterical. Take the following statement by a British government minister in 1982:

'Who can be certain of the future? Can we disregard totally even the possibility in years to come of a disintegrating Soviet empire, with, as an act of desperation, the dying giant lashing out across the central front?'[2]

With demonology dressed up as political analysis, the 'Soviet empire' becomes the force of darkness behind all upheavals in the world. In France, anti-Sovietism has become a moral crusade — often led by former leftists. Best-selling authors like Glucksmann, Morin, Ellenstein, Castoriadis and Besançon peddle a vision of the Soviet threat which expresses an almost pathological hatred for the Soviet Union.

## 'The evil empire'

The more apocalyptic Western visions of the Soviet menace are produced for popular consumption. Nevertheless even scholarly or policy-orientated debates are often influenced by perceptions of the unpredictability and irrationality of the Soviet Union. Former American foreign affairs chief Kissinger warned in 1981 of 'the tendency of the Soviets to escape their dilemmas by foreign adventures'.[3] Often the 'adventurist' behaviour of Soviet foreign policy is put down to the Kremlin's commitment to Marxist ideology. Even Ulam, a relatively balanced analyst, has endorsed this view:

'The thirteen or so men at the apex of the Soviet power structure have to think of themselves not only as rulers of a national state, but also as high priests of a world cult, which in turn is the source of legitimacy for the system as a whole and for their own power in particular.'[4]

In fact, it is difficult to detect any ideological considerations in Soviet foreign policy. Hence Western experts are obliged merely to assume or assert their existence.

The difficulty of detecting any special ideological factors in the conduct of the Soviet Union's external affairs has led to a growing tendency among policy analysts to emphasise the traditional element in Kremlin diplomacy. In practice Western strategists do not take seriously the notion that ideology plays an important role in Soviet foreign affairs. One participant in a recent Nato discussion outlined a different view:

'The Soviet Union will continue to develop along the lines of a traditional rather than an ideological power. Although ideology may be used under appropriate circumstances as a foreign policy tool, the Soviet view of world developments will be dictated increasingly by Russian national security interests. Similarly, Soviet instrumentalities such as military power, economic aid, and diplomacy will greatly resemble those of traditional powers.'[5]

The pragmatic element in Soviet foreign policy certainly appears to confirm this view.

Traditional geo-political considerations do exert a considerable influence on the Soviet Union's relations with China and Eastern Europe. Such factors go a long way towards explaining specific events — such as the 1979 invasion of Afghanistan. But if this argument is taken too far it inevitably becomes one-sided. To treat the Soviet Union merely as another capitalist nation state is to ignore what is distinctive about its relationship to the world. In recent years a tendency has developed which explains the Kremlin's foreign policy as following an unbroken line from the days of Peter the Great. Instead of seeking an explanation of Soviet foreign policy in the specific features of the Soviet social formation, commentators try to understand today's events as the result of an inexorable process of historical development.

Two American analysts are typical in drawing on Russia's imperial tradition to explain Soviet militarism today. In all seriousness, they claim that 'the now much-discussed Soviet preference for the offensive was laid in the eighteenth century by the talented General Aleksander Suvorov'.[6] Reading history backwards in this way, they seek to explain the manoeuvres of Stalin or Khrushchev as the continuation of Tsarist intrigue. This spurious use of history ends up drawing superficial parallels between Soviet foreign policy and Western postures in international relations.

There is some correspondence between Soviet foreign policy and the Tsarist imperial tradition. Continuity in geo-political considerations, however, cannot explain the unique features of modern Soviet foreign policy. In contrast to the external relations of Western powers, those of the Soviet Union are highly contradictory. Although in general the Soviet Union has played a profoundly conservative role in world affairs, it has occasionally backed radical challenges to the imperialist world order — in Cuba, Vietnam and Angola, for example. Its contradictory role makes it quite distinct from other global powers. Only by extending our analysis of the Soviet social formation can we come to a full assessment of its contradictory foreign policy.

## The East-West clash

Since 1917 the relationship between the Soviet Union and the capitalist world has gone through a series of distinct phases. Periods of open hostility have given way to more relaxed episodes, only to revert back to discord. Even in times of relative harmony, East-West contacts are always tense. This was the case even with the exceptionally intimate relations forged in the wartime Grand Alliance. It is clear that there is an underlying and irresolvable conflict in East-West relations, one of a different order from the rivalries that wax and wane in relations among imperialist powers. The fundamental conflict between the Soviet Union and the capitalist world is rooted in the different forms of economic regulation that prevail in the two blocs. The elimination of the market in the Eastern bloc acts as a barrier to the expansion of capitalism. The capitalist world feels this restriction on the world-wide movement of capital particularly acutely at a time of economic crisis. From the point of view of the Soviet Union, on the other hand, the world-wide operation of the law of value is a permanent and major threat.

If world market forces penetrated the Soviet Union they would undermine its integrity. The higher levels of productivity achieved through the capitalist international division of labour would lead to a flood of cheap imported goods, thus destroying Soviet manufacturing industry. This in turn would draw the Soviet Union closer into the world economy and deprive its state of the power to direct investment, establish new points of production and control the distribution of resources.

The Bolsheviks' appreciation of the power of the capitalist international division of labour led them to dismiss the strategy of building socialism in one country. Lenin's prediction that war between the Soviet Union and capitalist countries was inevitable has often been quoted; yet it has been less widely grasped that he saw this development, not merely as a military matter, but as the result of a deeper antagonism between two different social systems. In Lenin's view two factors lay behind the East-West conflict. First and foremost, he anticipated that inter-imperialist rivalries would, one day, break out into open conflict and drag the Soviet Union into war. Second, there was a basic clash between two contradictory forms of economic regulation.

Lenin was willing to establish trade agreements and other economic links with the capitalist world. This was for pragmatic reasons: an isolated and impoverished Soviet Union could hardly undertake economic reconstruction, never mind build socialism. Lenin's pragmatism was always qualified by the view that all such policies were a short-term expedient in a rapidly changing situation, as he explained in 1920:

> 'We must seize the opportunity and lend every effort to achieve trade relations even at the cost of maximum concessions, for we cannot for a moment believe in lasting trade relations with the imperialist powers; the respite will be temporary....The existence of a Soviet Republic alongside of capitalist countries — a Soviet Republic surrounded by capitalist countries — is so intolerable to the capitalists that they will seize any opportunity to resume war.'[7]

Unlike Stalin and others, Lenin saw the threat from the West primarily in economic terms. In the long run he hoped to minimise this threat by extending the revolutionary process to other parts of the world. In the short run, Lenin looked to the Soviet state's monopoly over foreign trade as the essential line of defence against the impact of the capitalist world economy. The monopoly over foreign trade — close state supervision and control over exports and imports — was designed to minimise the influence of the capitalist world market and to strengthen the power of the Soviet state over the economy as a whole. It aimed to subordinate the Soviet Union's links with the world economy to the objectives of the state and to curb the disruptive effects of the international law of value.

Preobrazhensky explained how the monopoly over foreign trade could allow state objectives to prevail over commercial considerations:

> 'Exports which are unprofitable commercially may be highly advantageous to the interests of the state economy as a whole, if the foreign exchange so obtained be used for importing machinery for industry which it is more expensive to manufacture here than abroad.'[8]

For Preobrazhensky as for Lenin, the monopoly of foreign trade was a prerequisite for the preservation of Soviet power.

By contrast, Stalin emphasised the military side of the threat from the capitalist world. His approach, which eventually crystallised into the theory of socialism in one country, underestimated economic obstacles and tended to reduce the threat from the West to that of armed intervention. Stalin's underestimation of the dangers of the operation of the law of value led him at one stage to consider dismantling the monopoly of foreign trade. Indeed, one of Lenin's last political struggles was with Stalin over this very question. When Lenin discovered that Stalin and his collaborators were contemplating measures that would undermine the monopoly over foreign trade, he wrote from his death-bed to Trotsky, urging him to take up the issue:

> **'At any rate, I earnestly ask you to take upon yourself at the coming Plenum, the defence of our common opinion of the unconditional necessity of preserving and reinforcing the monopoly of foreign trade.'**[9]

Lenin added that it was 'impossible to yield on this question' and 'that in case of our defeat we must carry the question into the party congress'.

The debate over the monopoly of foreign trade in the early twenties anticipated future developments. The classical Bolshevik position regarded national boundaries as a barrier to socialist development. For Lenin, progress depended on establishing a division of labour with other revolutionary states. He recognised the serious threat of military attack, but regarded the danger of economic isolation as a problem of deeper significance. For Stalin, economic problems could be resolved within the confines of a single state; the main concern of foreign policy was to prevent military intervention.

Both wings of the Bolsheviks sought peace with the capitalist world. This was a necessity for a nation facing major problems of survival. However, 'peace' meant different strategies to the two sides. For Lenin, peace offered a breathing space during which the Soviet Union would attempt to survive, while relying on the international revolution for its long-term development. For Stalin, peace was an essential condition for a national strategy of development — the Soviet Union could strike out on its own, so long as it was spared military interference. In the early twenties these differences remained at the level of emphasis. It was only through the subsequent evolution of Stalin's foreign policy that their consequences became clear.

## Stalin abroad

The foreign policy of the Soviet Union today shows a remarkable degree of continuity with the approach established by Stalin in the twenties. The Stalinist line in international affairs followed directly from the strategy of building socialism in one country. In contrast to the classical Bolshevik approach, the Stalinist leadership at first downplayed and eventually ignored the link between the development of the Soviet Union and the success of the international revolution. Moscow still encouraged revolutionary movements and communist parties, but only insofar as they could be used as a tool of Soviet strategy. As the years passed it became increasingly difficult to distinguish the methods of Stalinist diplomats from those of their Western counterparts.

The only element of the Leninist system of foreign relations that was preserved under Stalin was the monopoly of foreign trade. Despite Stalin's early doubts about the policy, he quickly changed his mind. It soon became clear that, to keep control over the Soviet economy, the Kremlin needed all the protection it could get against the threat posed by the higher levels of productivity of the capitalist world system.

Between 1926 and 1927 the Stalinist regime evolved a new approach to external events. Under Stalin's regime Lenin's 'breathing space' became a period of indefinite duration during which the bureaucracy could pursue its domestic industrialisation plans. Stalin maintained that the survival of the Soviet Union depended on 'co-existence' with the capitalist world and a 'policy of peace' towards the imperialist powers. He hoped that rivalry among the Western powers would take the pressure off the Soviet Union and provide it with an opportunity to grow.

Stalin aimed to take advantage of conflicts among the major capitalist powers by establishing diplomatic relations with some of the rivals and thus overcoming the Soviet Union's isolation. This is how he explained his strategy in December 1927:

**'We must take into account the contradictions in the imperialist camp, postpone war, buying off the capitalists and take all measures to preserve peaceful relations....The basis of our relations with the capitalist countries is the acceptance of the co-existence of two fundamentally different systems.'**[10]

Exploiting 'contradictions in the imperialist camp' was the point of departure of what later became known as the policy of peaceful co-existence.

Stalin's new line held that foreign intervention was the only obstacle to building socialism in the Soviet Union. Hence foreign policy had one overriding objective — to prevent foreign intervention. From this point of view, collaboration with foreign capitalist powers appeared to be the best guarantee of keeping the Soviet Union on course towards communism. But collaboration marked a wholesale reversal of the previous policy of relying on the international revolutionary movement to safeguard the Soviet Union.

Since 1927, the Soviet leadership has consistently pursued the following foreign policy objectives:

1 **Peaceful co-existence: while the Kremlin is prepared to launch military interference in other countries, this is very much an exceptional departure from its pursuit of stability.**
2 **Taking advantage of imperialist rivalries: the Kremlin desperately fears a united bloc of imperialist powers which would compound its isolation.**
3 **Fear of encirclement: the fear of becoming surrounded by adversaries leads to the pursuit of the same geo-political objectives as earlier Russian regimes. The proliferation of nationalist movements within the Soviet Union and the development of hostile relations with China has further complicated problems of border security.**
4 **Access to foreign technology: to compensate for its lack of internal dynamism, the Soviet bureaucracy has sought access to foreign technology. This was critical in the thirties and was one of the main motives behind détente in the seventies.**
5 **Trading off international influence for diplomatic objectives: the Soviet Union has used its influence over communist parties, liberation movements and other radical forces to press Western negotiators into making concessions. The Soviet Union's capacity to bargain in this way has allowed it to act as an arbiter in a number of international flare-ups.**

For 60 years the Soviet bureaucracy has stuck to these foreign policy objectives. It is ironic that the Soviet Union has acquired a reputation for expansionism — when in fact it has always sought to calm things down. The only exceptions to this rule have been Soviet interventions in countries on its borders, particularly in Eastern Europe. Here, the Soviet Union has defied Western hostility to establish a buffer zone against military incursions.

The continuity of Stalinist foreign policy results from the persistence of the underlying problems facing the Soviet social formation. The weakness of the Soviet economy remains as big a constraint on military adventures today as it was in the thirties. One of the striking features of studies of Soviet external relations is that, in the face of overwhelming evidence of continuity, experts continue to deny or ignore it. Thus studies discover major differences between the policies of Stalin, Khrushchev and Brezhnev.

For example, Carlo's generally useful survey of the policy of co-existence refers to the period between 1928 and 1932 as one which saw the 'extension of the foreign policy of the USSR'.[11] It is true that in these 'third period' years there was a revival of radical rhetoric in Moscow — and that Stalin and his lieutenants warned the international communist movement to prepare for imminent revolution. Yet, while the Soviet bureaucracy lectured the international communist movement about the impending collapse of capitalism, it continued to churn out pacifist statements. Its 'policy of peace' was pursued throughout the phase which critics have inaccurately characterised as 'extremist' or 'ultra-left'.

Rykov, one of the Kremlin's main foreign affairs spokesmen, explained why Soviet society needed peace, even in the third period:

**'Comrades, the fulfilment of the five year plan is bound up with an enormous development in our exports and imports, the import of a vast mass of equipment for our industry, agriculture and transport. Therefore we are not less but more interested than before in the development of peaceful relations and trade agreements.'**[12]

Rykov's pragmatism was typical of Soviet diplomacy throughout the third period. Indeed it was during these years that the Kremlin began to consider abandoning the remnants of revolutionary policy that survived from Lenin's era.

One of the first signs that even the formalities of Leninist policy had been dispensed with was the Kremlin's new attitude to the League of Nations. In the early twenties, the new Soviet government dismissed the League of Nations as a 'thieves' kitchen', arguing that it was a tool of imperialism. In response to the pressures of isolation and the rise of fascism, however, the Soviet bureaucracy began the search for new allies. Stalin regarded entry into the League of Nations as an act of goodwill which could open the way to better relations with Western capitalist countries. Magyar, a leading Stalinist functionary, signalled a change of line in 1934, explaining that although the League was still 'an instrument of imperialist policy', a new situation had arisen 'in which precisely that imperialist group which at present...is not in favour of immediately letting loose the dogs of war, has decisive influence in the League of Nations'.[13]

Six months later, the League was no longer an instrument of imperialist policy but the 'organiser of peace'. Litvinov's speech marking the Soviet Union's entry into the League of Nations complimented delegates for 'their struggle against aggressive militarist elements'. Litvinov concluded his sycophantic statement by hailing the League's attempt to enforce peace:

**'Could there be a loftier and at the same time more practical and urgent task for the co-operation of all nations?'**[14]

Soviet entry into the League was the bureaucracy's way of saying that it accepted the world order established through the Treaty of Versailles at the end of the First World War. The treaty the Bolsheviks had denounced as an attempt to consolidate the forces of counter-revolution was now accepted as a fact of life. For the first time the Soviet regime was prepared to go beyond 'pragmatic' relations with its imperialist opponents. To demonstrate that it could be a reliable ally, the Kremlin came out in support of the carve-up of the world ratified at Versailles. Recognising Versailles was part of the price that the Soviet bureaucracy was prepared to pay to establish diplomatic relations with France. The Franco-Soviet pact of May 1935 showed just how far Stalin was prepared to go.

Lenin recognised that the Soviet state was obliged to enter into treaties and other agreements with imperialist states. For Stalin, however, such deals were not merely pragmatic expedients. Whereas Lenin retained a consistent hostility to the imperialists, Stalin extended political support to the Paris government and gave the French ruling class his vote of confidence. The communiqué issued after the Stalin-Laval talks of May 1935 summed up the new approach:

**'Comrade Stalin expressed complete understanding and approval of the national defence policy pursued by France with the object of maintaining its armed forces at a level consistent with its security requirements.'**[15]

Stalin's explicit commitment to the defence of an imperialist power revealed how conservative Soviet foreign policy had become. This was the Soviet bureaucracy's first public statement of its preparedness to subordinate the international class struggle to its foreign policy objectives.

Khrushchev's 1956 speech to the twentieth congress of the Soviet Communist Party is often cited as a major departure because it advocated peaceful co-existence and rejected the inevitability of war. In fact, the outlines of this approach were already evident in the thirties. To uphold the League of Nations and the Franco-Soviet pact, the Stalinists had to redefine the Bolshevik analysis of imperialism. In a major revision of Lenin, they argued that imperialism need not be militaristic.

The bureaucracy distinguished carefully between 'peaceful' imperialist powers, which could be supported, and 'aggressive' imperialists, which all had to oppose. Leading Stalinist official Manuilsky told the seventh congress of the Communist International in 1935 that the world could now be divided into two camps: the 'camp of war' and the 'camp of peace'. Lenin's critique of pacifism, which was directed explicitly against the notion that the less aggressive imperialist powers were more peaceful than their rivals, was discreetly abandoned.[16]

Once the view was accepted that imperialism need not be militaristic, it followed that war was no longer inevitable. Stalin did not need Khrushchev to draw this conclusion — he had reached it himself in 1944:

**'The alliance between the USSR, Great Britain and the United States of America is founded not on casual, transitory considerations, but on vital and lasting interests.'**[17]

Even if Stalin was only paying lip-service to 'lasting interests', he clearly assumed that imperialist rivalries could now be suppressed and the danger of war overcome.

Another episode which is often cited as evidence of an aggressive turn in Soviet foreign policy is the opening of the Cold War in the late forties. Zhdanov's speech in September 1947, which proclaimed the division of the world into hostile camps, is said to prove that the Soviet Union is bent on world domination. In reality Zhdanov's speech was a reaction to Western pressure. Malenkov's report to the nineteenth congress of the Soviet Communist Party in 1952 showed that, despite the rhetoric, the Kremlin never lost sight of the goal of peaceful co-existence: 'The peaceful co-existence of capitalism and communism are quite possible, given a mutual desire to co-operate, readiness to carry out commitments undertaken, and observance of the principle of equality and non-interference in the internal affairs of other states.'[18]

The draft programme of the Soviet Communist Party issued in 1985 repeats Malenkov's call:

'The party proceeds from the belief that the historical dispute between the two opposing social systems, into which the world is divided today, can and must be settled by peaceful means.'[19]

A cynic might object that peaceful words do not necessarily mean peaceful deeds. But while Soviet declarations can be trusted no more than those of any world power, the continual repetition of the slogans of peaceful co-existence shows, at least, a consistent disregard for the principles of Leninist foreign policy. Moreover, it is a matter of historical record that the Soviet bureaucracy has never refused any serious Western offers of peace, détente or other durable diplomatic arrangement.

The continuity of Stalinist foreign policy seems to be contradicted by the sharp shifts and turns that appear to mark East-West relations. The underlying approach of Soviet foreign policy is one thing; how it works out in practice, another. In this context the decisive factor is the influence of the West.

## The evolution of foreign policy

The Soviet bureaucracy has been forced to adapt its external conduct to the changing attitudes of the West. It is no exaggeration to state that the different phases of Soviet foreign policy have largely been determined by the main Western powers. Western influence has created both problems and opportunities for the Soviet bureaucracy. The ambivalent character of its relationship with the West was already evident in the Soviet Union more than 50 years ago.

In the thirties Soviet policy was dominated by the fear of foreign intervention.[20] This fear was the decisive influence behind the frantic drive to industrialise. Stalin's well-known speech of February 1931 summed up the mood of the bureaucracy:

'We are 50 or 100 years behind the advanced countries. We must make good this distance in ten years. Either we do it, or they crush us.'[21]

Defence determined key decisions on industrial growth, enabling arms-related industries to mushroom.[22] By 1938 the arms sector consumed a third of the Soviet Union's structural iron and steel and 42 per cent of high-grade rolled steel.[23] The armaments build-up put a major strain on investment resources and ensured that consumption was curtailed.

The Soviet Union's limited scope for alliances with Western

powers provoked the instability that was the hallmark of its foreign policy in the thirties. Stalin hoped that rivalries among Western states would create some diplomatic openings, and at different times courted virtually all the major European nations. In the end the hostility of the Western bourgeois democracies drove Stalin into a short-lived and nearly fatal pact with Hitler in 1939.

Western commentators often cite the twists and turns of Soviet foreign policy as evidence of its insincerity. The Stalin-Hitler pact in particular is held up to demonstrate the infamy of the Kremlin. There can be no doubt that Stalin was a cynical manipulator of foreign affairs. But it is hypocritical for Western commentators to contrast Soviet policy unfavourably with that of the Western powers.

The ambivalent attitude of the Western powers to Nazi Germany was no less infamous than the Stalin-Hitler pact. Indeed the Western powers' hesitant criticisms of fascism stood in stark contrast to their tirades against communism. It was this very policy of appeasement which left the Soviet bureaucracy isolated and forced Stalin to consider forming an alliance with Hitler.[24] The Stalin-Hitler pact indicated how the Soviet Union was hostage to changing rivalries within the imperialist camp.

While imperialist rivalries did not open up much opportunity for diplomatic agreements, they did create considerable scope for economic deals. During the Depression years Western firms were anxious to extend their markets abroad and were indifferent to their customers' political persuasions. To secure deals, Western capitalists were prepared to make concessions and provide the Soviet Union with cut-price technology. This was an important development for the Soviet bureaucrats, who took advantage of the crisis of the capitalist world to obtain essential technology and industrial know-how. The influx of Western technology helped to reduce the Soviet Union's isolation and contributed to the high growth rates of the thirties.

It was only after the outbreak of the Second World War that the Soviet Union could derive major diplomatic benefits from inter-imperialist rivalries. After the German invasion of the Soviet Union in 1941, Stalin became a much sought-after partner in the anti-Hitler alliance. The war weakened the capitalist world enough for Stalin to be able to set the terms on which he would join the Allies. The breakdown of capitalist Europe and major upheavals in the colonial world allowed the Soviet bureaucracy to make major gains at the expense of other powers. By 1942 it was widely understood that there could be no return to the pre-war status quo. The collapse of the authority of the capitalist states of Eastern and Central Europe, and the disgrace of their ruling classes, provided the Soviet Union with an excellent opportunity to extend its sphere of influence and establish a protective zone around its borders.

The claims of the Soviet bureaucracy were backed by millions under arms. Through the international communist movement, its influence extended to radical resistance forces throughout the world. Stalin had no compunction about trading off this influence to advance his diplomatic objectives. In 1943 he dissolved the Communist International as an indication to the Allies that the Soviet Union was not bent on world revolution, but was rather merely a traditional world power interested in securing its own geopolitical advantage. In public, at least, American president Roosevelt and British prime minister Churchill embraced Stalin as one of their own. The conference of the 'big three' at Yalta in February 1945 ratified the division of the world into distinct spheres of influence and marked the high point of Stalin's diplomacy. For a brief moment the Soviet bureaucracy was accepted by the Western powers as a legitimate partner in running the world.

Stalin's foreign policy in the forties combined pragmatism with a determination to defend the Soviet Union's sphere of influence. The Soviet bureaucracy was prepared to keep its side of the bargain: Stalin refrained from supporting the revolutionary movement in China. He recognised that Greece was Britain's patch and willingly betrayed the Greek communists to the British forces. In France and Italy, Stalin made a significant contribution to the restoration of post-war capitalist stability by encouraging the influential communist parties to collaborate in the post-war reconstruction of the capitalist order. Stalin's flexible approach did not however extend to Eastern Europe. The Soviet bureaucracy was prepared to be pragmatic only insofar as this was consistent with its objective of establishing a protective zone in Eastern Europe. When Western powers attempted to interfere, notably in Poland in 1945, they were met with a firm rebuff. In a message to Churchill and to Roosevelt's successor Truman in April 1945, Stalin reiterated the basic position of non-interference in each other's sphere of influence:

> **'You evidently do not agree that the Soviet Union is entitled to seek in Poland a government that would be friendly to it, that the Soviet Union cannot agree to the existence in Poland of a government hostile to it....I do not know whether a genuinely representative government**

has been established in Greece, or whether the Belgian government is a genuinely democratic one. The Soviet Union was not consulted when those governments were formed, nor did it claim the right to interfere in these matters, because it realises how important Belgium and Greece are to the security of Great Britain. I cannot understand why in discussing Poland no attempt is made to consider the interests of the Soviet Union in terms of security as well.'[25]

Stalin had carried out his side of the bargain and, in return, he expected Truman and Churchill to respect Soviet domination in Eastern Europe. From the end of the Second World War until the outbreak of the Cold War in earnest in 1947, Soviet foreign policy was entirely responsive to Western initiatives. As long as the Western powers required Soviet co-operation, Stalin was willing to go along with the carve-up. But as the post-war settlement took shape, the attitude of Western powers began to change. Britain took the lead in the realignment of relations with the Soviet Union. In his famous speech at Fulton, Missouri in 1946 Churchill warned that an 'iron curtain' was descending across Europe. Churchill expressed Britain's uneasiness at its own decline and the fear that the Soviet Union would divide up the world with the USA and squeeze Britain out.

It was not until after the defeat of Japan that the USA began to reappraise its relations with the Soviet Union. In its new role as the dominant global power, the USA sought to neutralise the Soviet Union. As General Strong put it, the USA needed a 'world settlement' after the war which would enable it to impose its own terms, 'amounting perhaps to a Pax Americana'.[26] The US ruling class could no longer behave as just a regional power: world domination was now its historic duty. McCloy, chief delegate to the conference which established the United Nations, explained:

'I've been taking the position that we ought to have our cake and eat it too: that we ought to be free to operate under this regional arrangement in South America, at the same time intervene promptly in Europe.'[27]

From this point of view, the Soviet Union was a rival — a barrier to the establishment of Pax Americana.

From the middle of 1945 onwards, American policy was directed towards eliminating all obstacles to world hegemony. There is considerable evidence to suggest that the US decision to drop atomic bombs on Hiroshima and Nagasaki was motivated as much by the desire to put the Soviet Union in its place as it was to bring the war in the Pacific to a rapid conclusion.[28] While the motives behind the bombings remain a matter of interpretation, in 1945 Washington's monopoly over nuclear arms was clear for all to see. Truman used the terrifying destructive capacity of nuclear weapons to boast that America had become 'the most powerful nation in the world — the most powerful nation, perhaps, in all history'.[29]

The immediate obstacle to the restructuring of the world economy under US domination was the instability of Europe and of a large part of the colonial world. The 'communist menace' in Europe and Asia had to be crushed if the capitalist system was to be rebuilt out of the ruins of war. In the view of US policymakers, the menace could not be fought unless the Soviet Union itself was contained. The disintegration of capitalist rule in China and the dramatic rise in support for the Communist Party there was seen as a major threat to Pax Americana. The fear that insurgency in China might spread stimulated a growing mood of anti-communism in Washington. It provided a convenient pretext for American intervention throughout the world.

Western historians often claim that the Cold War originated as a response to Soviet expansionism in Central and Eastern Europe. In fact, although the USA was keen to curb Soviet influence in these areas, and especially in Germany, its main concern was instability elsewhere. The Truman Doctrine, proclaimed in March 1947, was particularly directed at establishing US influence in Greece, Turkey and the eastern Mediterranean. This was the opening salvo of the Cold War. Within weeks Truman widened the attack, calling for the communist parties of Western Europe to be banned. In May 1947, communist ministers were kicked out of coalition governments in France and Italy.

The anti-Soviet campaign unleashed a chain of action and reaction. In response to the expulsion of communists from office, the Soviet bureaucracy tightened its control over Eastern Europe. In Hungary, non-communist politicians were purged from government in May 1947. But Stalin still held out hopes that relations with the West could be stabilised. Only the announcement of the Marshall Plan in June 1947 finally shattered his hopes.

Ostensibly an economic aid package, the Marshall Plan had the effect of drawing Western Europe directly into the US sphere of influence. Although in principle aid was also to be made available to the Soviet Union and Eastern Europe, Washington knew that, because the plan amounted to an assertion of the economic power of the USA, Moscow had no alternative but to reject it. If US power had expanded into Eastern Europe, it would have seriously loosened the Soviet bureaucracy's grip. In Yergin's assessment of the squabble over Eastern Europe, the Marshall Plan aimed to use 'the powerful and attractive magnetism of the American economy to draw these countries out of the Soviet orbit'.[30]

The Soviet rejection of the Marshall Plan, and the pressure the Kremlin placed on its East European satellites to follow suit, are generally adduced as evidence of Moscow's hostile intentions towards the West. But from the Soviet point of view, these were defensive responses to a disruptive economic policy masquerading as a benign aid programme. Soviet attitudes only hardened as a reaction to the US-inspired partition of Europe. When, later in the year, the Western powers consolidated the division of Germany to minimise Soviet influence, the Cold War appeared unstoppable.

After the breakdown of the wartime alliance, the Soviet Union adopted an increasingly defensive posture and concentrated on consolidating its sphere of influence. The establishment of a new international communist body — the Cominform (Communist Information Bureau) — in September 1947 was one indication of the new approach to foreign affairs. In propaganda, the emphasis shifted from the virtues of co-existence to the parting of the world into two hostile camps. Zhdanov's speech to the founding meeting of the Cominform is another statement often produced as evidence of the Soviet Union's responsibility for the outbreak of the Cold War:

**'A new alignment of political forces has arisen. The more the war recedes into the past, the more distinct become the major trends in post-war international policy, corresponding to the division of the political forces operating on the international arena into two major camps; the imperialist and anti-democratic camp, on the one hand, and the anti-imperialist camp, on the other.'**[31]

In fact Zhdanov's speech was a belated recognition of the failure of the Kremlin's strategy of partnership with the West. For some time, US policymakers had been thinking aloud about the division of the world into rival camps. The major US policy statement of the period, Kennan's article 'The sources of Soviet conduct', published two months before Zhdanov's speech, had already anticipated the irreconcilable conflict of interests between the two blocs.[32] Zhdanov was merely acknowledging, rather late in the day, a state of affairs created in Washington.

Despite Zhdanov's strident rhetoric, the Cold War was not a fight picked by the Soviet Union, but a burden imposed on the Soviet bureaucracy by the USA. In the late forties the Soviet Union was in no position to take on the United States. The Medvedevs have argued convincingly that the inferior military position of the Soviet Union put the bureaucracy on the defensive.[33] One of the most thorough studies of Soviet politics in this period emphasises the conservative approach of the Soviet leadership:

**'Most authors on the subject seem to agree that the Soviet Union began the post-war era on a cautious note. Opportunities to extend communist influence in Greece, Iran and Austria were not taken up by Moscow in 1946 and 1947.'[34]**

The full Soviet clampdown in Eastern Europe followed the announcement of the Truman Doctrine and the Marshall Plan.

The shift in Soviet foreign policy in 1947 was a defensive response to Washington's monopoly of nuclear weapons and its overwhelming economic power. From Moscow's point of view, the worst part of the post-war scenario was that the USA could use its hegemony to suppress the rivalries among the Western powers that the Soviet Union had previously tried to exploit. Not since the early thirties had the Soviet bureaucracy faced such a concerted barrage of Western hostility. Although the Soviet Union's global influence grew as a result of the breakdown of the capitalist world order during the war, within a few years it was again out on a limb. During the Cold War the USA imposed a virtual economic blockade on the Soviet Union (see table) while trade with the West declined sharply.

| US exports to the Soviet Union (in $ million)[35] | | | |
| --- | --- | --- | --- |
| Year | Value | Year | Value |
| 1944 | 3475 | 1948 | 30 |
| 1946 | 358 | 1949 | 7 |
| 1947 | 149 | | |

The USA pressed its allies to join the economic boycott and the export of virtually all capital goods to the Soviet Union was restricted. The US Battle Act of 1952 placed an embargo on all items 'representative of significant technological advances of strategic value'.

The breakdown of economic links with the West was a blow to the Soviet bureaucracy. Foreign technology had played an important role in stimulating industrial development. Without foreign technology the Soviet Union was forced to mark time. It was unable to develop its natural gas reserves or make any advances in newly designated priority areas such as chemicals, plastics and synthetics. At the same time Western pressure forced the bureaucracy to divert considerable resources into arms production. As a result, the Soviet Union succeeded in exploding its first nuclear device in August 1949 — but at a heavy cost to its limited resources.

In the fifties the Soviet Union made numerous attempts to overcome its isolation. In 1954 a leading British business journal noted the Soviet bureaucracy's quest for closer economic ties with Western countries:

'Now one by one the Western industrial nations are being approached, first France, then Italy. The most recent is Belgium.'[36]

In general Soviet diplomats were cautious. Even at the height of the Cold War they showed an interest in trying to relax East-West tensions.

In standard Western accounts, the Korean War from 1950 to 1953 is held up as conclusive evidence of the Soviet Union's aggressive intentions. In reality, however, it shows just the opposite. A recently disclosed statement by the notoriously militaristic US General MacArthur reveals his conviction that the role of the Soviet Union in Korea was marginal: 'No evidence had been found of any close connection between the Soviet Union and the North Korean aggression. The only possible link was the Russian equipment being used.' MacArthur also commented that 'if it had really inspired North Korean aggression, the Soviet Union would not have abandoned the North Koreans so completely, giving them no assistance whatever'.[37] The Korean War reflected the prevailing state of East-West conflict — American posturing and Soviet caution.

The Soviet Union displayed its careful handling of external affairs at the 1954 general conference on Vietnam. Despite the fact that communist-inspired forces were on the verge of a total victory over the French, the Soviet bureaucracy was prepared to endorse a compromise involving the partition of the country. A year later, on a different front, the Soviet Union withdrew its troops from Austria, indicating a willingness to accept a negotiated settlement to the outstanding post-war issues in Europe.

The USA was not receptive to the Kremlin's peaceful overtures. Despite its cautious diplomacy, the Soviet Union was still an obstacle to Pax Americana. Yet, while it faced a solid wall of hostility from the West, the Soviet Union received an unexpected boost from the third world. The victory of the Chinese revolution in 1949, and the proliferation of anti-colonial struggles in Asia and North Africa, reflected the decline of Western control in the third world. This allowed the Soviet Union to overcome its isolation and strengthen its influence despite the Cold War. Thus Western leaders came to see the malevolent hand of Moscow behind every anti-colonial uprising. The revolution in Cuba in the late fifties underlined the Soviet Union's potential to expand its influence.

Under Khrushchev, the Soviet bureaucracy renewed its efforts to secure détente in international relations; but again the USA was not responsive. A number of international conflicts, notably the Berlin and Cuban missile crises in 1961, exposed the high level of East-West tension. In retrospect it is clear that American attitudes were shaped by the need to keep the Western alliance under firm control. In this important respect, the Cold War provided the perfect cover for flexing American muscle.

It was in the sixties that the USA invented the arms race, carefully fostering the idea that the Soviet Union was outstripping the West in nuclear missile stockpiles. For Washington it was vital to assert the primacy of Nato to keep in check potential rivals such as West Germany, Japan and France. MacNamara, US defence secretary in the Kennedy administration, later explained how the Americans fabricated the myth of Soviet nuclear superiority:

**'We overstate the Soviets' force and we understate ours, and we therefore greatly overstate the imbalance.'**[38]

Such a fraudulent strategy could not keep Western rivalries in check for long.

By the mid-sixties the stronger West European nations had begun to strengthen their economic links with the Soviet Union. At the time, an American study of this development concluded that the trade restraints embodied in the 1952 Battle Act had imposed 'additional restrictions on American exporters attempting to do business in that part of the world':

**'Most of these restrictions now fail to accomplish their original purpose. They no longer deny the Soviet Union and Eastern Europe**

access to goods embodying advanced industrial technology, obtainable only in the USA. Today such goods are generally available to Soviet and East European buyers in Western Europe and in Japan.'[39]

The Soviet Union's economic isolation was slowly coming to an end. It was only a matter of time before the USA recognised this fact of life. A combination of motives finally pushed Washington to adopt the policy of détente. One important consideration was the need to get the Soviet Union to play its part in maintaining the status quo in the third world. One writer has suggested that 'the essence of the Nixon and Ford administration's approach to the USSR at the summit meetings of the seventies was a trade-off between nuclear parity and the containment of third world revolution'.[40] Whatever Washington's motives, Brezhnev jumped at the chance — détente was what the Soviet bureaucracy had wanted all along.

Different phases of Soviet foreign policy have largely been a reaction to Western attitudes. In all stages of its development, the Soviet bureaucracy has sought to establish stable diplomatic relations and reduce military tensions. It has followed this approach, not in pursuit of any lofty principle, but because of the crippling effect of international tensions on the Soviet Union. The present Soviet leadership is only too aware of its reliance on Western technology and hence on détente. Despite the USA's reversion, in the eighties, to a more anti-Soviet posture, Gorbachev and his colleagues live in hope of a return to détente.

## The limits to Soviet global power

In transforming itself into the world's second strongest military power, the Soviet Union has made a major achievement. Rivalries among the imperialist nations and the instability of the backward capitalist world have played a crucial role in the rise of Soviet power. In recent years the Soviet bureaucracy has displayed considerable skill in exploiting tensions between the United States and Europe.

Soviet foreign interests are backed up by an impressive military capability. Although Western analysts have consistently exaggerated Soviet military strength, it is evident that the Soviet Union has managed to keep up in the arms race. However the heavy demands made by the military sector on the rest of the economy severely limit the scope for diversifying industry. Western strategists have often claimed that forcing the Soviet Union into an all-out arms race could destabilise its economy. While this outcome is unlikely, it is clear that the Soviet economy will be hard pushed to expand as long as vast resources are diverted into the military sector.

The Soviet Union's success at the expense of the West can easily disguise the real limits to its power. It is one thing to derive some advantage from the instability of the capitalist world order, but quite another to consolidate these gains. The Soviet Union lacks the economic strength to back up its international ambitions, so that its external influence is constantly restricted by its domestic difficulties. This is particularly evident in its relations with the backward capitalist world.

Soviet successes in the third world have been seriously tarnished by setbacks. The overthrow of allies such as Lumumba in Zaire, Nkrumah in Ghana, Ben Bella in Algeria and Sukarno in Indonesia amounted to a whole succession of diplomatic reverses. The Soviet Union's economic weakness gives it only a fragile hold over its allies, a fact spectacularly exposed by the breakdown of its close relations with Egypt. In 1971, Sadat took Egypt into the orbit of the United States and expelled some 20 000 Soviet military personnel. The Soviet Union cannot compete with the Western powers for economic influence. For the rulers of countries like Egypt, economic links with Western powers, not the Soviet Union, appear to provide a rational solution to the problems of development.

The Soviet Union has not even succeeded in keeping a firm grip on the Eastern bloc. Both Yugoslavia (1948) and China (1960) broke with what they regarded as Moscow domination. The breakdown of relations with China has been a major setback for the Soviet Union. Sino-Soviet rivalries have been used by the West in much the same way as the Kremlin attempts to take advantage of imperialist rivalries. The millions of Soviet troops tied down on the Chinese border underline the difficulties this conflict causes for the bureaucracy.

Only direct political domination keeps the rest of Eastern Europe in the Soviet camp. It is a testimony to the economic weakness of the Soviet Union that it can only exercise authority over Eastern Europe by means of force or the threat of force. Despite Soviet pressure, tendencies towards fragmentation are evident in Eastern Europe. The permanent instability of Poland and the periodic reassertion of nationalist sentiment in Rumania reveal the deep tensions within the countries of the Warsaw Pact. One of the paradoxical features of the 'Soviet empire' is that living standards in the satellite countries are in general higher than they are in the Soviet Union. Despite 40 years of domination, Eastern Europe has still not been integrated into a workable division of labour with the Soviet Union.

The growth of Soviet power is often exaggerated, or at least confused with the decline of Western imperialism. In historical terms the Soviet Union has passed its peak. Yet it is often claimed that the emergence of the Soviet navy has given Moscow a new influence over world events. American analysts argue that the navy gives the Soviet Union the status of a world rather than a regional power. Aspaturian, for example, suggests that the Soviet airlift of Cuban troops into Angola marked a new stage in Moscow's foreign influence:

**'The fact that Moscow could logistically conceive and execute such a military operation was a tangible confirmation of its global reach.'**[41]

There is no doubt that the Soviet navy has extended its global reach. However, it is also clear that it is no major threat to Western naval power, as a specialist French publication has conceded:

**'Despite continuous diplomatic efforts, the Soviet navy has not yet succeeded in finding a foreign base worthy of the name, and the few staging posts and other facilities it has acquired here and there cannot compensate for what would in wartime be a very serious handicap.'**[42]

No navy can control the seas without a network of bases. In fact the Soviet Union has lost a number of important naval bases since the forties.

The split with Albania in 1946 led to the loss of port facilities, and the break with Yugoslavia cost it Cattara in 1948. The rupture with Egypt led to the loss of Alexandria and, in 1977, Moscow was forced to give up the Berbera base in Somalia. Gaining access to ports in South Yemen and Ethiopia did little to offset these losses. The coup in South Yemen in January 1986 showed that Moscow's position in that country is far from secure. The Soviet Union's global activities present a highly uneven picture. Its military strength has undoubtedly grown enormously, but it has not succeeded in translating this into wider political influence. A revealing study conducted by the Washington-based Centre for Defence Information showed that of 155 countries surveyed, the Soviet Union had influence in just 19. The authors noted that outside Eastern Europe, the Soviet Union 'lacked staying power': they concluded that setbacks in China, Indonesia, Egypt and Iraq outweighed Soviet gains in more peripheral areas.[43]

This study also revealed that, despite all the American rhetoric about the Soviet threat to the third world, US advisers have a shrewd awareness of Moscow's limited influence. In recent years the American Rand Corporation has produced evidence which suggests that the costs of maintaining influence in countries like Cuba and Vietnam are so high that they are likely to force the Soviet leadership to think twice before embarking on any similar initiatives elsewhere.[44]

Many Western observers fail to grasp that the fortunes of the Soviet Union abroad are proportional to the decline of the West. The Soviet Union has not gained influence in the third world through forceful military interventions. Its advances have taken place at points where the Western powers are weakest. It is significant that the war in Afghanistan has provided the Soviet armed forces with their first combat experience since the Second World War.

## Is the Soviet Union imperialist?

Many left-wing critics regard the Soviet Union as an imperialist power. Since Moscow's invasion of Czechoslovakia in 1968, the Chinese leadership in particular has levelled this charge repeatedly. Many Western commentators offer the Soviet invasion of Hungary in 1956 or the occupation of Afghanistan in 1979 as proof of Moscow's imperialist designs. Others point to the Soviet Union's domination of Eastern Europe as typically colonial.

It is understandable that observers should have a negative reaction to Soviet foreign policy. The oppressive rule of the Soviet bureaucracy is evident to any observer of Eastern Europe. The Soviet invasion of Afghanistan can only be regarded as a cynical and reactionary move. But the fact that the Soviet Union has a sordid record in foreign policy does not make it an imperialist power.

For Marxists the term imperialism has a specific meaning. In the course of history the most diverse regimes have built empires, established colonies and engaged in military occupations. The aim of scientific analysis is to specify the social forces that give rise to expansionism and militarism, to create a precise understanding of different historical phases. The ahistorical approach, which lumps together all forms of foreign aggression and labels them imperialist in an attempt to explain the whole course of world history, in the end explains nothing. Lenin's theory of imperialism, by contrast, applies specifically to the capitalist mode of production: it only makes sense in relation to the development of capitalist societies.

For Lenin imperialism could not be reduced to colonialism, annexation, or any other particular aggressive policy. Imperialism was a form of social organisation that capitalism was obliged to assume to counteract the effects of its decline. Marx had argued that, at a certain stage of its development, capitalism was forced to restrict free competition and reorganise itself so that accumulation could continue.[45] Lenin drew out the implications of this analysis and argued that, for the most developed capitalist countries, the only way to escape tendencies towards crisis was to expand internationally.

Lenin drew particular attention to the way the tendency for the rate of profit to fall at home forced capitalist countries to export capital abroad.[46] This compulsion to operate globally stimulates rivalries among the major capitalist powers, as they divide and redivide the world into separate spheres of influence. In the imperialist era, military adventures and colonial occupations are not arbitrary acts of foreign policy, but the inescapable outcome of capital accumulation on a world scale. Militarism and colonialism are not therefore the defining features of imperialism. These features are not the starting point, but the consequences of the form of social organisation that decadent capitalism is forced to adopt to guarantee its survival. To what extent does this analysis apply to the Soviet Union?

Most writers who characterise the Soviet Union as imperialist simply sidestep the issues raised by Marx and Lenin. Cliff, for example, accepts that the export of capital is the typical feature of imperialism, concedes that the Soviet Union does not export capital, but proceeds to argue that there can also be atypical imperialist countries. To justify this argument, Cliff contends that, in the thirties, Japan was an imperialist country which did not export capital.[47] If Japan could be imperialist without exporting capital, the argument goes, so could the Soviet Union. Besides displaying an indifference to the fact of Japanese capital export in the thirties, Cliff's method remains purely assertive.[48]

Lenin explained expansionism by identifying the contradictions inherent in the capitalist system. By contrast, theories of Soviet imperialism resort to exogenous factors. In Cliff's view the quest for plunder, the pressure to catch up with the West, the need for more labour and strategic considerations all enter into the explanation of

Soviet expansionism.[49] In fact none of these factors is specific to capitalist society. Instead of demonstrating an inherent drive towards expansion in Soviet society, Cliff offers a shopping-list of arbitrary factors and motives. In this sense the term imperialism could be used to describe aggressive behaviour throughout history, from Alexander the Great, through Attila the Hun, to Napoleon Bonaparte. This is not merely a terminological dispute. The question at issue is whether or not expansionary tendencies are inherent in the Soviet social formation.

Unlike Western capitalists, the Soviet bureaucracy has no difficulty in deciding what to do with surplus investment resources. Given the constant problem of shortages, it has no inclination to invest precious assets abroad. The structural crisis of the Soviet social formation means that the bureaucracy has no impulse towards economic expansion. Indeed the activities of the bureaucracy in the international sphere are continually held back by its lack of economic clout. The Soviet Union experiences immense difficulties in bringing even its close allies in Eastern Europe into a collective division of labour.

The Soviet Union's third world allies have derived little economic benefit from their links with Moscow. Cuba is one exception — but the American embargo has given Castro no choice but to maintain close links. Soviet relations with Angola and Ethiopia are more revealing. Both countries rely on Soviet political and military support, yet their economies are heavily dependent on the West. According to Zeebroek, in 1981 only 9.8 per cent of all Angola's imports came from the Soviet Union, while 56.6 per cent came from Western Europe and a further 11.1 per cent from South Africa. In that year 27 per cent of Angola's trade was with the USA and the EEC.[50]

The figures indicate that Soviet influence in the third world is based on military aid, not on economic domination. In the early seventies the radical Chilean leader Allende summed up the dilemma facing third world countries:

'**Chile cannot supply its own needs, it must purchase machines, engines, petroleum, replacement parts and raw materials. Some people will say: "then buy them in the socialist world." That is not possible, because it does not produce them.**'[51]

The Soviet Union's lack of economic power explains why third world allies can so easily leave its orbit. Short of direct military occupation, the Soviet Union cannot really dominate its allies. The

Western powers, on the other hand, are able to use their control over the world economy to sustain influence in the third world. One of the key features of imperialist domination is that it can be exercised indirectly, through the operation of economic forces. Thus the Western powers, unlike the Soviet Union, do not have to rely on direct political control. The domination of third world countries by a small number of imperial powers is automatically reproduced through the operation of the world market.

The ruling classes of third world countries have been happy to accept military assistance from the Soviet Union — but they have treated this as a temporary expedient before moving on to establish closer economic links with Western powers. Apart from weapons, the Soviet Union has very little to offer third world countries. Indeed the trade patterns of the Soviet Union resemble those of a developing nation: it exports raw materials and imports manufactured goods and food. There is little demand in the third world for the products of Soviet industry. Even a longstanding ally like India prefers to import its manufactured goods from the West.

The Soviet Union's lack of economic influence limits Soviet power in Eastern Europe. Though the Stalinist bureaucracy plundered Eastern Europe after the war, Moscow no longer retains an exploitative relationship with its satellites today. East European countries are still under Soviet political control, but are very different from imperialist colonies. Moscow's main concern is to ensure the stability of its buffer zone. On several occasions it has shown its preparedness to use any means to crush opposition to its rule. But because the Soviet bureaucracy has realised that repression only breeds resentment, it has become more discriminating in its use of force. Jaruzelski's Poland is the main beneficiary of this change in approach.

Far from plundering Eastern Europe, the Soviet Union subsidises its satellites. Since the seventies, Moscow has supplied cut-price oil to Eastern Europe to promote economic stability. East European manufacturers produce goods of a much higher quality than Soviet factories and export large quantities into the Soviet Union. When Gorbachev talks of 'horizontal integration', he means that the Soviet Union needs all the high-technology products it can get from Eastern Europe. The Soviet 'superpower' imports its floppy disks from East Germany and even from Bulgaria. The growing dependence of the Soviet Union on Eastern Europe means that Moscow can no longer rule by dictat. Although the threat of force is always in the background, the Soviet bureaucracy is forced to rely on the more traditional means of diplomatic pressure.

If the Soviet Union is not an imperialist country, then what are the motives behind its military and diplomatic postures? The central objective of Soviet military mobilisation is to secure its borders and to prevent instability from spilling over into the Soviet Union. The fact that Soviet militarism is prompted by considerations of national security does not make it any less aggressive. But the defensive geo-political considerations behind Soviet military activity explain why it has in general been restricted to Eastern Europe. The only exception to this is Afghanistan.

Afghanistan has become a major focus of anti-Sovietism in the West. Commentators have claimed that the invasion of Afghanistan in December 1979 marked a new phase of Soviet expansionism. It has even been suggested that the Kremlin's motive was the desire to move one step closer to the Persian Gulf. Informed experts, however, quickly dismissed such explanations, pointing out that the route to the Gulf from Soviet Central Asia does not lie through Afghanistan, but through Iran. In fact the invasion of Afghanistan was motivated by more mundane domestic considerations.

For decades Afghanistan had been a close ally of Moscow, providing a measure of stability on the Soviet Union's southern border. As the revolt against the government in the late seventies exploded out of control and significant forces began to move towards the West, the Soviet bureaucracy had to act to protect its own interests. Any shift by Afghanistan away from the Soviet alliance was perceived as a direct threat in Moscow.

The Soviet-inspired coup in Kabul was not a simple invasion of one country by another. Even before the coup there were more than 5000 Soviet troops in Afghanistan fighting the rebels on behalf of the government. The aim of the invasion was to stabilise matters by installing a more popular government and by extending counter-insurgency sweeps. Although the Soviet Union was subsequently forced to step up its military presence, its original aim was to mount a defensive operation. In a rare moment of candour, leading Soviet bureaucrat Zamyatin explained that Moscow had to invade a state that would otherwise 'be hostile to us, that would endanger our security — a state not thousands of miles away from us, but that is right on our doorstep. Herein lies the crux of the matter.'[52]

Afghanistan is a good example of a military intervention that has nothing to do with imperialism. Imperialist countries do not launch foreign invasions simply to safeguard their own borders. Unless the term imperialism is used in a general ahistorical sense —

to mean no more than the obnoxious behaviour of one state towards another — tanks in Kabul represent something else. Indeed it is clear that the expansionist and militaristic behaviour of the Soviet state reveals its inability to exert influence in surrounding areas except by force of arms.

In other countries cited as evidence of Soviet expansionism — South Yemen, Nicaragua, Angola, Ethiopia — the Soviet role cannot be characterised as imperialist. In these countries, regimes formed through popular radical revolts were forced to turn to the Soviet Union to counteract Western pressure. The hostility of the imperialist order towards such regimes has forced them to look to the Soviet Union for support. The fact that the Soviet Union appears as an obvious source of support for anti-imperialist movements is one of the main distinguishing features of its role in world affairs. This role ensures a constant state of tension in East-West relations. However the Soviet Union's approach to third world liberation movements is not motivated by commitment to world revolution, but by concern to overcome its own isolation.

For Moscow every third world upset for the West provides it with another bargaining counter at the international conference tables. The Soviet Union's role in Vietnam shows that its support for anti-imperialist revolt is always negotiable. Angola, Ethiopia and South Yemen show that the Soviet Union is always prepared to seize opportunities to bolster its diplomatic position against the West.

## The myths of the new Cold War

The period of détente between 1970 and 1976 conferred considerable advantages on the Soviet Union. Washington's acceptance of Soviet progress in strategic nuclear weapons stabilised the arms race and allowed the bureaucracy to reduce its investment in the defence sector. As the military posturing declined, diplomatic activity burgeoned, bringing stability to Europe through the West's formal recognition of the frontiers established in the post-war period.

Détente provided the Soviet Union with an unprecedented opportunity to acquire Western technology, goods and investment. This gave the flagging Soviet economy a much needed boost. The twenty-fifth congress of the Soviet Communist Party in 1976 emphasised the importance of Western technology. The development of new priority areas, particularly energy, depended heavily on imported technology.[53] The persistence of the Sino-Soviet conflict reinforced Moscow's desire for good relations with the West. Indeed the relaxation of East-West tensions helped the Soviet Union to compensate for the heavy burden of securing its Far Eastern borders. Contrary to conventional wisdom in the West, the Soviet leadership desperately wanted détente to last.

For the USA and the Soviet Union détente ratified the division of the world established after the Second World War. It stabilised international power relations and curbed the arms race. What then brought this mutually convenient arrangement to an end?

The invasion of Afghanistan in 1979 is often cited as a landmark in the breakdown in détente. But détente was dead long before the tanks rolled into Kabul. As early as 1976 the consensus of support for détente within the American establishment was already beginning to crumble. In the following year president Carter stepped up the arms race with his decision to produce Cruise missiles. In January 1978 defence secretary Brown directed the Pentagon to set up a rapid deployment force for overseas assignments and, by December, Carter was demanding a substantial increase in the military budget. From mid-1979 US defence expenditure was set on an upward curve.

The December 1979 Nato decision to deploy long range nuclear weapons in Europe was the culmination of the first phase of the Western rearmament drive. In the strident tone that became the hallmark of US foreign policy in the late seventies, Carter's 'State of the Union' message in January 1980 asserted the right of the USA to intervene militarily in the Middle East.

As well as initiating a new arms race, Carter launched a new anti-Soviet crusade. In a remarkable policy switch, the USA embarked on a diplomatic rapprochement with China, so that by 1978 a new anti-Soviet alliance seemed to be in the making. American apologists provided two justifications for re-opening diplomatic hostilities against the Soviet Union. They claimed that Moscow had used the cover of détente to extend its influence in the third world, and that it had made furtive efforts to establish a first-strike nuclear capability. Even a superficial survey of the evidence shows that these justifications had little basis in fact.

Washington became preoccupied with the Soviet threat in the third world because, in the seventies, Western-sponsored regimes fell to popular radical movements in Vietnam, Angola, Mozambique, Ethiopia, Iran, Nicaragua and South Yemen. For Washington, it was easier to explain these defeats as the result of Soviet subversion than to confront their indigenous causes. The Soviet Union certainly benefited from the wave of third world revolts, but they were the direct result of the decline in Western control in these countries, not the outcome of Soviet intervention. The gravest blow of all to Western interests — the fall of the Shah of Iran in 1979 — took place in defiance of Soviet intentions, not in accordance with them.

Under Reagan, the myth of Soviet expansionism acquired absurd proportions. The first major foreign policy statement of the Reagan administration, made in 1980, was the claim that Cuban and Soviet 'aggression' were responsible for the revolts in El Salvador and the rest of Central America. Over the next two years the Reagan administration put considerable resources into fabricating evidence that would confirm Soviet aggression in America's 'backyard'. In February 1981 the US State Department published *Communist interference in El Salvador,* presenting 'evidence' of Soviet and Cuban involvement. Within a month, however, the evidence was exposed as a tissue of lies. The *Wall Street Journal* observed that the authors of the report on insurgency in Central America 'probably were making a determined effort to create a "selling" document, no matter how slim the background material'.[54] Such crass manoeuvres led former defence secretary Brown to criticise the Reagan administration's 'simplistic view of all world problems as Soviet inspired'.[55] Simplistic or not, similar tales served as pretext for the subsequent invasion of Grenada and for US backing for right-wing rebel forces in Nicaragua and Angola.

Washington's arguments about the growing Soviet military threat were equally absurd. The Soviet bureaucracy could ill afford to divert resources into a new arms race. Its supposed programme for military superiority was a myth similar to the 'missile gap' tales of the sixties. As the Medvedev brothers have argued, it is a matter of historical record that all innovations in post-war weaponry have been American:

**'Every significant new technology of nuclear warfare — nuclear missile submarines, MIRVs, cruise missiles, the neutron bomb, and so on — has been introduced into the arms race by the United States.'**[56]

Launched in 1985, the Strategic Defence Initiative — 'Star Wars' — is the latest addition to this list. This point is not a matter of interpretation but of incontrovertible fact. *The Economist* has conceded that, in the military sphere, 'the United States has pioneered all major recent advances'.[57] The same observations apply to the alleged superiority of Soviet naval power, as McGuire, a leading Western expert, has noted:

> 'Most specialists in the field now accept that the initial shift to forward deployment was a response to the threat to Russia from sea based nuclear delivery systems...triggered by President Kennedy.'[58]

A quick glance at an atlas reveals the absurdity of the notion of a Soviet naval threat to the West. The Soviet navy has no foreign base worthy of the name; a mere 15 ports provide it with facilities. By contrast, the USA has 360 major bases and 1600 installations in 36 countries.[59]

Spurious allegations about Soviet military supremacy have provided the excuse for American rearmament. An unusually candid CIA study of East-West relations in the seventies admitted that 'attacks on the USSR were used to muster public support for large increases in expenditure for strategic and conventional weapons systems'.[60] But if the Soviet Union was not a threat to the USA, why did Washington reject détente and precipitate a new era of East-West tensions?

The anti-Soviet shift in American foreign policy had nothing to do with the Soviet Union as such. The real reasons for this shift lay in the USA's difficulty in preventing its own decline as the dominant global power. During the seventies America's influence in the world declined steadily, causing consternation within the ruling class. At the time this fall from grace was perceived subjectively as the result of the 'Vietnam syndrome' — as an inability to deal with problems in the third world. Influential American right wingers denounced successive presidents as appeasers who had failed to stand up for national interests.

The downfall of the Shah of Iran in 1979 brought home to Washington how fragile its grip was over even its closest allies. The subsequent protracted crisis over the American hostages detained in Tehran was a painful reminder of the limits of American power. Third world setbacks like this provided the main impetus to the growth of US militarism and an interventionist foreign policy.

Although the decline of American power was most tangible in the third world, this was not the most serious threat to Pax Americana. The USA was losing its grip, not merely in relation to the third world, but also with other Western nations. From the late sixties the world order created under American domination was steadily undermined by the deepening recession. The American economy ceased to be all powerful, as its share of total OECD industrial output fell from 44.4 per cent in 1963 to 34.9 per cent in 1975. By then the industrial output of the EEC exceeded that of the USA. Declining productivity became such a serious problem for America that, in the seventies, it lost 23 per cent of its share of the world market. By the mid-eighties, West Germany and Japan accounted for about 50 per cent of world exports.

The decline of US imperialism has been paralleled by the growth of tensions within the Western camp. The more dynamic Western states have begun to resent the arrogance of American power. For West Germany and Japan the old alliances have increasingly become something of a straightjacket. Yesterday's allies have come to regard one another as rivals in a shrinking world market. Moreover, as the crisis of US industry has forced American capitalists to increase their dependence on the world market, trade conflicts have intensified. While tensions have not yet reached the pitch of the thirties, they put the question of how long Pax Americana can last firmly on the political agenda.

Since the mid-seventies, a number of key conflicts have emerged in the Western alliance. In the economic sphere there have been disputes over imports, export credits and interest rates. In the diplomatic sphere there have been open disagreements over Iran, Israel and Libya. Even relatively minor events, such as French arms sales to Egypt, have struck a raw nerve in Washington:

**'Down the road is the worry that the French connection may loosen Mubarak's ties to US policy, steering him towards radical Arab politics.'**[61]

There have also been acrimonious disputes over European defence, Central America and Western policy towards the Soviet Union. The failure of Washington to obtain solid backing from its Western partners over the boycott of the Moscow Olympics in 1980, and over economic sanctions against the Siberian pipeline project, indicates the decline of American authority.

The rise of anti-American nationalism in Europe is a clear expression of the tensions within the Western alliance. Drawing attention to this trend, the editor of the West German newspaper *Die Zeit* has contrasted the unanimous European sympathy for the USA over the 1962 Cuban missile crisis with the uneven response to the USA's campaign against the Soviet Union over the invasion of Afghanistan. His conclusion is sober:

'In foreign policy then, the traditional ideological chasms between left and right are narrowing: the two camps are drawing together on the joint platform of "Little Europe" nationalism and resistance to American leadership.'[62]

In the early eighties the Western alliance came under serious internal strains for the first time since it was established after the Second World War. Divisions over economic matters and other conflicts of interest have begun to threaten the coherence of the Western alliance. In 1982 British industry minister Jenkin warned that measures to keep European steel out of the USA 'could lead to trade war' which 'would be a major source of bitterness and acrimony within the alliance'.[63] 'Economic relations between the USA, the European Community and Japan', *The Times* commented on the same day, were 'worse today than at any time since the war'.[64] The lack of support for Reagan's economic sanctions against the Soviet Union was a major source of embarrassment. A report from the influential Trilateral Commission suggested that the main consequence of Reagan's sanctions was to 'strain severely relations within the Western alliance'.[65]

The decline of the USA, the rise of its rivals and the re-emergence of open inter-imperialist conflict have become the main challenges facing American foreign policymakers. The new Cold War has provided the central axis of Washington's response. Its objective is to compensate for the USA's economic decline through displays of political and military might. This is a rational policy because, although Europe and Japan are catching up economically, in the military sphere America's predominance is still unquestioned. Hence US politicians are bent on militarising all aspects of international relations — particularly economic aspects. The USA's drive to impose 'strategic consensus' on Nato means forcing its Western rivals to accept its leadership. A growing emphasis on intervention in the third world, plus paranoia about 'international terrorism' and 'terrorist states', supplement the overall militarisation of America's international relations.

Cold War policies and anti-Soviet propaganda provide the most effective way of maintaining the integrity of the Western alliance, as *The Economist* explains:

'Of all the threats that now hold Western Europe and the United States together, the two strongest are the threat of attack by a common potential enemy and the alliance that was created to meet that threat.'[66]

The revitalisation of Nato against the 'evil empire' counterbalances the centrifugal forces now tearing the Western alliance apart. The Soviet Union is not the active partner in either the build-up of the arms race or the deterioration of East-West relations. It is continually forced to respond to US pressure. The Soviet bureaucracy can only match the 40 per cent increase in the US defence budget between 1980 and 1984 by paying a terrible price. Any attempt to compete with the Star Wars programme would have a devastating effect on the Soviet economy. As a CIA commentary on the Reagan-Gorbachev summit in Geneva in 1985 indicates, Washington has a shrewd grasp of the issues at stake:

**'The chief pressure on Moscow to reach a new compromise arrangement with Washington is likely to come from a perception of Soviet technological inferiority to the USA in the new realm of space defence.'**[67]

Although the USA is responsible for the new era of East-West conflict, the Soviet Union has been forced to reply. Yet the Soviet bureaucracy remains committed to extricating itself from this conflict. Even more than in the first Cold War, the Soviet leadership has sought to avoid provocative statements — in the hope that it can reduce tensions. The upsurge of American hostility since the seventies has set back Soviet diplomatic aspirations. However, the growth of frictions within the Western bloc in the eighties has also presented the Kremlin with opportunities for the future.

## Future trends

The pursuit of stable diplomatic and economic links with the West has been a constant theme of Soviet foreign policy. Success or failure has always depended on the Western response, which has therefore played a decisive role in shaping Soviet conduct. Western foreign policy has been much more unstable than that of the Soviet Union, a factor Moscow has sometimes been able to exploit to its advantage. Rivalries among the Western powers, and their insecure grip in certain parts of the third world, have allowed the Soviet bureaucracy to assimilate Western technology and to extend its global influence. Indeed were it not for the internal tensions within the imperialist world, the Soviet social formation could not have survived.

From this perspective the Cold War of the fifties stands out as a unique period — one in which imperialist rivalries were suppressed.

Recent events have shown that the unity of old can no longer be sustained. The decline of the USA and the ascendancy of its imperialist rivals have turned its attempts to relaunch the Cold War into a charade.

Current commentary on East-West tensions is misplaced. It ignores the emerging pattern of conflict within the capitalist world and the tendency of economic rivalries to give way eventually to military conflict. There is certainly a basic contradiction between the modes of economic regulation in the Soviet Union and in the West. This contradiction ensures the Soviet Union's separation from the capitalist world economy and allows it to act as a focus for radical movements around the world. As long as the Soviet Union plays this role, its relations with the West will be fraught with tension. However, East-West tensions cannot explain the current drive towards Western rearmament, which originates in the capitalist world itself.

The contradictions within the Western camp are more profound than those between East and West. Imperialist rivalries are rooted firmly in the capitalist system and are only tempered by the dominant influence of the USA. It can be only a matter of time before these rivalries reassert themselves with full force. In contrast to the explosive contradictions contained within the imperialist world, East-West rivalries are episodic and conjunctural. Washington's attempts to militarise international relations can only postpone its decline and the West's descent into militarism and war.

The Soviet bureaucracy's hope for the future lies in rising inter-imperialist competition. This will weaken the external threat to the Soviet Union and allow the bureaucracy to forge new alliances and play opponents off against one another. Gorbachev has already embarked on this course — though so far with limited results. However in the early eighties the Soviet leadership has had considerable success in getting hold of Western technology, for Washington's economic boycotts have been the first casualties of the rifts within the Western alliance. The USA has failed to translate the military consensus behind Nato into the economic sphere.

Deepening recession in the West will enable the Soviet Union to strike useful deals in the realm of foreign technology. But the extensive dependence of the Soviet social formation on the imperialist world order reveals its regressive features. Despite the many points of East-West conflict, the Soviet Union is committed to preserving the existing division of the world. Its diplomatic efforts are directed merely towards improving the terms on which it operates in the international order. As a result, it cannot but act as a conservative force in foreign affairs.

## Notes

1. Cited in Delwitt & Dewaele (1984), p324.
2. Cited in Chomsky, Steele, Gittings (1984), p12.
3. *The Times,* 30 July 1981.
4. Ulam (1983), p350.
5. Cited in Chomsky, Steele, Gittings (1984), p20.
6. Strode & Gray (1981), p13.
7. Lenin 'Report on concessions', *CW31.*
8. Preobrazhensky (1967), p105, footnote 1.
9. Trotsky (1971b), p60. See also Lenin's letter to Stalin in *CW33,* p460.
10. In Stalin (1968), p3.
11. Carlo (1978), p65.
12. 'Extracts from the report by Rykov, chairman of the Soviet council of people's commissars, to the fifth Soviet congress',20 May 1929, in Degras (1952), p374.
13. Magyar (1934).
14. See Degras (1953), pp93-4.
15. Cited in Claudin (1975), p180.
16. See Lenin 'The question of peace', *CW21.*
17. Stalin (1950), p112.
18. Cited in Noyee & Donaldson (1984), p17.
19. CPSU (1985), p93.
20. See Haslam (1983), chapter 3.
21. Stalin 'The tasks of business executives' in Stalin (1940), p366.
22. Harrison (1985), p7.
23. Harrison (1985), p8.
24. See Fleming (1961), pp106-34 for illustrations of this process.
25. Cited in Claudin (1975), p422.
26. Cited in Shoup and Minter (1977), p164.
27. Kolko (1970), p470.
28. See Alperovitz (1965).
29. *The Times,* 10 August 1945.
30. Yergin (1978), p119.
31. In Noyee & Donaldson (1984), p1.
32. See Kennan (1947).
33. Medvedev & Medvedev (1982), p159.
34. Dunmore (1984), p104.
35. Cited in Adler-Karlsson (1968), p156.

36  *The Economist*, 8 February 1954.
37  Cited in Halliday (1984), pp140-1.
38  *The Guardian*, 9 August 1982.
39  Cited in Alden Smith (1973), p262.
40  Davis (1982), p51.
41  Aspaturian (1980), p3.
42  *Flottes de combat 1983* cited in Zeebroek (1984), p290.
43  'Soviet geo-political momentum: myth or menace — trends of Soviet influence around the world from 1945 to 1980', *The defence monitor*, January 1980.
44  Rand Corporation (1983).
45  See Marx (1973), p651.
46  See Lenin 'Imperialism, the highest stage of capitalism', *CW22*, p300.
47  Cliff (1970), p177-8.
48  The crisis of profitability in the Japanese economy in the thirties and its relationship to the invasion of Manchuria is documented in Farl (1974).
49  Cliff (1970), pp180-2.
50  Zeebroek (1984), p294.
51  Carlo (1978), p79.
52  *The Guardian*, 10 December 1980.
53  See the interesting observations of Ticktin (1978b).
54  *Wall Street Journal*, 8 June 1981.
55  *New York Times*, 20 September 1981.
56  Medvedev & Medvedev (1982), p162.
57  *The Economist*, 6 February 1982.
58  Cited in Steele (1983), p33.
59  See Zeebroek (1984), p290.
60  Gelman (1985).
61  *Business Week*, 8 February 1982.
62  Joffe (1981), p836.
63  *Financial Times*, 14 January 1982.
64  *The Times*, 14 January 1982.
65  *The Times*, 9 September 1982.
66  *The Economist*, 27 February 1982.
67  Cited in *the next step*, 22 November 1985.

# Conclusion

In the months leading up to the twenty-seventh congress of the Soviet Communist Party in February 1986, the Soviet press was full of calls for change and for radical solutions to the country's problems. Discussion of the drafts of the revised party programme and statutes emphasised the need for a decisive break with the past. Gorbachev declared his aim of achieving 'a qualitatively new stage of Soviet society'. He argued that nothing short of a fundamental change would suffice, because the old ways were 'the root of the matter...the essence of our problems'.[1] Both the new party programme and the draft guidelines on social and economic development over the next decade held out a vision of a new society.

A yearning for change is evident in all sections of Soviet society. Even the more conservative bureaucrats recognise that the scope for traditional solutions is exhausted. There is widespread acceptance, at least in theory, that further development requires steady improvements in the productivity of labour. All commentators agree that more investment without higher efficiency can only lead to further stagnation. Soviet experts openly admit that administrative measures are of little use in stimulating growth. They freely concede that the system of priority allocation and massive resource investment can keep things ticking over, but only at the cost of storing up problems for the future.

The Soviet leadership wants change, but does not know how to achieve it. Gorbachev's keynote speech to the 1986 party congress revealed the emptiness of the Kremlin's reform programme. He challenged past practices and went further than any Stalinist leader in questioning the relevance of official 'Marxist-Leninist' dogma. Yet, after five and a half hours of exhortation, delegates were no wiser about how they could proceed towards a 'qualitatively new stage of Soviet society'. Gorbachev's speech, given 30 years to the day after Khrushchev's famous denunciation of Stalin, contained no major departures from the strategy offered by the leadership in 1956. The tone and emphasis were different but, in all essentials,

Gorbachev merely repeated past leadership performances. For all its commitment to reform, Gorbachev's harangue was an eloquent testimony to the irreformable nature of Soviet society.

The Soviet social formation can survive, but it cannot move forward. Given the lack of any internal impetus to develop, its future prospects depend heavily on external factors. Foreign technology and openings on the world market allow the bureaucracy to keep going. The chronic weakness and instability of the capitalist world order provide what has become a permanent 'breathing space' for the Soviet Union. For the Soviet leadership, the best thing that happened during the 1986 congress did not take place in Moscow at all, but 4000 miles away in the Philippines. Whether or not the overthrow of president Marcos proves a long-term setback to US influence in South-East Asia, it indicates the opportunities for the Soviet Union in the region, despite the Kremlin's opportunist support for Marcos in the past. Here, as in other third world trouble-spots, Soviet success depends on the weakening grip of the West, not on the dynamism of its own system.

The Soviet Union has come a long way under its Stalinist leadership. However, its transformation into a superpower owes little to any inherent drive within the Soviet social formation. The stagnation of Soviet society reveals its failure to evolve a developmental dynamic. From the point of view of historical materialism, it is necessary to conclude that the Soviet Union contains no progressive tendencies. Its very survival owes more to rivalries among the imperialist powers than to its own form of social organisation. The destiny of the Soviet Union will be largely decided by events in the international arena.

While Marxists recognise that the capitalist system is the main barrier to the progress of humanity, the Soviet regime plays a significant role in perpetuating the existing world order. The Soviet bureaucracy is committed to preserving the status quo both at home and abroad. The regressive character of the Soviet social formation is shown by its basic failure to raise the productivity of labour. The cultural and moral backwardness of Soviet society corresponds to its wider failures of social development. In this sphere, the Soviet system can claim no superiority over capitalism. Writing in the nineteenth century, the French socialist Fourier argued that any society could be judged by the way it treated women. Engels endorsed this view and Trotsky applied it to the Soviet Union in 1938:

'The position of *woman* is the most graphic and telling indicator for evaluating a social regime and state policy.'[2]

The inferior social standing of women and the strength of irrational prejudices about family life remain an indictment of Soviet society today. The Soviet bureaucracy promotes chauvinist attitudes towards women, just as it cultivates Great Russian nationalism and other reactionary sentiments. In such a society, progress is inconceivable without a social revolution.

Western apologists for the Kremlin have generally avoided the cultural backwardness of the Soviet Union. Most attempts to defend the Stalinist system select one or two features of Soviet society in an attempt to demonstrate its progressive character. For example, some argue that the Soviet Union is more progressive than capitalism because all industry is nationalised. But, as we have observed, there is nothing inherently progressive about nationalisation. By this criterion, Burma or Syria would be more progressive states than Nicaragua under the Sandinista government. Nationalisation brings progress only insofar as it assists the socialisation of production.

Others point to particular achievements such as the existence of full employment in the Soviet Union, which they contrast favourably with unemployment in the West. Mass unemployment is indeed a major indictment of the capitalist system and a compelling argument for social change. However, full employment does not in itself constitute progress. Workers in the slave camps of Nazi Germany and on the estates of feudal Europe were fully employed, but nobody would argue that these systems were superior to modern capitalism.

As a result of the declining influence of Stalinism in the West, left wingers are no longer so inhibited about criticising the Soviet bureaucracy as they once were. Indeed a critical attitude to the Soviet bureaucracy is commonplace among anti-establishment movements around the world. Whereas, in its early years, the Soviet Union was an inspiration to the oppressed, the bureaucratic regime which has supplanted the October Revolution now inspires more revulsion than respect. Reacting against the degeneration of the Russian Revolution, many on the left have concluded that revolutionary Marxism is not a realistic option.

For more than half a century the Soviet bureaucracy has appropriated the name of Marxism. Millions regard the official dogma of the Kremlin as bona fide Marxism-Leninism, and the Soviet Union as a society engaged in the transition to communism.

As a result, Marxism has been discredited and the perspective of revolutionary change has become widely regarded as unattractive and impracticable. The existence of the Soviet Union in its modern form provides Western apologists for the capitalist system with their strongest argument against Marxism.

*The Soviet Union demystified* is both an exposure of the Soviet social formation and a critique of Stalinism. It is also a restatement of the original project of Marxism. The current trend for dismissing the possibility of creating a communist society in response to the negative experience of the Soviet Union makes such a restatement essential. It has now become a virtual article of faith on the left that Marx's views on socialism are out of date. Hall notes that the 'Marxist conception of socialism' is 'grounded in an earlier grasp of the historic tendencies of capitalist development'. He takes this view to justify his recommendation that the left today should restrict its horizons to the quest for moderate reforms.[3]

Rustin is right when he states that 'few Marxists now favour a "command economy" of the Soviet kind, or a monopoly of economic powers in the hands of the state'.[4] He notes, with evident approval, that there has been 'increasing recognition, even in communist countries, of the value of market mechanisms, in measuring comparative economic performance and in assuring the efficient allocation of resources'. In this perspective, Marxism has been thrown out together with the Soviet Union. While many regard such views as anti-Stalinist, in fact they represent a concession to the outlook of the Soviet bureaucracy.

Gorbachev and his colleagues would heartily agree with Western radicals on the virtues of the market. Even the new-found faith in parliamentary democracy proclaimed by Hall, Rustin and others has its origins in the Stalinist tradition. The Soviet bureaucracy has insisted on monopolising power only in Eastern Europe; elsewhere it has endorsed pluralism and other forms of capitalist rule. From their advocacy of the Popular Front in the thirties to Eurocommunism in the seventies, the Stalinists have always been ready to come to terms with capitalist states and pro-capitalist political parties.

The fact that left-wing critics are still constrained by the Stalinist tradition shows that Marxists still have a score to settle with the Soviet bureaucracy. We must learn from the devastating experience of the Soviet Union, without making the slightest concession to those who regard it as an argument against revolutionary change. The Soviet Union should serve, not as an argument against revolutionary change, but as a grim reminder of the price to be paid for failing to carry through the revolutionary transformation of society. By demystifying the Soviet social formation, our aim is to retrieve the vision of Marx and Lenin and the vitality of October 1917, and to reassert their relevance for today.

## Notes

1   *Pravda,* 16 October 1985.
2   Trotsky (1970b), p10.
3   Hall, S. 'Realignment for what?' *Marxism Today,* December 1985.
4   Rustin (1985), p2.

# Selected Bibliography

*Periodicals*
Critique
Current Digest of Soviet Press (CDSP)
Ekonomicheskaya gazeta
Ekonomika i organizacia promyshlennogo proizvodsta (EKO)
International Press Correspondence
Izvestia
Kommunist
Planovoye khozyaistvo
Pravda
Problems of Communism
Problems of Economics
Sotsiologicheskiye issledovania
Soviet Studies
Voprosy ekonomiki
Voprosy filosofii
In Britain, the periodicals listed above can be found at the School of Slavonic and East European Studies, University of London, the British Museum and the Marx Memorial Library.

*Articles and books*
Adler-Karlsson, G. (1968) *Western economic warfare 1947-67: a case study in foreign economic policy*, Stockholm
Alden Smith, G. (1973) *Soviet foreign trade, organisation, operations and policy 1918-1971*, New York
Alperovitz, G. (1965) *Atomic diplomacy: Hiroshima and Potsdam*, New York
Amann, R. (1982) 'Industrial innovation in the Soviet Union: methodological perspectives and conclusions' in R. Amann and J. Cooper (eds.), *Industrial innovation in the Soviet Union*, London
Arnot, B. (1981) 'Soviet labour productivity and the failure of the Shchekino experiment', *Critique*, No 15
Aspaturian, V. V. (1980) 'Soviet global power and the correlation of forces', *Problems of Communism*, May-June
Bailes, K. E. (1978) *Technology and society under Lenin and Stalin*, Princeton
Barsov, A. A. (1969) *Balans stoimostnykh obmenov mezhdu gorodom i derevnei*, Moscow
Baykov, A. (1947) *The development of the Soviet economic system*, Cambridge
Bellis, P. (1979) *Marxism and the USSR: the theory of proletarian dictatorship and the Marxist analysis of Soviet society*, Brighton
Bergson, A. (1961) *The real national income of Soviet Russia since 1928*, Cambridge, Mass.
Bergson, A. and Levine, H. (eds.) (1983) *The Soviet economy: towards the year 2000*, London
Berliner, J. (1957) *Factory and manager in the USSR*, Cambridge, Mass.

Berliner, J. (1983) 'Planning and management' in A. Bergson and H. Levine (1983)
Binns, P. and Haynes, M. (1980) 'New theories of East European class societies', *International Socialism,* No 7
Bond, D. L. and Levine, H. (1982) 'The 11th five year plan 1981-85' in S. Bialer and T. Gustafson (eds.) *Russia at the crossroads: at the 26th congress of the CPSU,* London
Bottomore, T. (1983) 'Sociology' in D. McLellan (ed.) *Marx: the first hundred years,* Oxford
Brown, A. (1985) 'Gorbachev, new man in the Kremlin', *Problems of Communism,* May-June
Bukharin, N. (1980) *Notes of an economist,* Belfast
Bunce, V. and Echols, J. M. (1980) 'Soviet politics in the Brezhnev era: "Pluralism" or "Corporatism" ' in D. R. Kelley (ed.) *Soviet politics in the Brezhnev era,* New York
Bushnell, J. (1980) 'The "New Soviet man" turns pessimist' in S. F. Cohen, A. Rabinowitch and R. Sharet (eds.) *The Soviet Union since Stalin,* London
Campbell, R. W. (1983) 'The economy' in R. F. Byrnes *After Brezhnev,* London
Carlo, A. (1978) 'Structural causes of the Soviet co-existence policy' in E. Jahn (ed.) *Soviet foreign policy: its structural and economic conditions,* London
Carr, E. H. (1966) *The Bolshevik Revolution,* Vol 2, Harmondsworth
—(1969) *The interregnum 1923-24,* Harmondsworth
—(1970a) *Socialism in one country,* Vol 1, Harmondsworth
—(1970b) *Socialism in one country,* Vol 2, part 2, Harmondsworth
—(1978) *Foundations of a planned economy 1926-29,* Vol 3, part 1, London
Carr, E. H. and Davies, R. W. (1974) *Foundations of a planned economy 1926-29,* Vol 1, part 1, Harmondsworth
Carrère D'Encausse, H. (1981) *Stalin: order through terror,* London
Carrillo, S. (1977) *'Eurocommunism' and the state,* London
Castoriadis, C. (1980-81) 'Facing war', *Telos,* No 46, winter
Chapman, J. G. (1979) 'Recent trends in the Soviet industrial wage structure' in A. Kahan and B. A. Ruble *Industrial labour in the USSR,* New York
Chomsky, N., Steele, J. and Gittings, J. (1984) *Superpowers in collision,* Harmondsworth
Claudin, F. (1975) *The communist movement,* Harmondsworth
—(1979) 'Some reflections on the crisis of Marxism', *Socialist Review,* May-June
Cliff, T. (1970) *Russia: a Marxist analysis,* London
Cocks, P. (1983) 'Administrative reform and Soviet politics', *Soviet economy in the 1980s,* part 1
Cohen, S. F. (1973) *Bukharin and the Bolshevik Revolution,* New York
Communist International (1980) *Theses, resolutions and manifestos of the first four congresses of the Third International,* London
Congress of the United States (1983), Joint economic committee *Soviet economy in the 1980s: problems and prospects,* (in two parts), Washington (referred to as *Soviet economy in the 1980s)*
Cook, P. K. (1983) 'The political setting', *Soviet economy in the 1980s,* part 1
CPSU (1985) *The programme of the Communist Party of the Soviet Union (draft),* Moscow

Davies, R. W. (1980) *The industrialisation of Russia: the socialist offensive*, London
Davis, M. (1982) 'Nuclear imperialism and extended détente' in NLR (ed.) *Exterminism and Cold War*, London
Day, R. B. (1981) 'Leon Trotsky on the problems of the Smychka and forced collectivisation', *Critique*, No 13
Degras, J. (ed.) (1952) *Soviet documents on foreign policy 1925-32*, Vol 2, Oxford
—(1953) *Soviet Documents on foreign policy 1933-41*, Vol 3, Oxford
Delwitt, P. and Dewaele, J. M. (1984) 'The Stalinists of anti-communism', *Socialist Register*, London
Deutscher, I. (1970) 'The twentieth congress of the Soviet Communist Party' in F. Halliday (ed.) *Isaac Deutscher: Russia, China and the West 1953-66*, Harmondsworth
Dunmore, T. (1980) *The Stalinist command economy: the Soviet state apparatus and economic policy 1945-53*, London
—(1984) *Soviet politics 1945-53*, London
Dyker, D. A. (1983) *The process of investment in the Soviet Union*, Cambridge
—(1985) *The future of the Soviet economic planning system*, London
Ellman, M. (1975) 'Did the agricultural surplus provide the resources for the increase in investment in the USSR during the first five year plan?', *The Economic Journal*, December
Engels, F. (1968a) 'Ludwig Feuerbach and the end of classical German philosophy', *Marx Engels Selected Works (MESW)*, London
—(1968b) 'Socialism: utopian and scientific', *MESW*
—(1975) *Anti-Dühring*, London
Fainsod, M. (1958) *Smolensk under Soviet rule*, London
—(1961) *How Russia is ruled*, Cambridge, Mass.
Fal'tsman, V. and Kornev, A. (1984) 'Rezervy snizheniia kapitaloemkosti mashchnostei promyshlennosti', *Voprosy ekonomiki*, No 6
Farl, E. (1974) 'Is the USSR an imperialist country?', *International*, Vol 2, No 3
Feshbach, M. (1979) 'The structure and composition of the industrial labour force' in A. Kahan and B. A. Ruble *Industrial labour in the USSR*, New York
Fil'ev, V. (1983) 'Sootnoshenie rosta proizvoditel nosti truda i srednei zarabotnoi platy', *Voprosy ekonomiki*, No 12
Fitzpatrick, S. (1979) *Education and social mobility in the Soviet Union 1921-34*, Cambridge
Fleming, D. F. (1961) *The Cold War and its origins, 1917-60*, Vol 1, Garden City
Gelman, H. (1985) 'Rise and fall of detente', *Problems of Communism*, March-April
Gidwitz, B. (1982) 'Labour unrest in the Soviet Union', *Problems of Communism*, November-December
Glucksmann, A. (1983) *La force de vertige*, Paris
Goodman, A. and Schleifer, G. (1983) 'The Soviet labour market in the 1980s', *Soviet economy in the 1980s*, part 2
Gordon, A. and Nazimova, A. K. (1980) 'The productive potential of the Soviet working class: tendencies of development' reprinted from *Voprosy filosofii*, No 11 in *Soviet sociology*, Vol 19, part 4, 1981

Granick, D. (1954) *Management of the industrial firm in the USSR,* Cambridge
—(1967) *Soviet metal-fabricating and economic development,* Madison
—(1983) 'Institutional innovation and economic management: the Soviet incentive system, 1921 to the present' in G. Guroff and F. V. Carstensen (eds.) *Entrepreneurship in Imperial Russia and the Soviet Union,* Princeton
Grossman, G. (1983) 'The party as manager and entrepreneur' in G. Guroff and F. V. Carstensen (eds.) *Entrepreneurship in Imperial Russia and the Soviet Union,* Princeton
Grossman, H. (1943) 'The evolutionist revolt against classical economics', *The Journal of Political Economy,* Vol 51, Nos 5 & 6
—(1948) 'W. Playfair, the earliest theorist of capitalist development', *The Economic History Review*
—(1967) *Das Akkumulations- und Zusammenbruchsgesetz des Kapitals,* Frankfurt
Halliday, J. (1984) 'Anti-communism and the Korean War', *Socialist Register,* London
Harrison, M. (1985) *Soviet planning in peace and war 1938-45,* Cambridge
Haslam, J. (1983) *Soviet foreign policy 1930-53: the impact of the depression,* London
Hedlund, S. (1984) *Crisis in Soviet agriculture,* London
Hosking, F. (1985) *A history of the Soviet Union,* London
Hough, J. F. (1979) *The Soviet prefects,* Harvard
—(1983) 'Pluralism, corporatism and the Soviet Union' in S. Solomon (ed.) *Pluralism in the Soviet Union,* London
Hutchings, R. (1984) *The structural origins of Soviet industrial expansion,* London
—(1982) *Soviet economic development,* Oxford
Ilyenkov, E. V. (1982) *The dialectics of the abstract and the concrete in Marx's Capital,* Moscow
Jasny, N. (1961) *Soviet industrialisation 1928-52,* Chicago
Joffe, J. (1981) 'European-American relations: the enduring crisis', *Foreign Affairs,* spring
Karcz, J. F. (1971) 'From Stalin to Brezhnev: Soviet agricultural policy in historical perspective' in J. R. Miller (ed.) *The Soviet rural community,* Urbana
Kelley, D. R. (1980) 'The Communist Party' in D. R. Kelley (ed.) *Soviet politics in the Brezhnev era,* New York
Kennan, G. (1947) 'The sources of Soviet conduct', *Foreign Affairs,* July
Kheiman, S. A. (1984) 'The development of machine building: organisational and structural factors', *EKO,* No 6, translated in *Problems of Economics,* May 1985
Kolko, G. (1970) *The politics of war: the world and United States foreign policy, 1943-1945,* New York
Kotliar, A. (1984) 'The job placement system in the USSR', translated in *Problems of Economics,* December
Kronrod, I. (1984) 'Sovershenstvovanie mekhanizma khoziaistvovaniia i zakon stoimosti', *Voprosy ekonomiki,* No 5, translated in *Problems of Economics,* February 1985
Kushnirsky, F. I. (1982) *Soviet economic planning 1965-80,* Boulder

Kux, E. (1984) 'Contradictions in Soviet socialism', *Problems of Communism*, November-December
Kuznets, S. (1963) 'A comparative appraisal' in A. Bergson and S. Kuznets *Economic trends in the Soviet Union*, Cambridge, Mass.
Lane, D. (1985a) *Soviet economy and society*, Oxford
—(1985b) *State and politics in the USSR*, Oxford
Lane, D. and O'Dell, F. (1981) *The Soviet industrial worker*, Oxford
Lapidus, G. W. (1983) 'Social trends' in R. F. Byrnes (ed.) *After Brezhnev*, London
Leggett, R. (1983) 'Soviet investment policy in the 11th five year plan', *Soviet economy in the 1980s*, part 1
Lenin, V. I. (1962-80) *Collected Works (CW)*, Vols 1-45, Moscow
—(1972) *Marxism on the state*, Moscow
Lewin, M. (1962) 'The disappearance of planning in the state', *Slavic Review*, Vol 21, No 2
—(1973) *Political undercurrents in Soviet economic debates*, London
—(1978) 'Society, state and ideology during the first five year plan' in S. Fitzpatrick (ed.) *Cultural revolution in Russia 1928-31*, Bloomington
—(1985) *The making of the Soviet system*, London
Magyar, L. (1934) 'War, fascism and the policy of the Soviet Union', *International Press Correspondence*, Vol 14, No 8
Malish, A. F. (1983) 'The food programme: a new policy or more rhetoric?', *Soviet economy in the 1980s*, part 2
Malle, S. (1985) *The economic organisation of War Communism, 1918-21*, Cambridge
Mandel, E. (1974) 'Ten theses on the social and economic laws governing the society transitional between capitalism and socialism', *Critique*, No 3
—(1977) 'The Soviet economy today', *International Socialist Review*, June
—(1984) 'What is the bureaucracy?' in T. Ali (ed.) *The Stalinist legacy*, Harmondsworth
Marshall, K. (1983) *Real freedom: women's liberation and socialism*, London
Marx, K. (1968) 'Critique of the Gotha Programme', *Marx Engels Selected Works*
—(1970) *A contribution to the critique of political economy*, Moscow
—(1971) *Capital*, Vol 3, Moscow
—(1973) *Grundrisse*, Harmondsworth
—(1974) *Capital*, Vol 1, Moscow
—(1976a) 'The German ideology', *Marx Engels Collected Works (MECW)*, Vol 5, Moscow
—(1976b) 'Poverty of philosophy', *MECW*, Vol 6, Moscow
Marx, K. and Engels, F. (1975) *Marx Engels Selected Correspondence*, Moscow
—(1983) 'Correspondence 1852-55', *MECW*, Vol 39, Moscow
McAuley, A. (1981) *Women's work and wages in the Soviet Union*, London
Medvedev, R. and Medvedev, Z. (1982) 'The USSR and the arms race' in NLR (ed.) *Exterminism and Cold War*, London
Miller, J. (1964) 'Soviet planners in 1936-39' in J. Degras and A. Nove (eds.) *Soviet planning: essays in honour of Naum Jasny*, Oxford
Molotov, V. (1939) 'Third five year plan for the economic development of the USSR' in *The land of socialism today and tomorrow: reports and speeches of the eighteenth congress of the Communist Party of the Soviet Union (B)*, Moscow

Narkiewicz (1970) *The making of the Soviet state apparatus*, Manchester
Nove, A. (1982) *An economic history of the USSR*, London
Noyee, J. L. and Donaldson, R. H. (1984) *Soviet foreign policy since World War II*, Oxford
Poulantzas, N. (1973) *Political power and social classes*, London
Pravda, A. (1982) 'Is there a Soviet working class?', *Problems of Communism*, November-December
Preobrazhensky, E. (1967) *The new economics*, Oxford
Rakovsky, C. (1980) *Selected writings on opposition in the USSR 1923-36*, London
—(1981) 'The five year plan in crisis', translated in *Critique*, No 13
Rand Corporation (1983) *The costs of the Soviet empire*, Santa Monica
Richards, F. (1979) 'Revisionism, imperialism and the state: the method of *Capital* and the dogma of state monopoly capitalism', *Revolutionary Communist Papers*, No 4
Rigby, T. H. (1968) *Communist Party membership in the USSR, 1917-67*, Princeton
—(1979) *Lenin's government: Sovnarkom 1917-22*, Cambridge
Rosdolsky, R. (1977) *The making of Marx's* Capital, London
Rousset, D. (1982) *Critical history of the USSR*, London
Rubin, I. I. (1972) *Essays on Marx's theory of value*, Detroit
Rumer, B. (1981) 'The "second" agriculture in the USSR', *Soviet Studies*, No 4
—(1984) 'Structural imbalance in the Soviet economy', *Problems of Communism*, July-August
Rustin, M. (1985) *For a pluralist socialism*, London
Rutland, P. (1984) 'The Shchekino method and the struggle to raise labour productivity in Soviet industry', *Soviet Studies*, Vol 36, No 3
Schroeder, G. (1972) 'The "reform" of the supply system in Soviet industry', *Soviet Studies*, Vol 24, No 1
—(1983a) 'Soviet economic "reform" decrees: more steps on the treadmill', *Soviet economy in the 1980s*, part 1
—(1983b) 'Soviet living standards: achievements and prospects', *Soviet economy in the 1980s*, part 2
—(1983c) 'Consumption' in A. Bergson and H. Levine (1983)
Schwartz, H. (1965) *The Soviet economy since Stalin*, London
Schwarz, M. (1953) *Labour in the Soviet Union*, London
Shoup, L. H. and Minter, W. (1977) *Imperial brain trust: the council on foreign relations and United States foreign policy*, New York and London
Sirianni, C. (1982) *Workers control and socialist democracy: the Soviet experience*, London
Stalin, J. (1940) *Leninism*, London
—(1947) *Problems of Leninism*, Moscow
—(1950) *War speeches: order of the day and answers to foreign correspondents during the great patriotic war*, London
—(1968) 'Political report of the central committee to the fifteenth party congress' in X. J. Eudin and R. M. Slusser (eds.) *Soviet foreign policy in 1928-34: documents and materials*, Vol 1, Pennsylvania
—(1972) *Economic problems of socialism in the USSR*, Peking
Steele, J. (1983) *World power*, London

Strode, R. V. and Gray, C. S. (1981) 'The imperial dimension of Soviet military power', *Problems of Communism*, November-December
Sutton, A. C. (1971) *Western technology and Soviet economic development*, Vol 2, Stanford
—(1973) *Western technology and Soviet economic development*, Vol 3, Stanford
Ticktin, H. H. (1973) 'Towards a political economy of the USSR', *Critique*, No 1
—(1978a) 'The class structure of the USSR and the elite', *Critique*, No 9
—(1978b) 'The relation between détente and Soviet economic reforms' in E. Jahn (ed.) *Soviet foreign policy: its structural and economic conditions*, London
Trotsky, L. (1970a) *In defence of Marxism*, New York
—(1970b) *Women and the family*, New York
—(1971a) *Writings of Leon Trotsky 1934-35*, New York
—(1971b) *The Stalin school of falsification*, New York
—(1972a) *Revolution betrayed*, New York
—(1972b) *Writings of Leon Trotsky 1932-33*, New York
—(1972c) *Writings of Leon Trotsky 1933-34*, New York
—(1973) *Writings of Leon Trotsky 1930-31*, New York
—(1975a) *Documents of the 1923 Opposition*, London
—(1975b) *Writings of Leon Trotsky 1929*, New York
—(1975c) *Writings of Leon Trotsky 1930*, New York
—(1976) *Writings of Leon Trotsky 1937-38*, New York
—(1979a) *The challenge of the Left Opposition 1923-25*, New York
—(1979b) *Writings of Leon Trotsky Supplement 1934-40*, New York
—(1980) *The challenge of the Left Opposition 1926-27*, New York
—(1981) *The challenge of the Left Opposition 1928-29*, New York
Ulam, A. B. (1983) 'The world outside' in R. F. Byrnes (ed.) *After Brezhnev*, London
Voslensky, M. (1984) *Nomenklatura: anatomy of the Soviet ruling class*, London
Weitzman, M. L. (1983) 'Industrial production' in A. Bergson and H. Levine (eds.) *The Soviet economy: towards the year 2000*, London
Werth, A. (1961) *The Khrushchev phase*, London
Wright, E. O. (1978) *Class, crisis and the state*, London
Yergin, D. (1978) 'Shattered peace: the origins of the Cold War and the national security state' in C. S. Maier *The origins of the Cold War and contemporary Europe*, New York
Zaslavskaya, T. (1984) 'The Novosibirsk Report', *Survey*, Vol 28, No 1
Zaslavsky, V. (1982) *The neo-Stalinist state: class, ethnicity and consensus in Soviet society*, Brighton
Zeebroek, X. (1984) 'Soviet expansionism and expansive anti-Sovietism', *Socialist Register*, London
Zelený, J. (1980) *The logic of Marx*, Oxford

# Index

Afghanistan 213, 234, 238-40, 243
Aganbegyan A. 99-100, 190
agriculture
   collectivisation 31, 39-41, 43, 48, 97, 173
      Trotsky on 53
   *kulaks* 15, 27-31, 33
      liquidation of 31, 35, 39
   peasantry 14-5, 28-9, 32, 41, 95, 180
      Lenin on 94
   productivity 31, 37*n9*, 65, 154-8
      private plots 132
      ruralisation of towns 200
Allende, S. 236
Andropov,Y. 1, 2, 109, 121, 123, 125-6, 133, 138, 183, 187-8
anti-American nationalism 243-4
anti-semitism 205
anti-Soviet prejudice 1-2, 7, 68-9, 211-3, 251-2
   Afghanistan 238
   Cold War 226-30, 239-42, 244-6
apparatus 17-24, 27, 31-3, 36
   appointment system, *see nomenklatura*
   internal disputes 24
   on peasantry 29-30, 39
   *see also* bureaucracy
arms race 119, 175, 222, 229-31, 239, 245
   Cruise missiles and 240
   Soviet navy and 233, 241-2
   Star Wars and 241, 245
atomisation
   in pre-capitalist society 87
   in Soviet Union 134, 199-202, 204-5
   under capitalism 88
autarchy 112-3, 132-3
   in enterprises 105-6, 116-7, 153
   in regional ministries 105, 132, 142, 154
   'localism' 143
barter 106, 116
black market 116, 157, 201, 207
Bolshevik Party 7, 16-7, 27, 37*n12*, 53-4
   appointment system 18-9, 184*n28*
   fusion with state 17-8, 20, 31
   material privileges for members of 23
   on NEP 93-4
   party for private peasant enterprise 32
Brezhnev, L. 69, 75, 122, 132, 146, 231
Bukharin, N. 29, 95-6

bureaucracy
   central 40, 47, 65-6, 117, 140
      adaptation to autarchy 133, 152
      attempts to prevent disintegration 118, 132
      lack of control over economy 42, 47, 49-50, 59, 101-3, 113, 124-6, 143
   ruling stratum 22, 31-2, 44, 48, 71-4
      appointment system *see nomenklatura*
      attitude to market 149
      in agriculture 156-8
      barriers to transformation into a class 163, 172-7, 179
      conflict within 47, 70, 177
      conservatism of 76, 110, 147
      consumption of 111-2, 177
      control over working class 160-1, 178, 180-3, 187-90, 196-9, 201-7
      ideology of 137, 184*n3*, 203-5
      on the family 202-3
      left turn of 1929 35-6, 39, 96
      nature of 179
      preservation of foreign stability 211
      support for pluralism 252
      terror 42-3, 97
      Trotsky on 55-6, 59
      social base of 17-8, 31-2, 36, 43-5
      changes in thirties 52
      in regions 144
      turnover of 75, 178
Carter, J. 240
centralisation
   decentralisation 142-3, 146
   need for more 143-4
   of material allocations 49-51, 99-100, 110, 112, 116-8, 148
Chernenko, K. 189
China 213, 224, 226, 230, 232, 234, 239-40
Churchill, WS. 224-5
class, Marxist theory of 166-72
class structure of Soviet Union 172-80
Cliff, T. 92, 168, 172, 235-6
Cold War
   new 68, 239-42, 244-6
   old 221, 226-8, 230, 245
collectivisation *see* agriculture
Cominform 227
communism
   Soviet view 1-2, 138-9
   war communism, 12
   Western view 7, 9, 68-9, 81-4
Communist International 224
Communist Party of Soviet Union (CPSU)
   *see* Soviet Communist Party

consumer goods and services 64-5, 72, 83-4, 97, 112, 118, 155, 157, 194-6, 199-201, 206
   bureaucrats and 111-2, 177
   defective goods 128-30, 200-1
      conversion into use-values 130, 200-1
   defence sector and 132
   elimination of demand 63, 180
   starved of investment 64-5
co-operation 124, 133-4
corruption 111, 177-8
Cuba 230, 233-4, 236, 241, 243
defence sector 42, 48, 64, 100, 118, 128, 143, 192-3, 222, 231-2, 239
   consumer goods and 132
destalinisation 63, 68, 72-7
détente 222, 231, 239-40, 242
Deutscher, I. 73
developmental dynamic 172-5, 250
   see also Soviet social formation
dictatorship of the proletariat 7, 9-10, 12, 24n9, 27, 58
   Bolshevik 14-7, 27
   Lenin on 15-6
   Trotsky on 53
dissidents 68, 197
division of labour
   capitalist 94, 101, 124
      international 214
   national/technical 67, 102-3, 105-6, 111, 114, 116, 124, 131, 133, 154, 200
   social 86-7, 102, 114, 131, 133-4, 143, 154, 204
   under socialism 216
Eastern Europe 197-8, 213, 218, 224, 228, 232-4, 237-8, 252
   Albania 233
   Bulgaria 237
   Czechoslovakia 147, 234
   East Germany 237
   Hungary 3, 156, 207, 226, 234
   Poland 59, 195, 224-5, 232, 237
   Rumania 232
   Yugoslavia 232-3
economic experiments 113, 117, 141, 146, 153, 159-60, 173, 192
economic growth 64-5, 83, 120, 174
   crisis
      impasse 141
      symptoms of 122
      threat to social stability 206
   NEP 27-8, 40
economic reform see economic experiments, and reforms

economic regulation
   automatic 114, 152
   conscious 15, 58, 90-1, 101, 113, 143
   mechanism 69, 79, 97, 100, 137, 141
   Soviet 11-2, 93-8, 101, 163
      absence in 100-6, 119, 180
      elimination of 173
      failure of 109, 161
      improvisation 65
efficiency 104, 144
   capitalist, 89
   Soviet 63-5, 67, 98-9, 180
Engels, F. 9, 250
   on class 166, 169
   on materialist analysis 81
   on nationalised property relations 13
   on socialism 92
   on state 10-1
enterprises 65, 105, 110-2, 116-7, 126-8, 131, 142, 146, 206
   closed 192-3, 201
   co-operation 124
   empire-building 103
   hoarding 111-2, 150, 159
   lack of initiative 117-8
   production associations 152-3
   productivity of 144-51
   see also factory directors
Eurocommunism 9, 252
extensive growth 67, 109
factory directors 43, 45, 49, 61n18, 71, 111, 113, 116, 124, 126, 140, 148-51
   attitude towards new technology 117, 152
   initiative punished 134
   labour discipline 191, 197
   see also enterprises
family 187, 200, 202-3, 250-1
fascism 223
five year plan
   agriculture and 48
   first 39-43, 97, 104, 111-2
   fourth 64, 72, 119
   growth rates of 48
foreign policy 211-42, 245-7
   Soviet
      a world power 64, 231, 250
      détente 222, 231, 239-40, 242
      economic weakness undermines external influence 232
      foreign parties and 217
      objectives 218
      playing off imperialist rivals 217-8, 223, 228, 245-6
      response to Cold War 227-9
      Soviet 'expansionism' and 234-9

the West and 30, 64, 119, 163, 211-42, 245-7
  influence on Soviet policy 222-5, 231, 245
  Soviet influence due to Western weakness 234, 250
  third world and 213, 229-34, 236, 239-41
  Soviet loss of influence in 233-4
foreign trade 194, 214, 228, 230-1
  monopoly of 32, 51, 215-7
  planning and 61n34
  with Eastern Europe 237
  with third world 236-7
  US sanctions on 228, 243-4, 246
Fourier, C. 250
Germany
  1923 Revolution 27
  collapse of Communist Party 54, 62n48
  partition of 227
  Stalin-Hitler pact 223
  West German rivalry 243
Gorbachev, M. 76, 110, 129, 139-40, 153-4, 160, 189, 194, 231, 246, 249-50, 252
Grossman, H. 4, 84, 88, 167
gross value of output (val) 144, 155
growth rates 41-2, 48, 50-2, 58, 64-5, 119
  compared to West 52, 64
  decline in 67, 83, 122
health and safety 193
historical materialism 2-3, 7, 81, 84-6, 166, 168, 250
historical specificity 81-3, 234-5
hoarding 125-6
  enterprises and 111-2, 150, 158
  'reserves' 127
  labour 183, 191
  peasants' grain 95
housing 133, 194
Hungary see Eastern Europe
ideology 1-2, 32, 45, 76, 203-5
  cult of the individual 74
  foreign policy 212
  Marxism-Leninism 203, '249, 251
  non-antagonistic contradictions 138, 165
  pluralism'252
  traditional petit-bourgeois 204-5
Ilyenkov, EV. 4
imperialism 16
  American 64, 211-2, 224-31, 234, 239-46
    blockade on Soviet trade 228, 243-4, 246
    boycott of Moscow Olympics 243
    détente 231, 242
    Marshall Plan 226-7
  new Cold War 239-46
  Second World War 64
  weakness of 242-3
  British 30, 97, 99, 224-5, 244
  French 220
  Japanese 235, 243, 248n48
  theories of 234-9
    Lenin's 214-6, 219-22, 234-5
    Stalinist 221-2
incentives 43, 72, 97, 100, 105, 118, 140, 145-9, 160, 181, 193, 206
  agricultural 157
  co-operation and 133-4
  prevention of 118
industrialisation 28-30, 39-44, 48-52, 61n10, 64-5, 97-100, 102, 124, 173, 180
  debate on 29
  influence of West 222
  limited potential of 67
  Trotsky on 53, 56
industrial production 42, 48, 63-4
  inability to equip agrarian sector 156-7
  see also growth rates
intelligentsia 31, 39, 74, 176, 192, 195
  anti-semitism 205
  anti-working class 106, 183, 197
  new 43-45, 47
intensive growth 67-8, 109, 123, 152
intervention, danger of imperialist 16, 63, 97, 214-7, 222
investment
  control of 50-1, 63-6, 214
    consumption goods 72
    no drive to invest abroad 236
    over-investment 126
    productivity 123, 144
    diminishing returns on 67, 83, 121, 140-1, 152, 249
  in agriculture 154-6
  growth rate of 42, 51, 65, 115-6
  mobilisation of 40-1, 63, 121
KGB see secret police
Khrushchev, N. 1, 132, 140, 142-4, 146, 155, 249
  destalinisation and 63, 72-5
  foreign policy under 220, 230
Kissinger, H. 212
Kosygin, A. 120, 146
  see also reforms
kulaks, see agriculture
labour
  discipline 43, 74, 159-60, 180-1, 187-91, 193, 206
  limited social character of
    in agriculture 154
    in Soviet Union 102, 105-6, 114, 116,

126, 130-1, 133, 135, 201
  pre-capitalist society 87
  under capitalism 89-90
  manual 104, 110, 158, 183, 190-4
  market in 106, 160, 206
  mobility 43, 99, 192, 198, 200
  shortage 51, 158-60, 181-3, 187, 190, 198, 202, 205-7
  socialisation of 13, 86-8, 94, 102, 104, 106, 110, 123, 133-4, 173, 200
  in a planned economy 90
  *see also* workforce, *and* working class structure
labour-time, 87-91, 125, 161,163
  disposable 91
  distribution of 11-2, 40, 48, 50-1, 79, 102-4, 107, 112-3, 115, 141
  under capitalism 88, 148
  under socialism 176
  inefficient allocation of 63, 98-9
  no tendency to economise 125-6
  reduction of 86
  socially necessary 89
law of primitive socialist accumulation 29
law of value 29, 83, 88-91, 148
  destruction 101-2
  international 214-5
  rehabilitation 113-4
  struggle against 95-8
League of Nations 219-20
Left Opposition 19, 23, 27, 30, 33-6, 54
  industrialisation debate 29
  joint platform 22
  tied to state apparatus 24, 32-3
Lenin, VI.
  on monopoly of foreign trade 215-6
  on imperialism 214-6, 219-22, 235
  on internationalism 14
  on party renewal 21-2, 27
  on peasantry 14, 25*n*34
  on planning 11-3, 15, 25*n*27
  on problems of transition 5, 11-7, 25*n*23, 25*n*26, 28, 94
Lenin levy 23, 27
Litvinov, M. 219-20
MacArthur, D. 229
MacNamara, R. 230
Malenkov, G. 72, 75, 112, 139-40, 142, 221
Mandel, E. 81-3, 110-2, 168, 172, 177
market
  capitalist 11, 14, 83-4, 87-9, 101, 104, 124, 148, 173, 175, 252
    discipline of 102, 177
    elimination of 90-9, 214
    relation to classes 170
    world 215, 237, 243, 250

Soviet 14, 28-30, 39-40, 91, 94, 96-7, 173
  agrarian 156
  black market 116, 157, 201
  destruction of 50-2, 97-8
  market enthusiasts 114, 145, 252
  restoration of 113-4, 137, 147-8, 152, 154, 160-1, 206
Marshall Plan 226-7
Marx, K. 125
  *Capital* 83
  on capitalism 8
  on class 166-8, 170-1
  on communism 9, 90-1, 111, 125
  out of date on 252
  on dictatorship of proletariat 10
  on historical method 81-2, 174
  on property relations 58, 176, 184*n*27
Marxism
  discredited by Soviet bureaucracy 2, 7, 204, 251-2
  theory of class struggle 166-8
  theory of historical materialism 2-3, 81, 84-6, 166, 168, 250
  theory of transition 5, 9, 82, 125
Medvedev, R. & Z. 228, 241
military sector *see* defence sector
mobilisation of investment resources *see* investment
Molotov, V. 45, 72, 75
monopoly of foreign trade *see* foreign trade
nationalisation 11-4, 25*n*20, 57-8, 251
  denationalisation of land 28, 37*n1*
nationalised industries 15
national question 3
  nationalism 205, 251
Nato 230, 244-6
nature 85-6
  nature-imposed necessity 85-7, 101, 124
natural resources 51, 63, 67, 99, 141
  scarcity of 121
*nepmen* 14, 27, 31, 33, 36, 39, 52
New Economic Policy (NEP) 14-5, 18, 27-33, 40, 93, 95, 156
  end of 35
  Lenin on 28, 94
new technology *see* technology
*nomenklatura* 176-7, 179, 184*n28*, 194
Normed Net Output (NNO) 150-2
peaceful co-existence 217-8, 221-2
peasantry *see* agriculture
planning
  Soviet 13-5, 59, 65-6, 96-107, 112, 144-5, 174
  agriculture 48

foreign trade 61*n34*
planned anarchy 98
transitional society 11-2, 90-1, 104
Poland *see* Eastern Europe
population growth 158, 182, 190
Preobrazhensky, E. 22, 25*n23*, 92-4, 96, 112, 148-9, 215
    on industrialisation debate 29
priority allocation 66, 100-4, 106, 112-4, 118, 128, 153, 249
prison camps 68
    economic role 70
private plots 132, 156, 158, 199-200, 207
production associations 152-3
productivity of labour 9, 50, 58, 86-7, 118, 123, 125
    compared with West 58, 175, 214
    Soviet 51, 58, 65, 104, 120, 249-50
        tendency to stagnate 67, 141, 150-1, 158, 160-1, 190
profit
    capitalist category 51, 83, 98, 148-9
        law of tendency of rate of profit to fall 83, 235
    as an indicator 145-6, 149
property relations
    bourgeois/private 13
    nationalised 13, 55-9, 176, 251
purges 21, 39, 42-3, 47-8, 70-1, 178
quality of production 49, 51, 59, 84, 104, 127-31, 149, 181
racism 3
Rakovsky, C. 22, 36, 41, 61*n9*
Reagan, R. 211, 241
reconstruction
    after First World War 214
    after Second World War 64
redundancy 159
reforms 72-3, 137-62, 249-50
    1979 decree 141, 150
    agrarian 157-8
    Kosygin 120, 141, 146-8, 150
    Shchekino 159-60
    territorial reorganisation 132, 140, 143
    *see also* economic experiments
regions 65, 142
    localism 143
regulation *see* economic regulation
religion 205
repair sector 130-1, 142, 183, 190, 201, 207
restoration, capitalist 14, 29, 157, 173
Revolution, October 1917 1, 7, 11, 251, 253
    causes of its degeneration 13-24, 27-8, 34, 52, 60
Right Opposition 33
Rosdolsky, R. 4

Rubin, I. 4, 88-9
Russian Revolution *see* Revolution
Rykov, A. 35, 219
secret police 40, 71, 74-5, 176, 178
    as a unit of economic administration 70
Shchekino experiment 159-60
shock workers *see* Stakhanovites
shortages 83, 118, 127, 134, 236
    consumer goods 194, 196, 200
    food 96
    industrial goods 95
    inputs 65
    labour shortages *see* labour
showtrials 47-8, 70
    Shakhty 35, 53
social laws 84-6, 137
    forces of spontaneity *see* spontaneity
    fragmentation *see* tendency towards
    limited social character of labour *see* labour
socialism
    Marxism on 2, 7, 91, 139
    Soviet bureaucracy on 1-2, 91, 138-9, 217
    Western view 1-2, 9, 13, 81-4
socialism in one country 32, 34, 94-5, 214-5
social mobility 32, 37*n12,* 43-5, 47-8, 71, 75, 181, 194-5
social power
    capital as 170-1, 237
    of bureaucrats 36, 70, 168, 172
    of feudal lords 170
    of *kulaks* 28
social services 194, 206-7
social stability 73, 155, 194, 196, 205
Soviet Communist Party 43-5, 72, 178
    conference
        thirteenth 23
        fifteenth 34
    congress
        tenth 14
        eleventh 20
        twelfth 22
        thirteenth 19
        fifteenth 30
        eighteenth 45
        twentieth 72, 220
        twenty-second 1
        twenty-fifth 239
        twenty-seventh 249
    programme
        1961 2
        1985 (draft) 2, 165, 202, 221-2, 249
Soviet social formation
    accidental origin of 173-4
    cultural backwardness 250-1

durability 63-4, 73
emergence of 3, 5, 69, 76, 99, 180
labour in 104, 112
lack of dynamic of 75-6, 79, 118-9, 137, 172-5, 211, 218, 236, 250
    survival dependent on West 245-6, 250
limits of 100, 107, 133, 139
    historically bankrupt 200
    historically transient 139
reproduction of 79, 110
Soviet war economy 12, 63-4
Soviet working class 178-80, 187-209
    *see also* working class
soviets 16, 19-20
space sector 100
    *see also* Star Wars
specialists *see* Tsarist regime
spontaneity 91, 101-6, 110-7, 141, 143, 154, 174-5
bureaucracy unable to abolish 116, 148
recreating the form of a market 113
Sputnik 65
Stakhanovites 45
Stalin, J. 24, 27, 35, 37*n1*, 140
and purges 47-8
and theory of socialism in one country 32, 94
and Trotsky 22-3
control over society 69-71
foreign policy 215-226
head of administration 19
on imperialism 215-6, 220-3
on industrialisation and collectivisation 39, 49, 93, 95, 97, 110
on law of value 91
on monopoly of foreign trade 215-7
on new intelligentsia 44
Stalinism, theories of 1-2, 7, 68-9, 168-9
Western apologists for 251-2
Star Wars 241, 245
state capitalism 14, 25*n26*, 83
success indicators 102, 140, 150
    NNO 150-2
    profit 145, 147, 149
    sales revenues 149
super ministries 154
surplus
    mobilisation 97, 115
    problem of realisation 116-7, 124
targets, production 42, 48-9, 59, 65, 99, 127-8, 147-9, 151
    enterprises and 117, 124
    irrelevance of 114-5, 144-5
    Soviet obsession with 125
    tendency to overfulfil 115

technology
    foreign 41-2, 51, 61*n9*, 61*n10*, 61*n35*, 66-7, 118-9, 141, 174, 218, 239, 245-6, 250
    US sanctions on 228-9
    problems of assimilation 49, 66, 100, 182
    factory directors and 117, 150, 152
tendency
    towards atomisation of economic and social life 114, 134-5, 204
    towards autarchy 103, 105-6, 124, 132-3, 142, 148, 178, 183
    in agriculture 155
    towards dissolution of the division of labour 102-3, 111, 114, 131-3
    towards fragmentation 47, 118, 124-7, 134, 143, 148, 174, 177
    in Eastern bloc 232
terror 42-3, 47, 51, 70-3, 97, 118, 180-1
after destalinisation 74
against working class 197-8, 207
amnesties 71-2
drawbacks to 49, 207
Western view of 68-9
third period 219
    *see also* bureaucracy, 1929 left turn
third world 171, 236-7, 239
    *see also* foreign policy
Ticktin, H. 4, 130, 184*n14*
totalitarianism 1, 7, 68
trade unions 32, 198
transition to communism 5, 9, 13-4, 17, 82, 90, 95, 101, 111, 113, 175, 251-2
transitional societies 5, 9, 11-2, 24*n9*, 25*n23*, 57-8, 81-2
Trotsky 5, 22, 24, 34, 92, 112
critique of Soviet bureaucracy 23-4, 34-6, 52-60, 62*n62*
expulsion and exile 34, 37*n7*
on appointment system 19
on bureaucracy as 'centrists' 35-6, 55-6
on industrialisation 53, 95
on nationalised property relations 56-9
on Soviet Union and imperialism 60
on Stalin 35
on women 250-1
Truman, H. 226
Tsarist regime 20-1
specialists 19-20, 31, 33, 39, 43-4
alliance with bureaucracy 27
unemployment 28, 159, 195, 206, 251
val *see* gross value of output
value
    exchange value 83
    non-use values 118, 128-30

conversion into use values 130, 200, 202
theory of 50, 88
use value 50, 83-5, 88, 104-5, 129-30, 157
wage labour 28
wage levels 41-4, 73, 159-60, 181, 190-5
agrarian 157
irrelevance of money 196
women's 193
war communism 12
wars
civil war 16, 19
Korean War 229
Second World War 42, 48, 60
economic effects of German occupation 63-4
redivision after 223-6, 240
Star Wars 241, 245
Warsaw Pact 232
waste 106, 125, 128, 130, 145
of labour time 99, 118, 127, 134, 142
of raw materials 110, 126-7
Western technology *see* technology
women 3
as part of workforce 160, 189, 193
domestic work and 196, 202
family and 202-3, 250-1
work discipline *see* labour discipline
workforce 50, 64, 158, 160, 189-90
*see also* labour *and* working class structure
worker aristocrats 32, 36, 44-5
workers' control 11-2, 15
under NEP 14
workers' democracy 16, 50, 123-4, 144, 173, 175
workers' management 11-3, 58, 175
workers' state 11
deformed 57
working class
action 15, 27, 37n12
hostility to redundancies 159
moonlighting 201
response to raised norms 200
attitude to state 204, 206
culture 19, 195
enslavement 43, 180
individualism 134, 199-202, 204-5
alcoholism 189, 199, 202-3
living standards 28, 41, 51, 65, 72-3, 99, 194-6, 199
queuing 134, 191, 196
passivity 27, 118, 196-9, 205
structure 40-2, 50
decimation due to civil war 16

differentiation into bureaucracy 36
skilled/unskilled division 191-3
*see also* labour *and* workforce
Yalta 224
Zaslavskaya, T. 106-7, 109, 113-4, 123, 134, 183, 187-8, 198
Zelený, J. 4
Zhdanov, A. 221, 227-8
Zinoviev, G. 17, 34, 37